D0484150

Rogers'
Rules
for
Success

Rogers' Rules for Success

HENRY C. ROGERS

ST. MARTIN'S / MAREK

Design by Mina Greenstein

Library of Congress Cataloging in Publication Data

Rogers, Henry C., 1914–
  Rogers' rules for success.

  1. Success in business. 2. Psychology, Industrial.
I. Title.
HF5386.R5445   1984   650.1   84–13324
ISBN 0–312–68829–6 (hard)

10 9 8 7 6 5

To Roz and Warren—
without whose devotion,
patience, and understanding
this book would never have
been written.

Contents

Introduction

IMAGINE YOURSELF as a political candidate. You have decided to run for office. If you win, you will not only be called senator, congressman, mayor, governor, or president. No, you will carry an even more prestigious title. You will be called—*successful person.*

There will be other winners, and not only in politics, but they will be smaller in number compared to those who never even started the race. You will be among the privileged few.

In order for someone to enter the campaign for successful person, he/she must have the will, drive, determination, and energy to wage a long arduous war. This is not a one-day skirmish, the results of which will be determined when the sun rises in the morning. It is a long and demanding journey that can last for years. In my case, it has gone on for a lifetime. I campaign today as devotedly and as intensely as I did forty years ago.

Everyone in the race has doubts about his abilities and his talents. As he looks around at the other candidates, it becomes apparent, however, that the competition is not too formidable. There are few geniuses around. Most of the candidates are ordinary people just like you and me.

The candidate must develop a strategy that he hopes will help get him elected. He soon learns that a degree of talent coupled with hard work is not sufficient. An ability to relate to people—and for people to relate to him—is essential to win the necessary votes.

I use this analogy, relating the struggle for success to a political campaign, because I have always thought of my own life as one long crusade, a campaign that has never ended. For most of my adult life, I have been running for election. In a certain sense, I have won some campaigns, and have lost others. If someone were to ask me my secret for success, I would say that I have never stopped campaigning.

I am a battle-scarred veteran who is willing to pass his political know-how on to others. I am confident that I can help you to become a more successful person tomorrow than you are today, if that is what you really want.

When I was a teenager, my hero was Horatio Alger. In numerous inspirational works, Alger preached that clean living would bring riches and success within the grasp of earnest and ambitious youth. Any farmhand or clerk could become president; all you had to do was pull yourself up by your own bootstraps.

I believed him. I was fascinated by Ragged Dick, Tattered Tom, Squire Haynes, and the other heroes who peopled his novels. Night after night I read tales of Alger characters who bettered themselves through honesty, courage, and diligence. I was not alone. There were millions like me who helped establish Horatio Alger as one of the best-selling American authors of all time, in the process making *him* a wealthy and successful man.

I was ready to be honest, courageous, and diligent. Having found all of Alger's virtues in myself, I was also ready to settle back and let success come to me. It took many years before I realized that Alger told only a small part of the story. It was a sad day for me when I figured out that being Dudley Do-Right would make my mother happy but it wouldn't bring me fame and fortune.

In the years between my Horatio Alger pipe dreams and my emergence as a successful Hollywood press agent, I learned first to become a publicity expert and then taught myself to become skilled in the art of public relations. I discovered, however, that becoming schooled in my chosen profession still left something missing and that knowledge itself was not synonymous with success. I knew that I needed another dimension. I admired friends and acquaintances who had the knack of selling themselves to others. I said to myself, "They're skilled in *people* relations, and it is paying off for them."

People relations?—People. I watched my friends' interactions with others—their relationships with them—and I realized that this quality that was either genetic or acquired, conscious or unconscious, had as much to do with their success, or more, than all their professional knowledge.

I had read about power ploys and one-upmanship and realized that these approaches to developing relationships with others had a negative connotation. People relations, in contrast, was positive in nature. It brought out the best qualities in those who practiced it. I decided then that while I was working to become a more proficient public-relations person, I must also work simultaneously to become a better people-relations person.

As I was progressing along this path, I began to learn that the use of psychology was becoming a factor in the development of my relationships, both on the professional and the personal level.

Then one day I coined a word that described the program of thinking and behavior that I had been developing for myself: *psychorelations*. Psychorelations is the name I affixed to what I now consider to be a very critical skill. It is critical because it determines the quality of one's relationship with people, which in turn determines his level of success. Psychorelations is the tool by which we sell ourselves to other people. Psychorelations is people relations elevated to the highest level.

How well do you relate to others? How effectively do they relate to you? Do you make a good impression? A bad impression? Or no impression at all? Do people seem to gravitate to you or avoid you?

Do they seek out your opinions or dismiss them? Do you interest them or do you bore them?

Your awareness of and your sensitivity to your own behavior, your ability to discern it and do something to improve it, determine your ability to practice the art of psychorelations.

This ability to relate favorably to people may strike you as something intangible, but the results are altogether tangible. It is that trait in your personality that wins love and respect; enables your mate to forgive your sins, and your business associates to excuse your oversights, your mistakes, and your failures. It is that trait that makes you enjoy being with people and makes people enjoy being with you. It is the trait that will help you to become a successful person.

Developing your skills in psychorelations will be more important to your career than all the academic knowledge you acquire in college, more important in determining your future than a B.A., B.S., M.B.A., LL.D., M.D., or even Ph.D. Allow me to present it to you in the form of a maxim: *To the degree that you relate sensitively, appropriately—and, yes, even charmingly—to the people and events you face in both your business and personal life, you will be successful.*

In order to develop an ability in people relations you must first have an understanding that in order to be a success today, you must have the ability to *sell yourself.*

A successful total life is built gradually upon a series of daily interactions with other human beings, some exchanges being vital and some trivial, but each having a consequence. Indeed, your lifetime rating for business and personal success will be determined almost unerringly by how effectively you handle these interactions.

Who are the people in your life who are especially important to you? Your boss, your wife, husband, children, friends, community leaders, business associates, club members? If *real* success is your goal, then you must sell yourself to *all* of them. You must make them so receptive to you that they will help you to achieve your goals. The time has come for you to be a salesman for yourself.

... must consider your *image*, the
... e. For those who don't like the
... *age*, use the expression *true self*.
... ... ute it at will whenever I use the
... to explain what I mean here.
... r sense has only come into com-
... is the key that can unlock your
... es to you, rather than to corpora-
... s, or organizations, is defined by
... *cious impression you have about*
... *er people have about you (public*

... is made up of thousands of ideas
... around in your brain constantly
... you have of yourself. Improving
... process of self-analysis. You must

... yself?
... as a person?

... erman" or a "wonder woman" to
... e not going to give yourself just
... ou to look at yourself in the mirror
... yself today more than I did yester-
... shonest with you. You would be
... do that. Work at making yourself
... ike and respect yourself with good

... improving your *self*-image, we will
... public image is made up of a myriad
... e apparent when you act and inter-

act with others and determine the overall impression that others have of you.

How is your public image established?

If you relate effectively to others, and they like and respect you, then you have been successful in building a favorable public image. Having achieved that, and assuming that you have average talent and abilities, you have a better than even chance of getting what you want out of life.

The odds are in your favor.

That is what psychorelations is all about.

ROGERS' INSTANT DECISION MAKER FOR WARY BOOK BUYERS

This book is for you if:

- You have a fervent ambition to be more successful than you are today.

- You are willing to develop the will, the drive, and the energy that are necessary. These traits are not genetic. You can acquire them.

- You are ready to work hard to achieve your goals.

- You accept the fact that there will be many defeats along with the victories.

This book is not for you if:

- You never thought much about success until this very moment.

- You are satisfied with your present life.

- You prefer to play rather than work.

Rogers'
Rules
for
Success

1

How I got here

Just who is Henry Rogers? What does he know about success? Where does he get the cheek to write a book about it? These are fair questions that deserve answers.

Because I have no published record of helping people to become successful as does Dale Carnegie, or Dr. Norman Vincent Peale, or Clement Stone, I feel obliged to justify myself and my qualifications as the author of this book. I am a public-relations man. I am chairman and founder of Rogers & Cowan, one of the most successful public-relations firms in the country. For more than forty years I have been working at my craft, helping my clients to become more successful. I have worked intimately with many hundreds of people, many of whose names are familiar to you. I have been fortunate to represent as clients a cross section of important people and companies ranging from the world's most renowned movie stars to heads of industries and corporations.

Our diversified list of clients include Paul Newman, Sylvester Stallone, Dudley Moore, Nick Nolte, Gene Kelly, Danny Kaye; Ford Motor Company, R. J. Reynolds Tobacco, Arco Petroleum

Products, Texas Instruments; Redken Products, North American Philips; Braniff Airlines; Paul McCartney, Barry Manilow, Rod Stewart, David Bowie, and the BeeGees.

We work with our clients on a personal level. The client of a lawyer or an accountant has no need nor any wish to discuss his hopes, aspirations, goals, securities, insecurities, fears, ego problems, and a hundred other character traits that may concern him. He does, in contrast, confide in his public-relations representative. The public-relations person, because he is the link between his client and the public, is constantly brought into the intimate personal life of his client. In order for him to do his job most effectively, he must deal in the areas of psychology and human relations as much as he does with those purely textbook aspects of public relations. It has been my involvement with, not merely my observation of, these hundreds of people over a long period of years at Rogers & Cowan that has given me the knowledge and experience required to write this book.

I started my company. You could correctly say that I started from scratch. When it began, it was just me and an office and $500 of my father's money. Remember, though, that $500 then was the equivalent of $5000 today. Considering where I am now compared with where I started, I consider myself a success. Moreover, others consider me a success, too.

Did I have a head start? Was I a brilliant student? Did I come from a wealthy family? Did I marry the boss's daughter? The answer is "no" to all those questions.

I have on my desk an eight-by-ten photograph that is just beginning to fade. The year is 1941. Around me are Claudette Colbert, Jane Wyman, Jack Benny, George Burns and Gracie Allen, and several other Hollywood luminaries. I am seated between William Wilkerson, the editor/publisher of the *Hollywood Reporter*, and Charles K. Feldman, one of Hollywood's most important talent agents, who represented, among others in those days, Charles Boyer, Tyrone Power, and John Wayne. I am twenty-seven years old in the photograph, fashionably dressed, and just beginning to emerge as a Hollywood press agent on the way up.

How did I get there? *Six* years before the photograph was taken I had tried and failed to get a job as a shirt salesman; *five and a half* years before I had been fired from my first job. What had happened during those few intervening years?

To some extent, consciously but mostly unconsciously, I learned and then practiced psychorelations. Like many of you, I was not an ideal candidate for success when I began. However, through trial and error, I discovered some simple techniques that—in retrospect —made the difference between my anticipated life as a shirt sales-man and my actual life.

My beginnings were far from auspicious. I was born in Irvington, New Jersey, to middle-class European-born parents with little for-mal education. At the time of my birth, they were proprietors of Irvington's leading dry-goods store. Part five-and-dime, part men's and women's clothes and accessories, part household furnishings, the store is a key part of my childhood memories. I started working there when I was about ten. By the time I was in my early teens I was already selling merchandise.

To this day I still see red when I see lace—on anything or anyone. When we were about to close the store at 9:00 P.M., an elderly woman would inevitably come in and insist on seeing "some lace." I would bring out box after box in a variety of widths and colors. By nine-thirty or nine-forty-five she would finally make her decision. I would then measure out the yardage, cut it, bag it, ring up a forty-nine-cent sale on the cash register, and thank her through clenched teeth.

I grew up believing that I would eventually take over the store. Success, as I understood it at that time, was to follow in my fa-ther's footsteps (Alger approved wholeheartedly). Be brave, cheer-ful, clean, honest, and reverent, and watch the business grow. After graduating from high school, I automatically followed the course my father had planned for me: enrollment in Wharton School of Finance and Commerce at the University of Pennsyl-vania in Philadelphia.

To say that I did not apply myself to my studies at Wharton is an understatement. College to me was a social, not an educational experience.

I didn't think about Horatio during this period. After all, my father's business was waiting for me. I was the boss's son. I didn't have to concern myself with such mundane matters as seeking out a career, looking for a job, making ends meet. I opted instead to sow wild oats, an activity that seemed to accompany the Great Depression of the 1930s—for those who could afford it, of course. Despite the bread lines and the sight of mature, respectable-looking men standing on street corners selling apples for a nickel apiece, I was oblivious to the realities of life. Today I am a person of social conscience who cares and tries to do something about the troubles of the world. At the ages of seventeen, eighteen, and nineteen, I was unmindful of poverty, unemployment, a constantly falling stock market, and failed banks. Instead, with a weekly allowance check, I concerned myself with speakeasies, bootleg whiskey, prostitutes who could be bought for two dollars, and nice girls who could be seduced up to the point of a chaste kiss.

My carefree round of partying (occasionally punctuated by attendance at classes) was cut short one day when I learned that my father's business was in serious trouble. People who are hungry and out of work don't buy dry goods, or indeed goods of any kind.

Forced to lay off employees with many years of faithful service, my parents recalled me from Wharton and enrolled me in night school at New York University. NYU's Washington Square campus was a far cry from the elegant Pi Lambda Phi fraternity house in Philadelphia. Gone was the camaraderie, the proms, the dating, the crap games, the poker games. Penn-Cornell weekends with pretty girls and bootleg whiskey. I was now back home in Irvington working as a replacement for one of the long-term employees who had been discharged from the store payroll for economic reasons. I worked in the store as a salesman from nine to five—with no salary. There was just no money available for me to receive pay. At five, I walked two blocks to Irvington Center, and took the Springfield

Avenue bus to the Hudson tube station in Newark. There I leaped on the subway-type train to Journal Square in Jersey City, where I changed trains and eventually arrived at Ninth Street in New York, my destination. A five-minute walk took me to a lunch counter outside the Washington Square building where my classes were held. A quick sandwich, a glass of milk, and it was time for my first class at 7:00 P.M. Retailing, Advertising, and Accounting were my courses. At ten I was on my way back to Irvington. For five days a week this was my routine. On Saturdays I worked in the store from nine to nine. On Sundays I slept late, had dinner with my family, spent the evening listening to Jack Benny, Burns and Allen, and Eddie Cantor on the radio—and then to bed.

In retrospect, it is difficult for me to understand why I was not worried about my future. I did not complain, even to myself, about my change in life-style. I had enjoyed the lush life of living away from home, but now that I was back, I really wasn't suffering. We still lived in the same gracious home on the oak-lined avenue where I had spent all my teen years, the food was better than it was in Philadelphia, and although I knew that my father's business was near collapse, I still lived in the dream world of "nothing bad can ever happen to me or my family." Franklin D. Roosevelt had just become president of the United States. He would save us all. Herbert Hoover was responsible for all our problems. Roosevelt would solve them. I would soon be back at the University of Pennsylvania, and when I graduated, my future was assured in the family business.

But it didn't turn out that way at all. President Roosevelt didn't solve our problems, and one night at a family conference, father announced that he was about to close down the store. Creditors were hounding him, the banks had cut off his credit, and there was no other recourse but to declare bankruptcy. Father was choked up, mother was crying, I sat dumbfounded and confused, while sisters Estelle and Lillian were still too young to realize what was happening.

Where was my older sister Sylvia? She had married the year before and had gone off with her lawyer husband to start a new life in Los Angeles. I wondered what she was doing and whether I would ever see her again. I sat for a moment daydreaming about Sylvia among the palm trees, when my father's voice finally penetrated.

"Don't you understand?" he asked in a plaintive voice. "We're all finished here in Irvington. We're getting out. I just couldn't stand living in this town any longer, knowing that my creditors were looking over my shoulder, accusing me of cheating them. No, your mother and I have talked it over. We're going to move to Los Angeles. We're going to join Sylvia and Gus [my brother-in-law] and we'll be one family again, the way we used to."

I wasn't dismayed. I didn't cry. I wasn't even sad. My Horatio Alger dreams started anew. Los Angeles was to me the most glamorous city in the world. During my dissolute days at the University of Pennsylvania I spent many midnight hours listening to radio broadcasts "from the world-famous Coconut Grove in the Ambassador Hotel." Los Angeles, California! Hollywood!

I was going to Hollywood. What would I do? I hadn't the faintest idea. Should I go to school? UCLA was a new state university in Los Angeles. Tuition was very cheap and I could still live at home. I had completed three years of college, two and a half years at Penn and one semester at NYU. One more year at UCLA or another Los Angeles-based college and I would get my degree, a B.S. in Economics. What good would that do me in the present depression? Would the degree help me get a better job? I doubted it. The family agreed. On our arrival in Los Angeles I would look for a job, as would sister Estelle, who had just graduated from high school. Lillian would continue to go to school. Exhilarated by the Los Angeles sunshine, the palm trees, the beaches, the white stucco Mediterranean-style houses and the manicured lawns, I began looking for a position in retail sales.

After all, I had been selling merchandise in the family dry-goods store almost half of the twenty years of my life.

Every morning I beat the pavement—the May Company, Bullocks, Robinson's—downtown Los Angeles, the Miracle Mile, Hollywood—everywhere the answer was the same—no, thank you. I finally confronted the fact that I was unemployed and getting nowhere.

It was time to get some advice. My sister Sylvia and her husband, after bolstering my flagging spirits, suggested I go to secretarial school. Secretarial school? It was rumored that movie studios were looking for male secretaries because so many producers and executives worked nights. Most women didn't care to work nights.

With visions of starlets dancing in my head, I enrolled in Woodbury College, a secretarial school on Vine Street just north of Hollywood Boulevard. There were thirty of us in the class. I was the only male. I was evidently in possession of privileged information; obviously I was the only person who knew that movie studios were looking for male secretaries.

Sister Estelle found a job before I did. I didn't know it at the time, but she was responsible for my first lucky break. It came one evening when I went to pick her up at her office to go to a party. She had secured a secretarial job in a press agent's office not far from school. Finishing my daily bout with shorthand, I arrived at her office in the dowager Packard that the family had driven out from New Jersey. The car was a luxury for the evening; usually we rode the bus.

She introduced me to her boss, a red-haired, intensely rouged middle-aged woman named Grace Nolan. Miss Nolan asked after my health and education. I told her of my years at the University of Pennsylvania and NYU and my plans for a career at a film studio. (I left out the part about secretarial school.) She smiled, puffed on her cigarette, and offered me a job as an office boy at five dollars per week.

I thought quickly, weighing the merits of a bird in the hand versus the vague promise of secretarial employment in the movie studio bushes. I started the following day. I had a job! In Hollywood!

Grace Nolan ran a one-woman publicity business in a one-room office. The Brown Derby restaurant on Vine Street was a block away. I had heard that the walls were covered with caricatures of movie stars—some of them actually autographed by those fabulous mythical creatures of the silver screen. It was a heady environment for an impressionable kid from Irvington. I couldn't believe someone was actually paying me to be there.

The Grace Nolan publicity office represented a number of actors and actresses. Her job was to get her clients mentioned in the numerous Hollywood columns that appeared in the six daily newspapers and the two filmland trade publications that were published in Los Angeles at that time.

I didn't understand what she was doing, nor why her clients paid her for the seemingly mysterious services she rendered. "Why does Cesar Romero want the columnists to write about him?" I asked my boss a few days after I started my job. "Because he knows that the movie executives who can give him acting assignments all read the Hollywood columns and trade papers, just as everyone in the movie business does," she explained. "When they read Cesar Romero's name, they are reminded of him. When his agent walks into their offices to talk about a role for him in a film that is being cast, they don't ask 'Who is he?' He is already a familiar name to them." "Now I understand," I replied, but then I had another question. "Why don't the columnists dig up their own news instead of using so many items that come in from you and the other press agents in the business?" "They use material from us," she answered, "to supplement the news they get themselves. You see, Henry, these columnists work very hard. They go to the movie studios every day to get news. Then they go out every night to the parties, restaurants, and nightclubs where the stars congregate to get more news. But with all that, they seldom get sufficient material to fill up their columns every day. That's where the press agent comes in. If we can supply them with information about Hollywood celebrities that they are unable to get for themselves, we are doing them a good turn."

I was beginning to learn the Hollywood publicity business.

It was exciting. It was different. I had expected to spend the rest of my life in Irvington, New Jersey, in the retailing business. I thought about the first twenty years of my life with mixed emotions. I had left my friends, male and female, behind. Despite a speech impediment, I had been a gregarious teenager and never wanted for friends of my own age. I had started dating when I was fifteen. I had joined a high school fraternity, Upsilon Lambda Phi, when I was sixteen. During my high school and college years there were friends, parties, card playing, tennis, and ice skating. During the summers, there were camps in the mountains of Pennsylvania or long, sun-drenched weeks at New Jersey shore resorts. All that was gone, and although I didn't miss any of it because of the new intriguing life that I felt was in store for me, I was lonely. Being twenty years old, with no friends and a five-dollar weekly income didn't allow for very much fun. Evenings were long, usually spent with family. Occasionally I took a girl to a movie. That was all, but the excitement of the days compensated for the boredom and loneliness of the evenings.

My mornings were spent poring over the newspapers, reading the columns to see which of the items Grace Nolan had written about her clients had been used. When I saw one of her items in print, I circled it with a red pencil and placed it on Miss Nolan's desk.

Every afternoon I drove her car to downtown Los Angeles where I stopped at the *Times, Herald-Express, Examiner, Daily News,* and *Post* to deliver the envelopes filled with Grace Nolan's items about her clients to the columnists who wrote for those papers. Then I would double back to Hollywood where I would stop at the *Citizen News* and the two Hollywood trade papers, *Variety* and *Reporter.* Finally, I would return to the office late in the afternoon to prepare for the next day's work.

My boss hadn't told me that my five-dollar-a-week job also involved night work. Miss Nolan's aunt was Grace Kingsley, a frail white-haired woman in her late seventies who at one time had been the powerful movie critic and columnist of the *Los Angeles Times.* While now too elderly to handle the rigorous requirements of that job, she still free-lanced for the *Times,* often writing on movies and movie personalities. Miss Kingsley had no one to escort her to the movie premieres, the nightclub openings, and the filmland parties to which she was invited. Her niece's office boy solved the problem. I was presentable and had access to the still-shiny but slightly out-of-style family Packard.

At least two nights a week I picked up Miss Kingsley at her pussycat–infested Victorian home on North Broadway in downtown Los Angeles and whisked her off to a glamorous Hollywood event. I was never unduly uncomfortable about escorting Miss Kingsley. She could have been my grandmother, and wasn't it a sign of good character, I thought, to take your grandmother to parties? Besides, I was learning, I was looking, I was studying—studying much more intently than I ever had in college. At last I went inside the Brown Derby on Vine Street. Yes, there were caricatures of all the movie stars on the walls, and yes, I could see that some of them were personally autographed.

One of my first big nights was the premiere of a Jean Harlow movie at Grauman's Chinese Theatre. Searchlights lit up the sky for fifty miles around, as well as the faces of Cary Grant, Spencer Tracy, Robert Taylor, Norma Shearer, Wallace Beery, Alice Faye, Tyrone Power, and many, many more. I recognized them all. Six months before, I had been watching them on the movie screens back in New Jersey. Tonight I was standing only thirty feet away from them.

A tremendous cheer went up from the crowd that surrounded the theater entrance. From a limousine stepped Jean Harlow herself, a vision in white. I thought I was dreaming. There she was—platinum hair, a clinging white satin dress, diamond earrings and bracelets, a white fox coat thrown casually over her shoulders. She bent over to say hello to a friend. An inch of breast was exposed for only a moment, just a flash of white flesh. I was in ecstasy.

There came the day that my boss handed me an elegant, engraved invitation. It was addressed to Grace Kingsley. It read "You and your escort are invited to attend the opening of Guy Lombardo and His Royal Canadians at the Coconut Grove, Ambassador Hotel." At that moment I felt that my job was too good to be true.

If I could have afforded it, I would have paid Grace Nolan five dollars a week just for the privilege of working for her.

The great night arrived. I picked up Miss Kingsley at her home and helped her into my car. She had tried her best to look her most attractive. She had obviously gone to the hairdresser that afternoon, for her thinning snow-white hair was fashionably styled. Her shapeless chiffon dress dated from another era, probably the turn of the century. An unidentifiable fur was wrapped around her wrinkled shoulders and arms. I would naturally have preferred to escort Jean Harlow that night, but if this was the only way to get to the Coconut Grove, I was satisfied. Besides, everyone loved Grace Kingsley. She treated me very politely and graciously, and introduced me as her "niece's business associate." We were always seated at the best table at nightclubs and restaurants.

Tonight was no exception. We had arrived early, the guests had just begun to trickle in. The maitre d' bowed to Miss Kingsley, nodded condescendingly to me, and escorted us to a ringside table. I looked around in wonderment. It was as glamorous as I imagined during those college evenings when I listened to Guy Lombardo playing the Cole Porter, George Gershwin, Jerome Kern, and Rodgers and Hart hits of the day. There were the palm trees that rose from floor to ceiling. In my naiveté I thought they were genuine; it was not until years later that I realized they were plastic. Toy monkeys frolicked in the treetops; the ceiling was a night-blue sky, and stars winked at me. An artificial moon on the far side of the room shone down on the elderly woman and her youthful escort.

I asked Miss Kingsley to dance. I thought it would give me an opportunity to get closer to the young film stars I had been admiring from afar. We stepped onto the dance floor and I quickly realized that it wouldn't work. Miss Kingsley's feet went one way, mine another. The fifty-five-year age difference didn't make us the best of dancing partners. After a few moments of stepping on each other's feet, we both admitted that the experiment hadn't worked and that our dancing days were over.

After three months, Miss Nolan informed me that she was very pleased with the job I was doing, and that my salary was to be increased to twelve dollars a week. I was thrilled. That night I began to dream about my future. Publicity would be my career.

The dreams were lofty and my hopes were mountain-high, but my euphoria didn't last very long. The following Saturday afternoon I returned from my weekly tennis game to find that disaster had struck. My mother was waiting for me. "Grace Nolan called," she said. "She told me to tell you that you're fired. Don't bother to come in Monday morning."

I finally was able to put the pieces together. My normal procedure on Saturday morning was to drive my boss's car to the newspapers, return to the office, and leave her car keys on her desk. Then I would go home by bus. That day, I had inadvertently neglected to return her keys. They were still in my pocket. She had had an appointment in Santa Monica with a prospective client that she had been forced to break because she couldn't drive her car. She was furious. My carelessness, she had told my mother, was inexcusable.

She was right. I was heartbroken, but I knew I deserved to be fired. I was angry with myself. Gone was my career. Gone were the glamorous evenings at the Coconut Grove, the Trocadero, and Grauman's Chinese Theatre. I had to face up to reality: I had no job.

I wanted to continue to pursue a career in Hollywood publicity, if only because I had already established a relationship of sorts with many of the Hollywood columnists and trade press reporters. Whenever I delivered a press release to the newspapers, I tried to find an excuse to chat for a moment. Some of the reporters had begun to recognize me; occasionally I received a warm "Hello, Henry! What have you got for me today?"

The reception was somewhat chillier when I made the rounds looking for work at the other Hollywood publicity offices. Some of Grace Nolan's competitors were kind enough to see me. Others wouldn't let me through the door. In the end it didn't matter. There was not a job to be had.

No one was waiting for me. I was now twenty-one years old and my total experience in Hollywood publicity was a six-month stint as an office boy.

Economic conditions, my age and lack of experience were certainly formidable barriers, but there was another that was even worse. I scarcely mentioned before that I stuttered. When I was nervous, I stuttered badly. A job interview is a nerve-racking experience for an adult who speaks normally, but for me, it was a nightmare. My mouth locked tight, my jaws became rigid, and my eyes squeezed shut. I was not a very impressive candidate. The prospective employers who saw me were kind and sympathetic, but no one hired me.

What could I do? I still wanted to be a Hollywood press agent, but there were no jobs. There was only one answer. I would start my own business—stuttering and all. It was an immature, ridiculous thought. Few were less qualified than I. I knew little, if anything, about business. I had no money. If I did go into business, where would I get clients? Who would be interested in having me work for them? Realizing all this, I decided to go ahead anyway.

I never thought of it as a bold and a courageous step or as an irrational move. I simply had no choice. I couldn't get a job doing what I wanted to do, so there was only one alternative: become self-employed. I never bothered to think that I literally had no experience. I had met a few people by this time who were in or on the sidelines of the movie business. Would they help open up some doors for me? I didn't know, but I could ask them.

How much would it cost me to go into business? I began to make lists of what I required. Rent, telephone, bus fares, lunches, a typewriter, office supplies. There would be no personal expenses because I still lived at home with my parents. I computed that $500 was required to keep me in business for six months.

I had only one source of funds—my father. He was skeptical. He had just gone through bankruptcy and there were very few $500 bills lying around. But he generously made what appeared at the time to be the worst investment of his life. He loaned me the money to go into business. I have always been grateful to him and grateful, too, that he lived long enough for me to repay him and for him to enjoy my success.

Three days after I received his check, a one-inch ad appeared in *Daily Variety* and *Hollywood Reporter*. Each ad cost four dollars. It read as follows:

HENRY C. ROGERS
Announces the Opening of His

PUBLICITY OFFICES

at

6605 Hollywood Boulevard, Hollywood, Calif.

Phone HO 9–6146

I was in the publicity business. I had a one-room office on Hollywood Boulevard that I shared with another press agent, Hal Weiner. We paid twenty dollars a month rent—ten dollars each. I sat at my desk waiting for the telephone to ring, for Hollywood to break down my door. I sat for one day. Two days. On the third day, the telephone rang. It was Joe Fine, advertising director of *Daily Variety*. I had placed my four-dollar ad directly with him.

"Henry," he said, "I have a client for you." I could scarcely believe it. Now I was really in business.

The client was the dance team of Kirby and De Gage. They had just completed an appearance in a dance sequence in a Warner Bros. musical. They believed that if they hired a Hollywood press agent they would be on their way to stardom. To achieve it, they paid me fifteen dollars a week. My job was to get their names placed in the Hollywood columns and trade papers. When their agent went in to try to get them another job, the publicity would have made the potential employer more amenable to their cause.

Grace Nolan had trained me well. I began a publicity campaign for my new clients. I wrote material on them for the Hollywood columnists and for the trade papers. I tried to follow the writing style of each of the columnists. I studied the editorial style of *Daily Variety* and *Hollywood Reporter* and soon felt that the news items

I wrote for them could not be differentiated from those written by their own journalists. I wrote items and articles about how Kirby and De Gage had just completed a dance sequence for a Warner Bros. musical, that they had just signed a contract to appear in an Agua Caliente resort hotel in Tijuana, Mexico, that they had just had new costumes designed for them by a world famous couturier (not true), and that they were under consideration for another more important part in another Warner Bros. film (true). The columnists, knowing me from my office-boy days, and feeling empathy for this young kid who was struggling to get his first client into print, used my material. My clients were happy with my efforts but there were no movie producers knocking down their dressing room door with lucrative contracts. The impending deal for them to appear in another musical fell through. It wasn't too long before Kirby and De Gage disappeared from my life.

In my first year, I grossed three-hundred sixty-three dollars in fees. It is difficult to understand now in the 1980s that I survived that first year and was still not discouraged. As I said, I lived at home and had no rent to pay. The bus fare to my office was ten cents, lunches cost thirty-five to fifty cents, my office rent was ten dollars monthly, and the telephone bill cost about four dollars a month. I moved around Hollywood, Los Angeles, and Beverly Hills by bus and streetcar. I managed without a secretary because I had originally learned to type in high school.

It is easy for me to say now that I was not discouraged. But each morning I gave myself a pep talk. "You can't quit," I kept telling myself. I didn't want to go back to the retail business, even if I could get a job at the May Company as a shirt or a shoe salesman. I didn't want to go into insurance or real estate, even though I could probably have made more money in those fields. I liked publicity. I got a charge out of it and wanted to stay in it. Maybe I wouldn't be all out successful as a publicist, but if I were able to earn a living at it, I would be satisfied. One day, when my father was trying to convince me to give it up for another career that would be more lucrative, I replied, "But, look Dad, if I can get two clients to each pay me twenty-five dollars a week, that's all I'll ever need." Dad indulged me, patted me on the head, and walked away, wondering how and if I would ever get two clients who would each pay me twenty-five dollars a week. Even that prospect seemed a long way off.

I met people, introduced myself as an up-and-coming Hollywood press agent, and managed to pick up an occasional client here and there. One person introduced me to another, and I began to make contacts who, I felt, could help me in the future.

Gossip columnists whom I had met in my office-boy days were helpful. They advised me that restaurants and nightclubs that catered to movie and radio personalities were my logical prospective clients. The owners of these establishments, anxious to get their place of business mentioned in the newspapers, were willing to pay me ten or fifteen dollars a week for my publicity services. They also allowed me a 50 percent reduction on my food and drink checks. Even though dinner cost only a dollar and a half I spent so much time in these places that very little money changed hands between me and my clients at the end of each week when the books were balanced. This didn't bother me, though, because I knew that I was learning something new every day. I didn't need immediate income. I needed experience.

My objective was to get actor and actress clients, for they were the substance of the publicity business in those days. I felt that at long last I had broken into the movie business when Marc Lawrence agreed to become my client. I was thrilled to represent this young character actor, but it didn't prove to be a particularly profitable relationship either. My agreement with Marc called for him to pay me fifteen dollars a week when he was working and ten dollars a week when he wasn't. However, he rarely, if ever, worked. Consequently, he rarely, if ever, had the ten dollars a week to pay me.

When Rosalind and I were married in 1937, I had been in business for two years. My income at that time was about seventy-five dollars a week, a sufficient amount back in those days for us to live a fairly comfortable existence—at least for a young man of twenty-three.

As I began to gain more experience and greater confidence, my fees began to increase. Phil Regan, known as "The Singing Cop," was the first performer to pay what was for me the astronomical sum of twenty-five dollars a week. A year later, some long-forgotten, extravagant actor actually paid me fifty dollars a week for my services. Progress was slow, but my little business was beginning to grow.

A dramatic turning point in my career came in 1939, when a stroke of fate brought me into contact with an unknown black-haired beauty named Rita Hayworth and her husband at the time, Edward Judson.

My wife and I met the Judsons through mutual friends on the tennis court at the Sunset Plaza Apartments, just off the Sunset Strip. Eddie Judson was an attractive, smooth-talking, well-groomed man who did not discourage people from thinking of him as a mysterious personality. It was said that he had been "in investments" in Texas, but no one seemed to know anything more than that. He was much older than his wife and she appeared to be completely subjected to his will.

Rita was raven-haired, with perfect features, olive skin, a sensuously rounded figure, ample breasts (which bounced seductively as she swung at a tennis ball), shapely legs, a tiny waist, and rounded buttocks. I had heard of her, but had never met her before. She was under contract to Columbia Studios, but at that moment her career was going the way of a hundred other beautiful girls in Hollywood: nowhere. Movie studios chewed up those girls like corn flakes. Pay them a few hundred dollars a week, put them in "B" pictures, get tired of them after a year or two (few if any of them had talent), drop their options, pick up a new batch of fillies, and begin the dance all over again. The hope was that some day a star would emerge from the flock.

The Judsons invited us over to play five-and-ten-cent poker a few days after our first meeting. After the game, Eddie asked if we would stay on for a while after the other guests had left. When Eddie said, "Henry, I'd like to talk to you about representing Rita,"

Rita nodded but didn't say anything. She let her husband do all the talking. He went on to explain that Columbia Studios had just given her a big break. She was to appear in a supporting role in a Howard Hawks film, *Only Angels Have Wings,* that would star Cary Grant and Jean Arthur. If Rita could give a convincing performance, and if her breakthrough into the big time were accompanied by a publicity campaign that brought her forcefully to the attention of the movie industry and the public, Rita would be on her way to stardom, Eddie said.

I agreed with him. His strategy made sense. Although Rita's success depended largely on her performances and the effect she had on the movie-going public, a lot depended too on the publicity campaign, which would be my responsibility. We made a deal, a three-year contract under which Rita agreed to pay me 5 percent of her income. She made $300 a week when we signed our agreement. Yearly options would take her to $600 a week at the time my agreement was due to expire.

I worked for Rita Hayworth for the full three years. When we started I received a fee of fifteen dollars a week. In the last year I received thirty dollars a week but it didn't matter. Rita Hayworth had become a star, and there were some in Hollywood who gave me the credit for her quick rise. I had made a contribution, but I was certainly not responsible for her success. No one becomes a star and remains a star through publicity. We both got lucky. Rita had star quality. I was one of those who helped it to emerge. People today still say to me, "Oh, you're the guy who made Rita Hayworth a star." For more than forty years I've been giving the same answer, "No, that's not true. She made *me* a star."

Through Rita and Eddie I met her talent agent, Tom Somlyo. Tom and I became golfing buddies, and one Saturday morning, he asked Charlie Wendling, another agent, to join us. Charlie and I also became friends. While this was happening, Rita's career was soaring. One day, Charlie, who happened to be Claudette Colbert's brother and manager as well, was asked by his sister to recommend a publicist to represent her. Charlie, bolstered by my newly acquired reputation as the "man who helped make Rita Hayworth a star," was not reluctant to recommend his friend Henry. A few days later, Claudette Colbert, at that time Hollywood's highest-paid star, agreed that I would become her publicist. With Rita Hayworth and Claudette Colbert as clients, my career as a Hollywood press agent was at long last fully launched.

Charlie Wendling not only introduced me to his sister, he also introduced me to his boss, the head of the agency, Charles K. Feldman. In the early 1940s, Charlie Feldman was one of the most influential men in the motion picture industry. He was the head of one of Hollywood's major talent agencies and represented dozens of the most important actors, actresses, directors, and writers. He was a lawyer, turned agent, turned businessman, turned movie producer. He was the first "movie packager." It was he who first conceived the idea of purchasing a script himself and committing one or more of his star clients to appear in it. He and the actor/actress would jointly decide who among Mr. Feldman's clients was best suited to direct the film. He would then go to Jack Warner at Warner Bros., Darryl Zanuck at Twentieth Century-Fox, or one of the other major studios, and sell the "package" at an enormous profit for himself. Thus, he not only provided excellent new opportunities for his clients, but also brought packaged film properties to the studios. Many of these packages became major box-office successes. Everyone loved Charlie Feldman because his deals made profits for his clients and the studios alike. An elegant man, he had an air of success about him.

Soon after I met him he became my mentor, and started sending me his clients for publicity representation. Thanks to his recommendation, I began to represent Marlene Dietrich, Dick Powell, Joan Blondell, and a number of his other important clients. I never had to sell myself to them. By the time I met with them, Charlie had already convinced them to hire me, and they would never question his judgment. It was through Charlie Feldman that I came to be seated at the dinner table where I began my story.

That eight-by-ten photograph of me sitting with the biggest

entertainment stars of 1941 illustrates that in about five years I had
begun to formulate the principles of psychorelations. The people
around that table—Claudette Colbert, Jane Wyman, Jack Benny,
George Burns and Gracie Allen—were Charlie Feldman's friends.
Even as we sat there, some of them were becoming *my* friends too.
My mentor was chairman of the Hollywood Victory Committee, a
forerunner of the USO that was the motion picture industry's
contribution to the war effort. I had been asked by Feldman to
volunteer my services as the publicist for army camp shows that the
Hollywood Victory Committee was staging for the troops. It was
an exciting way to serve my country, meet the great performers of
the day, and give my business a big boost—all at the same time.

Why me? Why did he select me? Was I lucky? Luck is the art
of being in the right place at the right time. Horatio Alger said that
luck comes to those who deserve it, but here he was plain wrong.
I didn't just "deserve" luck in some moral sense. I was lucky because
I put myself in situations where "lucky" things could happen and
because I worked hard to make myself someone whom others could
like and respect. In other words, I practiced psychorelations.

We should now take another look at how I came to be in that
photograph. With the benefit of twenty/twenty hindsight, I can
pinpoint the keys to my success up to that point in my life.

Have a Goal

I started without a goal, but stumbled luckily in the right direction. When Grace Nolan hired me, I had only the vaguest idea
about getting a job "in the movie business." This concept was good
enough to get "a job," but not focused enough for "a career." The
distinction is all important. Psychorelations can help pave the road
for you, but only if you know which road you are on.

If you are undecided about what career to pursue, some introspec-
tion is in order. This topic is worth a book in itself; many good ones
have been written. I recommend one with a sense of humor, *What
Color Is Your Parachute?* by Richard Bolles (Ten Speed Press,
$9.95). It provides a series of exercises to help you narrow the list

of possible career choices to those you might *really* like to follow. It's hard to be a success at something you hate doing.

Make Connections

By the time I was first introduced to Charlie Feldman, I had discovered that my future success in the Hollywood publicity business depended on my ability to meet the right people. For me, the right people were those who were associated with or who represented in some capacity the luminaries of the entertainment world whom I hoped one day to represent.

I set out to win the professional respect of agents, business managers, and lawyers who worked for those stars. I saw it as a game, but you had to be accepted as a member of the team before you could play. The lawyer recommends an agent to his client. The agent recommends a business manager. The business manager recommends a press agent. The press agent completes the circle by recommending a lawyer.

Work at Being Likable

It may sound simplistic, but it is one of the fundamentals of psychorelations. I not only had to meet artists' representatives, but I also had to establish a relationship with them on a personal level. I didn't want them to know me as Henry Rogers, the press agent. I wanted them to recognize me as Henry Rogers, the person, a man they would enjoy spending an evening with, or a lunch, the person who incidentally happened to be successful in the Hollywood publicity business. When I began in the business, there was a social stigma attached to being a press agent. We were known as flacks, and were never invited to the same parties as were the actors, actresses, producers, directors, and writers. If we appeared at industry functions, it was usually in a working capacity, rarely if ever as guests. I decided that if I could raise my social level, it would help me to achieve recognition in the publicity business.

Being likable is the flip side of making connections. I never said to myself, "Playing politics in the movie business is as important as playing politics in Washington," but I began to realize that meeting people, establishing relationships with them, and getting them to like and respect me would help me build a career. I figured that if people in the movie business liked me, if they respected me as a person and as a publicist, and if they believed that recommending me to their friends, acquaintances, or clients would not compromise their own relationships, then they would refer me to prospective clients.

How do you get to be likable? What about personal faults—physical and otherwise? I was a stutterer, for example, yet I was able to overcome my disadvantage.

Be Visible

You would see me every day—somewhere. I spent mornings in my office. I would have lunch at a fashionable restaurant or at one of the studios—where I would be seen. I would drop in on movie sets to see my clients and find that I would be introduced to other prospective clients. My acquaintanceship with producers, directors, and screenwriters broadened, and I made a point of dropping in to see them just to say hello. The word is *visibility.* The more people saw me and became conscious of me, the better chance I had that my name would be considered when the question was asked, "Whom should I hire as a publicist?"

My campaign to develop relationships with the agents, lawyers, and business managers in the film community resulted in another advantage that I discovered during those early years. As I lunched and had dinner at the best restaurants in town, I found myself being accepted on an equal social basis with the people I sought out. Everyone I met had an income ten, twenty, or fifty times greater than mine, but the fact that we dined at the same places, bought our clothes at the same tailor, and played gin rummy at the same tables, gave me a measure of social acceptance that I otherwise would have never attained. It was that social recognition, combined with my recently attained professional acceptance, that, I am confident, accelerated the growth of my publicity business.

Be Courteous and Considerate

In this area, Horatio Alger had it right. I made a point of being nice to secretaries and receptionists, switchboard operators, mailroom clerks, office boys, and other "unimportant" people whom I was in daily contact with. My apprenticeship in my parents' dry-goods store and my experience escorting Miss Kingsley stood me in good stead here. I was brought up with the idea that you are cordial to others —such cordiality is essential in any service business where you wait on customers. Remember the old lady buying forty-nine cents' worth of lace? It killed me, but I was nice to her. It didn't help advance my career to be pleasant to her while she dawdled over her choice, but then again it wouldn't have helped to be nasty to her either.

Miss Kingsley was probably a greater help than I knew at the time. Not only was she my "ticket" to many functions that would have been off limits to me, she was also someone who, in her day, had been prominent and powerful. There were still people who remembered her, people for whom she had done a favor or two. I certainly didn't hurt myself by being solicitous of her on our "dates." Those who were fond of her or indebted to her in one way or another were favorably impressed by the way I treated her.

After I was on my own, I tried very hard to remember names and faces of the "gatekeepers" in any business. In the early days I spent a considerable amount of time in waiting rooms, which I used to exchange a few pleasant words with the "support staff." It cost me nothing to do this and the next time I telephoned I had a much better chance of having my call put through.

Let's stop for a moment. Does all this sound calculating? It probably does. The fact is that it *was* calculating, it was planned, it was thought out, but there is a big *but* that went with all the calculation. It would never have worked if I hadn't liked doing it. I enjoyed it. It came natural to me. I liked Grace Kingsley. I never regarded going out with her as a business chore. Of course, I would have enjoyed taking a beautiful eighteen-year-old starlet to the Coconut Grove much more but that was not to be. Escorting Grace Kingsley on the town served a double purpose for me. I was furthering my budding business career and having a pleasant time doing it. You can't fake it. It shows through very quickly. If I hadn't liked what I was doing at the time, I'm sure there would never have been a Rogers & Cowan.

Mix Business with Pleasure

You will find yourself spending a lot of time working to be successful. This doesn't mean it can't be fun. I met Rita Hayworth on the tennis court. It *is* true that many business deals are made on the golf course.

My wife and I began entertaining business contacts in our home shortly after we bought it in 1945. We lived just a few blocks from Joan Crawford, Robert Preston, Fred MacMurray, Lloyd Nolan, and a number of agents, lawyers, and others with whom I did business. I wasn't the only businessman who was able to make business contacts at parties at my home. Other guests were able to make connections there too, which made them want to attend. They became aware of the importance of other invitees and this gave me, both as an individual and the head of a business, an added prestige and importance in Hollywood. Our guests usually reciprocated by inviting us to *their* homes, and soon my feet were planted under the best tables in town.

I found that entertaining at home had a tremendous advantage over taking a group to dinner at a restaurant. I was on my own turf, and on equal social terms with my client, prospective client, or the person I hoped would someday send me an important client. I quickly discovered that when I had a business meeting with someone who had been a guest in my home, my relationship with that person had acquired personal overtones, which always proved to be advantageous. I became accepted as a player on the team, and that was the status I had long been seeking.

Be Persistent, but Don't Push

Professionally, I was trying to be a better publicist than my competitors, but I knew that simultaneously I had to meet the players who were in the game I wanted to play. I knew that in order to meet them, I would have to become visible at the places where they congregated.

I would have lunch with a friend at the Brown Derby, Vendome, Romanoff's. Someone would stop by and say hello to my luncheon guest. I would be introduced. Two days later I would call this person and ask him to have lunch with me.

My approach on the telephone was forthright. "I'm new in this business," I would say, "and I feel it would be very valuable for me to know you. I don't want anything from you. I don't want to sell you anything. I would just like to get to know you. Would you have lunch with me one day this week?" Some people would put me off. They would not want to waste a valuable lunch hour on me. But I was *politely* persistent. I would propose meeting for breakfast or cocktails, or suggest that I drop by the office at the end of the day just to chat for a few minutes.

I don't recall ever having been rejected. I didn't seek out the head of the law firm or agency. That was shooting too high in those early days. I was after the second level. If I did well with them, then they would move me up to the "majors" when the time was right.

Once I met them, my next step was to get them on my team. My first rule was, "Don't sell." I used the approach that I was in a position to help them. I wanted nothing from them. "I have a very good relationship with the press," I would say. "If you ever need something in print, whether for yourself or for one of your clients, don't hesitate to call me. I'll be delighted to help you." I always felt that I was in a stronger position if I offered to do something for them, rather than appear to be asking them to do something for me. Whether or not they took advantage of my offer, the day would come when they could help. This was one of my early steps in tying psychology to a program of getting people to know me and regard me in a favorable light.

Look Like You're Worth the Money

I knew that I had to look good if I was to attract attention. I made a point of always being well dressed and well groomed. I developed a sense of color coordination and styling. By watching other people who commanded attention when they walked into a room, by looking at the cut of their clothes, the type of shirts and ties they wore, I selected what I considered the best traits of each, and developed a style of my own. I believe it put me a notch above my competitors, who gave little thought as to how they looked.

Expand Your Horizons

But why were my "targets" comfortable with me? They were well educated (some self-educated) and already successful. I was a kid, a beginner. Why was I so readily accepted by them on a social as well as a business level?

I was lucky in a number of respects. First, Roz, my wife, and I always looked to expand our horizons. I had been an avid reader since my early high school days. I had always enjoyed golf and tennis and played both games fairly well. Roz's aunt and uncle, Mildred and Sam Jaffe, introduced us to the world of art and music. We never thought of these activities in terms of business. We thought of them as mind expanders that we enjoyed.

But then I discovered that sports activities and cultural interests were also "door openers." I found myself on the golf course and the tennis courts with clients, prospective clients, and other important personalities in the entertainment world. When we talked over a drink, or at lunch or dinner, we discovered that we had read the same books, and we often discussed articles that had appeared that day in the movie trade papers.

As I became interested in the financial community, politics, and world affairs, I found that these were also topics for discussion with those people with whom I was now associating. As a result, I came to be recognized by important people in the movie colony as more than just a Hollywood press agent. I was on their intellectual level and was accepted as a member of their class.

By the time I met Charlie Feldman, my psychorelations aptitude (even though I was not conscious of it at the time) had developed to the point where I was able to converse freely with my mentor on his Impressionist paintings, his Chippendale furniture, and the latest Ernest Hemingway novel. I believe that he respected even my superficial knowledge of subjects other than publicity, and that our rapport stemmed from that. That rapport, coupled with my ever-growing ability as a press agent, was the reason—I am certain—that Charlie Feldman set his sights on me in those early days of my career.

Find a Mentor

When Charles K. Feldman started referring his clients to me, my career took off. Not only did I reap benefits from the actors and actresses whom I began to represent as a direct result of my association with him, but because of his stature in the movie business his implied endorsement opened doors for me with other agents, lawyers, and business managers who then started to refer their clients to me as well.

I learned a great deal from my mentor. I particularly remember the manner in which he handled his clients. When I was growing up, the agents I met appeared to be fawning sycophants who worked in an atmosphere of fear. They were afraid of losing their clients. They were quick to grab their suitcases, ever alert to open the door for them. I rebelled against such behavior. It was not in my makeup to work like this, but I thought that that was the way it had to be—until I met my mentor. He showed me that there was another way to represent clients, whether you are an agent or a press agent.

I asked him about this one day and he replied, "I start with the premise that I am as successful in my business as the client is in his. He is an actor and I manage careers. Unless there is a mutual respect for each other's talents, then I cannot do my job properly. If I am subservient to his wishes, if I permit him to tell me what to do, he doesn't need me. That doesn't mean I make arbitrary decisions. I don't tell the client what he should do. We talk, we discuss, and then we arrive at a mutually satisfactory solution to each situation." My attitude toward my clients was established the day that Charlie told me how he represented his.

I also learned from him how to deal with my associates, and how to work with people with whom you are doing business. In the days that Charles K. Feldman was at his peak as an artist's representative (he later became a successful motion picture producer), the studio bosses were potentates, czars, even robber barons. Louis B. Mayer, Harry Cohn, Jack Warner, Darryl Zanuck, and one or two others ruled Hollywood with the proverbial iron hand. They were despots who could make or break careers overnight. Charlie Feldman worked with these movie moguls as he did with his clients—with mutual respect. "You need me and I need you, so let's work together to our mutual advantage" was his motto. At one point L. B. Mayer, in a fit of temper, announced that MGM would no longer do business with Charles K. Feldman or his clients. The industry waited to see what Feldman's reaction would be. Would he capitulate? Would he go to see Mayer, hat in hand and beg for forgiveness. Charlie stood his ground. Eventually, Mayer recognized that they needed each other. He capitulated, paraphrasing Feldman's motto: "You need me and I need you, so let's work together to our mutual advantage." I remembered that incident a number of years later when Hedda Hopper announced that she would no longer do business with Henry Rogers or his clients. I also remembered it when we got into a tiff with Associated Press, and later, with Clay Felker, editor of *Esquire* at the time. I learned to retain my self-respect, but to always be ready to compromise.

Maybe Feldman saw characteristics in me that I now look for in others. Richard Kress, president of Norelco, put it very vividly when he said recently, "I never hire anyone who I wouldn't want to invite to my home to play poker." Charlie was evidently at ease with me. Informal in his business conduct, he would sprawl on a couch when I met with him in his office and invite me to smoke my pipe while sitting comfortably in an upholstered chair. When I was asked to

see him in his home, the butler would fix drinks for us, and as we
sipped them in front of a crackling fire, he would talk about the
publicity results he expected on the clients he had been responsible
for getting me. He was heavily involved in the management of their
careers, and believed that constructive publicity was important for
them. Let's keep it straight. I was not his friend. He lived in a social
world that was a zillion light years away from mine in those days.
He didn't invite me to his home for dinner nor to the races nor to
football games. We lived in different worlds, but he always treated
me with great *respect, warmth,* and *friendliness.* He evidently considered me as his protege. He was my mentor.

Be on the Ball
Although I came to understand that knowing the right people,
being visible, and playing the social game all contributed to my
success, I never overlooked the overriding importance of possessing
a certain degree of talent and developing that talent so that I could
get better and better at my job.

Early on, I had decided that the Hollywood publicity business,
as practiced by my competitors, was superficial and cosmetic. The
major effort seemed to be expended on getting the client's name in
print, without paying too much attention to what was written. The
clients' egos were massaged when they read their names in Louella
Parsons' or Hedda Hopper's columns, but I didn't believe in the old
adage "Any publicity is good publicity as long as you spell my name
right."

Even though my clients at the time were not sufficiently sophisticated to articulate what they hoped to achieve by engaging my
services, I figured it out for myself. I told them that publicity should
have an objective and a purpose. It should help build the client's
career. It should impress the movie moguls, the producers, and the
directors who were in the position to give my actor clients better
roles at higher salaries. If my publicity efforts were not directed
toward that goal, if I were content just to get my client's name in
print, then I would be just like my competitors. I wanted more than

that. I wanted to offer my clients something that was more intelligent and more constructive. I wanted to build a better mousetrap.
This was easy for me to tell a client, but how could I put my lofty
theories into practice?

Clients might "buy" my personality, my charm, and my well-
tailored clothes, but they would buy them more readily and be
willing to pay more for them if I were a better publicist than anyone
else. I had no formalized training in Hollywood publicity. There
were no textbooks to study or courses to take at that time. I had to
teach myself. I had to break new ground if I was to achieve the goals
that I had begun to define for myself.

I began to relate Hollywood publicity to corporate public relations as practiced by the early masters. I read about the careers of
the fathers of public relations, Ivy Lee and Edward Bernays. I
studied the methods and approaches used by John Hill and Carl
Byoir. I was introduced to and had tea time after time with Ben
Sonnenberg. I learned what the masters of corporate, political, and
industrial public relations did and applied some of their principles
and tactics to what I was doing in Hollywood. I believe that is one
reason why in the early days of my career I pulled away from the
pack.

The lessons to be learned from my early career are obvious. I
wanted to be better than anyone else. I realized that I was in a
political contest, a game, as it were, and I developed a program, a
campaign, to win the election. I learned the importance of developing business and personal relationships with people who could help
me, and was willing to devote the time and the energy it took to
accomplish this. I made it part of my life-style.

Before proceeding further, it is important to know that Henry
Rogers didn't make it on his own. Although I started in business
for myself in 1935 at the age of twenty-one, I was joined in 1945
by Warren Cowan, much younger than I, who began to work with
me when he was discharged from the army after World War II.
Warren was an immediate spark for me and the business, and by
1950, when it came time to change the name of the firm to Rogers

& Cowan, we were already established as the largest and most successful publicity business in Hollywood.

ROGERS' PROFILE FOR SUCCESS

As I look at the successful people I have known or observed and then look back at my own career over a period of many years, I ask myself if there are any common denominators that we all share. When I think through the answers to the question "Why me?" or "Why them?", I find that there are certain acquired characteristics that are essential components of a candidate for success. They are:

Self-Esteem
Energy
Drive
Will
Self-Control

Not everyone is in possession of these essential character traits, nor does everyone have a sufficiently strong desire to acquire them. You don't have to be born with them; very few of us are. Those who enjoy them worked hard to attain them. But it is clear that those who have self-esteem, energy, drive, will, and self-control are more successful than those who don't.

Self-Esteem

Self-esteem is all important in this profile for success, and I will have more to say about it later. For now, remember that too many of us spend unnecessary time worrying about the attributes we don't have. We're not good-looking. We don't have an M.B.A. from Harvard. We're a member of a minority. We live on the wrong side of the tracks. We don't look good in clothes.

Forget about flaws—for now, at least. Instead, concentrate on your good points. Don't tell me you don't have any. You do. It is time for you to begin to build your ego. You will need it in order to handle what's in store for you.

Energy

I have put energy near the top of my list, for so much in our psychorelations program stems from it. Energy, as it pertains to your success, has little to do with the physical. Unless you are among the unfortunate few who are anemic or who have some other strength-draining disease, each of you has sufficient physical energy to be successful. I describe energy as an emotional attribute. It is the desire to get up at six in the morning instead of at eight, because you want to get an early jump on your competitors. It is the desire to make fifty phone calls during the day instead of twenty-five, because you want to get the job done. It is what prompts you to call a Saturday or Sunday morning meeting with your associates because work is fun, and success is fun.

Do you feel that you lack the energy required to become successful? If so, the most likely explanation is that you regard your present work as drudgery. Take stock of yourself. If you find it easy to play eighteen or thirty-six holes of golf over the weekend but difficult to get through an eight-hour day at the office, it should be obvious that you regard your job as an exhausting, unpleasant struggle. In contrast, when you are putting for a birdie on the eighteenth green, after four hours of walking, a surge of adrenaline goes racing through your system.

You don't acquire energy for success just by going to a health club or jogging six miles every morning. It has been proven that a regular exercise program is essential to good health. It is good health plus a positive mental attitude about your job that will give you the energy required for a successful career.

Once you determine to become a more successful person, and once you regard your new campaign for success as an adventure— a glorious adventure—and as fun, not drudgery, you will find yourself working with just as much energy as you have when you're putting for that birdie.

Drive

Drive is a first cousin of energy. Someone inside of you is urging you on. "Move a little faster," he is saying, "accomplish a little more." "You can do better." "You're smarter than that guy down the hall. You can get a raise before he does." That little fellow is pushing you, shoving you, forcing you to climb higher and higher up the mountain. And something interesting is happening to you. You don't mind being pushed at all. You are beginning to acquire a drive that you never had before, and you seem to have the energy to sustain it.

Will

While all this is happening, you are also beginning to acquire the will to be successful. You are more ambitious. You want success more than you ever have before. It's no longer a struggle for you to get up at six in the morning instead of eight. You find yourself more aware, more alert. You see opportunities for achievement that you never noticed before. You no longer avoid responsibilities. You are looking for new ones. You walk into your office with your head held high, your stomach pulled in, and your shoulders thrown back. You are beginning to look like a West Point cadet. Your newly acquired will is beginning to reveal itself.

Self-Control

The last item on my list is self-control. I'm sure you can find successful people who lack it, but they are in the minority. An overwhelming percentage of people who are recognized as successful enjoy masterful self-control. A successful person breeds confidence in those around him. He assumes responsibility, and people feel comfortable when they give it to him. It is difficult to have confidence in a person who breaks into violent temper tantrums, who is rude and ill mannered, who thoughtlessly makes cruel and cutting remarks to his colleagues, who goes off on drunken binges, and smokes cigars in crowded elevators. It is difficult to equate people like this with the word success. The truly successful person is in control.

2

Getting your act together and taking it on the road

To the world at large, you are what you do. Your public image is determined by your behavior when you act and interact with others. In this chapter we will deal with the basics of psychorelations—how you can help yourself make a favorable impression on others.

WALKING IN THE OTHER PERSON'S SHOES

It is human nature to be self-centered, to spend most of our waking hours considering every event solely from an egocentric point of view. Yet, most of us have periodically resented others for this very attitude. Could it be that you, too, are thinking only of your own problems, only of your own interests? Do you ever stop for a moment to think of what it would be like if you were standing in the other person's shoes? You will become more skilled at psychorelations if you learn to deal with every situation from the other person's perspective.

Your boss may have scolded you today because your report didn't arrive on his desk when it was scheduled. Normally, you might be angry with him. Instead, put yourself in his shoes and consider the situation this way: He wanted to have a staff meeting this afternoon based on your report, as he is due to meet with the president of the company tomorrow morning to supply him with information he had expected to receive from you. Because you are late with your report, the staff meeting will be postponed, and he'll be in trouble with *his* boss.

When you put yourself in his place, you can't very well get mad at him. In fact, you can understand why he is peeved at you.

Recently, I noticed that an invoice for fees and expenses that was about to be mailed by our accounting department to one of our clients was very confusing. More details referring to previous payments were necessary in order for the client to understand the bill. I mentioned this to the accountant who was responsible. She replied that the statement was clear to her, and she did not know why I was concerned. I explained that she had the background on the billing procedure fixed in her mind, but if she were in the client's shoes, she would be as confused as I was.

I knew she wasn't convinced. "Sally," I said, "show the bill to Glen and ask him if it's clear to him. Then buzz me back and tell me what he says." A moment later she was back on the telephone. "You're right. Glen didn't understand it either, so I'm redoing it as you suggested." Glen had looked at the bill from the client's perspective.

Your own point of view in any given situation has a much greater chance of being valid if it includes the attitudes and perceptions of the other people who are involved. When you put yourself in the other person's shoes, you make him feel that you have a sincere regard for him. When you are able to instill that feeling in him, you have a greater chance of winning him over to your side.

Try to regard every encounter, every conversation, every letter, memo, or telephone call from the other person's point of view as well as your own. Remember: to "the other guy," you're the other guy!

Rogers' Exercises to See It Someone Else's Way

1) Write a profile of yourself as seen by those around you—your boss, your secretary, your spouse, your clients.

2) Write a job evaluation of yourself as if you were considering yourself for promotion.

3) Set up a series of problems and argue them from both sides, either aloud (when you're alone, in your car or elsewhere) or on paper. Some examples:

    a) As a "perk" of your job, you've had an expense account for entertaining clients. In an economy move, your boss has informed you that your expense budget has been cut in half.

    b) You've sent your client an invoice for services rendered. He hasn't paid it. He feels he hasn't received his money's worth. You think he got what he was entitled to.

    c) You've been asked to fire someone who is "not working out." He says he's suffered from a lack of direction, and asks for another chance.

MAKING THE OTHER PERSON FEEL IMPORTANT

Think about your reaction to the person who makes you feel important.

Your telephone rings. Your boss asks to see you. What does he want to see you about? What did you do wrong now? You walk into his office.

"Al," he says, "sit down. I have a serious problem, and I need your advice. I think you can help me."

When you walk out of his office you say, "What a great guy he is, and smart too. He knows where to look for advice when he needs it!"

On another day you walk into your home at dinnertime. Your wife grabs you, hugs you, and kisses you smack on the mouth.

"Darling, I'm so proud of you. My telephone has been ringing all day. All my friends have been complimenting me on my fabulous husband because of that absolutely sensational story that appeared on you in the morning newspaper." You beam with delight.

Another evening a friend walks up to you at a dinner party. He grabs your hand warmly and exclaims, "That speech you gave at the Rotary Club luncheon the other day was terrific. Your points were well taken and everyone was very enthusiastic about what you had to say."

You know how incidents like that make you feel. Pretty good. You feel proud of yourself when someone pays you a compliment, when someone makes you feel important. And what do you think of the person who is responsible? You like him, you respect him, you feel kindly disposed toward him.

Consider, then, how other people feel about you when you make them feel important. They will react just as you do. They will respect you, like you, and feel kindly disposed toward you. Simple, isn't it?

Most people will react to you exactly as you react to them. Your boss's opinion of you will skyrocket if you do something that will make him feel important. The same principle applies to your spouse and, for that matter, to everyone else. Look for opportunities to show people you consider them important—and when you do so, they will begin to think that you are more important.

I make a conscious effort every day to show people in my life that I recognize their importance. The only real assets that a public-relations firm has are the people who make up the organization. My associates who work with clients who pay us $50,000, $100,000, and $200,000 a year are not automatons. They must be treated in a positive and constructive manner. They are important people, and it is essential that I make them *feel* important. After all, most of our company's "assets" go down the elevator every evening.

When one of my associates comes in to see me, I usually ask him to sit opposite me on an L-shaped couch in one corner of my office. I have found that the intrusion of a desk sets up a psychological block between two people. Take the desk away and the relationship between employer and employee becomes easier, and less tense. Emotional barriers begin to evaporate. I have bolstered his confidence, given his ego a boost, and he realizes that I regard him as an important person.

The natural tendency of an employer who wants to see one of his employees is to buzz his secretary and have her ask the employee to come in to see him. Summoned to the boss's office, the employee feels intimidated before he walks in the door. To prevent this, I usually go to his or her office. I buzz him on the intercom to let him know that I'm on my way. With a simple gesture I have made that employee feel important, and I do it because I know how important I feel when a client insists that he will come to see me.

George Wolf, an old friend, called me from New York one day to tell me that Chuck Peebler would like to meet with me. Charles A. Peebler, Jr., is president and chief executive officer of Bozell & Jacobs, a very important advertising agency headquartered in New York, with offices in ten major cities throughout the United States. George explained that Mr. Peebler was interested in acquiring Rogers & Cowan. I told him that we had no particular interest in selling our business, but there was certainly no harm in talking and I would be delighted to meet with him the next time I was in New York.

"No," countered George, "Peebler wants to meet with Warren Cowan and you in your offices the next time he's in Los Angeles." A few telephone calls back and forth and we finally set up an appointment.

I was curious about why it was so important for Peebler to see us on our turf and, a few minutes after his arrival, I raised the subject.

"We could have had this appointment a few weeks ago in New York. I'm curious about why you insisted on making it here in Los Angeles."

Peebler smiled. "I came to see you in your office in your home city because I wanted to impress on you how important it is for me to establish a relationship with you. We want your company to be associated with ours, and I felt that you would consider our proposal more seriously if I came to see you personally."

He was right. I was impressed. And why not? He had made me feel very important.

Although we started out with no interest in the Bozell & Jacobs offer to buy our company Peebler's charm and persuasive manner eventually intrigued us to the point where negotiations actually got underway. Although the deal eventually fell through, it proceeded almost to the point of signature.

HOW WOULD YOU LIKE TO HEAR: "GREETINGS FROM THE WHITE HOUSE"?

When I discussed the theme "make the other person feel important" in a lecture at UCLA in 1982, I noticed that my students were particularly attentive. They each seemed to relate personally to the subject.

The following morning, Roberta, one of my associates, walked into my office, and half seriously, half in jest, said, "Well! I wish you'd practice what you preach. You certainly haven't made me feel very important lately!" I tried to laugh it off. "I wish you'd stop going to my lecture series. Before it's over I know you're going to make me eat every one of my words." The subject was dropped, and Roberta raised the topic she really wanted to discuss with me. But I was left feeling uncomfortable because I had noted a touch of seriousness in her voice. I had given her a difficult time recently and I determined to find an opportunity to make her realize that I did consider her important, both on the personal and professional level.

The following morning I left on a business trip for Washington. One of my appointments took me to the White House, where I met with Mike Deaver, one of the key men on President Reagan's staff. Morgan Mason, who had recently resigned from his position at the White House, where he had been assistant to the president for political affairs, to join our firm, had set up the appointment for me. I was seeking advice from Deaver on our planned opening of a Washington office, and he graciously gave me an hour of his time.

My meeting completed, I began to leave by way of the West Lobby of the White House when I noticed that it was 6:00 P.M., Eastern Standard Time, 3:00 P.M., Pacific Standard, a perfect time to call our Beverly Hills office. "May I use the telephone for a few minutes?" I asked the receptionist. "Of course, Mr. Rogers. There is one over there in the corner." I checked in with my secretary, and I spoke with Warren Cowan about a problem that had arisen earlier in the day. I was about to leave when I suddenly had a thought. I dialed Roberta's private number. When she picked up the telephone, I said, "Hi, what's new?" "Nothing exciting," she replied, "where are you?"

"I'm in Washington."

"What are you doing there?"

"I've had a couple of meetings and I'm about to take the shuttle up to New York." There was a pause.

"Where are you calling from? A phone booth?"

"No, I'm calling you from the White House."

"Where? What did you say?"

"I said I was calling you from the White House, from the West Lobby of the White House."

"Why? What are you calling about?"

"I'm calling to make you feel important. Do you get many calls from the White House?" She started to laugh.

"You're just impossible. Okay, okay, you've made your point."
Then we both laughed. " 'Bye now. I'll see you in a couple of days,"
she said and we both hung up.

There is a sequel to this story. A number of weeks later I had
another meeting at the White House. This time I was with Mabel
"Muffie" Brandon, whose official title was White House Social
Secretary. We had decided that we wanted her to head up our
Washington office and she had invited me to lunch to discuss it.
We chatted for a few minutes in her office and then left for one
of the small dining rooms reserved for staff members and their
guests. Our walk took us through the West Lobby, and I noticed
the same telephone I had used to call Roberta. I pointed it out to
Mrs. Brandon and said, "While we're having lunch, I'll tell you a
story about that telephone."

I did, and at the very moment I finished, a waiter approached our
table holding a telephone in his hand. "Mr. Rogers," he said, "there
is a call for you."

I was impressed. I don't usually have lunch at the White House
and I certainly don't expect to receive telephone calls when I do.
I picked up the phone. My secretary, June, was calling me from our
Beverly Hills office. She just wanted to tell me that one of my
afternoon appointments in Washington that day had been postponed. I thanked her, hung up, and turned to Muffie.

"That's very impressive. How did they ever track me down?"

Muffie smiled and replied, "That's easy. Your secretary knew that
you were meeting with me, and she called my office."

"I know that, but why was the call put through here? I could have
picked up the message when I went back up to your office."

Muffie laughed. "I guess Ramona, my assistant, wanted to make
you feel important!"

At that point I laughed too. If that was Ramona's objective, she
had certainly achieved it.

EVEN STARS NEED TO BE TOLD
THEY ARE IMPORTANT

I have friends who are reluctant to go backstage after a show to congratulate the cast on their performances. They feel that they are intruding on the actors' privacy. I tell them they're wrong. I discussed this subject with Rex Harrison during the height of his success in *My Fair Lady* on Broadway. I discussed it with Mary Martin many years ago when she was washing that man right out of her hair in *South Pacific,* with Rosalind Russell in *Wonderful Town,* Carol Channing in *Hello Dolly,* Angela Lansbury in *Sweeney Todd,* and Robert Preston in *Music Man.* Each of them told me they like having people come backstage after a performance. It confirms to them that the audience appreciates what they're doing, and they all confess that they, too, like to be made to feel important. Yes, even the most important stars in the world like to feel important. If they do, you do, I do, and the other fellow does too.

Making others feel important is so easy that I used to wonder why more people don't recognize its benefits and take advantage of it. The answer is that there are few people who feel big enough to make other people feel big. The person with little self-esteem is unable to give it to anyone else.

Rogers' Tips for Making People Feel Important

1) In conversation, devote the first few minutes to discussing *them.* When you say "How are you?" mean it.

2) Compliment them on a job well done.

3) Ask someone for advice on a subject you know he is knowledgeable about.

4) Bring someone a cup of coffee—whether it's your boss or your secretary or a coworker. Every so often bring a box of donuts or sweet rolls to the office.

5) Instead of doing business by phone, go to the other person's office.

6) When appropriate, make generous introductions of colleagues or employees to important visiting guests.

AT EASE!

Not only is it essential to make someone feel important, the art of psychorelations demands that we also make the other person feel at ease. As I reflect back on my life, I find that powerful and important people have always made an effort to make me feel comfortable. My experience has been that the more important they are, the more gracious they are. Could it be that their ability to reach out graciously to others has helped *make* them important? I believe so.

Prince Philip is a remarkable human being. He has great humor, he is bright, alert, aware, and well read. Despite the life he leads in Buckingham Palace and Windsor Castle, His Royal Highness has the common touch. He is innately kind and, realizing the position he holds, has the ability to make the other person feel at ease in his presence.

In 1966, I served as Prince Philip's public-relations representative on a twelve-day eight-city charity tour of the United States. It was midnight at the Fontainebleau Hotel in Miami Beach. We had just completed the first day of the tour. He had dismissed his aides, telling them it was time for them to get some sleep, but he had invited me to join him for a nightcap so that we might review the day's activities. I was somewhat tense about this personal, one-on-one meeting. Was I to be as formal with him in this late-night talk session as I had been all day when we were meeting the press and the public? I would have to take my cues from him.

As we approached his suite, he took the key from his pocket, unlocked the door, and walked in, with me following a step behind.

Without saying a word, he removed his dinner jacket, tossed it on the couch, took off his tie, and unbuttoned his collar.

"You, too, Henry. Get comfortable. We've both had a difficult day."

Following his lead, I took off my dinner jacket, laying it on the couch alongside his. I took off my tie, unbuttoned my collar, and accepted his invitation to sit in the upholstered chair that faced the one on which he had seated himself.

He had already put me at my ease. I felt no tension.

"Well, it's time for a drink," he said. "It's been a long day for both of us. We deserve it."

We both laughed.

"Good idea. I noticed some liquor bottles in the kitchen earlier. I'll fix the drinks. What would you like, sir?" I stood, but he motioned me to sit down again.

He had risen from his chair. "Stay there," he said, "I'm the host here. Would you like a whiskey and soda?"

"Yes, thanks. That sounds fine." I followed him into the kitchen.

Prince Philip took two glasses from the kitchen. Dropping ice cubes into them with his fingers, he poured generous slugs of whiskey, splashed in some soda, handed me my drink, clinked his glass against mine, smiled, and said, "Cheers. Now let's review the events of the day and discuss what tomorrow's schedule will be like."

We talked for a half hour. At one point he slipped out of his shoes, making the atmosphere even more easy and comfortable. We agreed on what had gone well on our first day and what could be improved on the next. Finally, when he yawned, I knew it was time to leave. We said goodnight; I slipped on my dinner jacket and walked down the hall to my own room.

Warm, easy to be with, intelligent, thoughtful, and with a touch of humility, Prince Philip displayed in that encounter his remarkable flair for putting a person at ease. He must have had the same effect on a thousand people in the past and will have the same effect on a thousand people in the future. He is a master at psychorelations.

When Roz and I had the good fortune to be invited to a party aboard HMS *Britannia* by Queen Elizabeth II of England during her recent visit to Los Angeles, we had no idea that we would even be introduced to her.

As we walked up the gangplank to board the royal yacht, which was moored at Long Beach, we noticed that we were two of only a few hundred guests. We were asked by an impeccably groomed, soft-spoken naval officer to line up on the deck, two by two. This was obviously the end of the receiving line. We moved slowly along the deck, step by step, to the salon where the reception was being held. A naval aide moved down the line handing each husband a card with his name and that of his spouse written on it. The man was asked to precede the woman with card in hand.

As we entered the drawing room there was the Queen, looking shorter, but much more attractive than the television news or newspaper photographs depict her, resplendent in an emerald and diamond necklace with earrings to match, elegantly dressed in a Hardie Amies white satin dinner dress, with a tight bodice and full skirt, personally greeting her guests. Standing a few feet away was Prince Philip, dressed in a dark gray suit, conservative blue-figured tie, white shirt, and just a speck of a white linen handkerchief peeking out of his breast pocket.

There were two couples in front of us, so we had an opportunity to watch the procedure. The husband handed his card to a smiling British naval officer, whose uniform, plastered with WWII battle ribbons, attested to his long years in the service of the Crown. He read the card aloud in a normal voice: "Mr. and Mrs. Michael Jackson." Our friends, Michael and Alana, were just in front of us. Michael went first. That was obviously tradition. I watched him and then Alana shake hands, exchange a few words with the Queen and then Prince Philip.

Then it was our turn. I handed my card to the naval aide. He read "Mr. and Mrs. Henry Rogers." I stepped forward to shake hands with the Queen of England. She smiled at me and extended her hand (didn't she ever get tired?). Her grip was firm. "I'm delighted to meet you, Mr. Rogers. Thank you so much for coming to our party."

It was no time to linger. Roz was right behind me and others were also lined up waiting to be introduced. "Thank you for inviting us," I murmured, and moved along to Prince Philip. "Henry," he said, "what a pleasant surprise!" He grabbed my arm in Nelson Rockefeller style and shook my hand vigorously. "Good evening, sir. I want to show you something." I extended the sleeve of my dinner jacket and showed him my shirt cuff. He took it in his hand, laughed, and then, still holding it in his hand, turned to the Queen and said, "Look, dear, Mr. Rogers is wearing the cuff links I gave him after the trip we took together sixteen years ago." She smiled, looked at me, and said, "How lovely!" then turned to greet her next guest.

Even though you're not royalty, you too can put people at their ease. Study the behavior of the successful people you know—the ones in whose presence everyone seems comfortable. Look for the little gesture, the wave of the hand, the crossing of a knee, the broad or even gentle smile, the tone of voice that makes you relax in their presence.

It's not easy to emulate another person. The wave of a hand or the crossing of a knee that comes so easily to someone else may be difficult for you. You must work at it. You probably have never thought of doing it before and the actual effort will be foreign to you. You must concentrate on what gesture at what particular time will put the other person at ease. It's not simple but if you keep working at it, you will begin to master the knack as others have.

An added effort in making people feel more at ease in your presence will quickly improve your public image and, hence, your opportunities for real success. With a concentrated effort it's not too difficult to achieve this quality—it's just another case of putting yourself in the other person's shoes. What makes *you* comfortable? What makes *you* feel at ease? If you keep those in mind, then you will gradually learn to make others comfortable.

You are at your desk and a woman comes into your office. It's unimportant whether she is a superior or a subordinate, whether she has an appointment or has just dropped in. How do you treat her?

Rogers' Ten Golden Techniques of Graciousness

1) Greet her with a warm smile and firm handshake.
2) Ask her to sit down and be comfortable.
3) Ask about her health and her family.
4) Offer her a cigarette, soft drink, or coffee.
5) Hold your phone calls.
6) Look her in the eye.
7) Treat her respectfully.
8) Ask questions and listen carefully to her answers.
9) Discuss subjects that are of interest to her.
10) Have a sense of humor about yourself.

PRACTICE BEING A LIP-SERVICE SANTA CLAUS

One of the most important elements in your psychorelations program is to learn to give compliments. Don't flatter—compliment. Flattery is suspect. A sincere compliment is appreciated. Your previous reluctance to praise someone probably stems from your uncertainty about how your compliment will be received. It will take a lot of practice to learn to deliver a compliment gracefully, with no awkwardness or even a hint of insincerity in your voice. There are many opportunities. Look for them and you will find them—and eventually your family, your friends, your business associates will accept them graciously.

There are many opportunities for me to give compliments because I seek them out. For example, I have always been conscious of clothes. I am aware of what people are wearing at a dinner party the moment I walk into the room. When I say to a wo-

man, "What a pretty dress you're wearing," I can see her respond.
I try to extend congratulations on special occasions. A friend may
have been promoted to a better job or he may have been elected
president of the local Kiwanis club. His sizable contribution to a
charitable cause may have just been announced or he may have
recently won the golf championship of the local country club. Everyone appreciates acknowledgment of his achievements. It is so
simple to take a few minutes during the day and—in person, by
telephone, or in a short note—extend your congratulations to someone who deserves it.

An expression of appreciation is all-important in keeping the
morale in an organization at a high level. An employee is not
satisfied with being well paid. He wants, expects, and deserves
recognition for his efforts—"psychic income." A quick note from
his employer saying "Well done" or "You did a great job. Congratulations" goes a long way toward making the day brighter and more
gratifying.

Then again, the boss appreciates a compliment as well. Do you
ever tell your boss what a good job he is doing? Do you ever write
him a memo complimenting him on something he did or said? Try
offering a sincere compliment. Your boss will become more aware
of you. He will be apt to recognize the contribution you are making
to the company. When your name comes up for a salary increase
or a new contract, your position with him is stronger than it might
otherwise have been.

I have often been asked whether this can be considered ass
kissing. The answer is "no." No more so than when you give a
compliment to a nonboss. You are practicing psychorelations. You
are building and developing your relationships with people. Why
leave your boss out? In fact, I suggest that you make him number
one on your "to impress" list.

Because the giving of compliments is so rare, the gracious acceptance of them is equally rare. You will probably find that a newly
acquired behavior pattern of giving compliments will at first be met
with confusion and suspicion. The recipient may retort with, "Oh,

stop kidding," or "Your flattery will get you everywhere with me." People often do not know what to say, so they resort to a wisecrack, or a self-deprecating remark. The proper response to a compliment is to say, "Thank you very much. That's very kind of you."

If someone answers your compliment with a smart-aleck answer, don't accept it. Reply, "No, I'm not buttering you up at all. I'm sincere" or "I mean it" or "That's my honest opinion." There might be a moment of embarrassed silence. The recipient, who has just laughed off your compliment, now reconsiders. He will look at you in a new light and perhaps will say, "Oh, I'm sorry. Thanks for the compliment." You will have emerged from this little byplay as a more admirable and more thoughtful person than you were just a few minutes before.

It will take some time before your friends, your family, and your business associates begin to accept the new you, the person who has overcome his reluctance to give a well-deserved compliment. In fact, it will also take you time to get used to it. At first you will be uncomfortable and unduly sensitive. Finally it will begin to come to you easily and naturally. Expect to encounter a certain degree of skepticism at first from others, because they won't recognize you in your new role. Gradually, however, as the giving of gracious praise becomes part of your normal behavior, people will accept your sincerity. You will find, too, that as you give, you will begin to receive.

DISPLAYING GOOD MANNERS

Some wag once said, "If manners were an animal, it would be an endangered species." I simply can't comprehend how everyone doesn't see that good manners are one of the most important keys to success in the world of business. From the waiter in a Chinese restaurant to the chief executive officer of a Fortune 500 company, everyone has something to gain from being polite and considerate. For the waiter, good manners will probably result in increased tips.

For the CEO, a gracious attitude toward his board of directors will result in a long list of perquisites that otherwise might be slow in coming.

I sit back in a dirty New York City taxicab and find it curious that the driver doesn't realize that he will get a bigger tip from me if he is courteous and affable rather than rude and sullen. I wonder if he blames *me* that he lives a tough life in the Manhattan jungle. But there is an old adage about biting the hand that feeds you; he should realize that I am a human being too, and that I will respond generously to a cheery "good morning" and a warm smile.

It is equally puzzling to me that some of our clients don't realize that they will get an extra effort rather than just a normal effort from me if they show better manners. Good manners are even more important when you are trying to get ahead within a corporate structure. When you are on your way up, you can't afford to be surly —to anyone.

One fundamental part of good manners is learning how to say thank you. Sherry Lansing, the former president of Twentieth Century-Fox Studios, accepted my invitation to appear as a guest speaker at a series of lectures I gave at UCLA. Early on the morning after her appearance, I sent an arrangement of flowers to her office with a note expressing my gratitude. Long before the flowers could have arrived, she telephoned me. She thanked *me* for having invited her and allowing her the privilege of speaking before my students. A few hours later she called me again. The flowers had arrived, and she thanked me again. That's good manners!

"Henry Dearest"?

Much has been written about Joan Crawford over the years. Her daughter's book, *Mommie Dearest,* and the subsequent movie on which it was based gave an unfortunately biased view of this remarkable woman. I represented Joan for ten years—years that started as a low period in her career, when Louis B. Mayer, head of MGM, fired her because she was "box office poison." I was with her during the time of her resurgence in the mid-forties when she won the Academy Award for her performance in *Mildred Pierce* and continued my representation of her until she married Pepsi-Cola boss Al Steele and moved to New York. I knew her almost as well as anyone. I knew her good points and her bad, her faults and her attributes. Only those who knew Joan Crawford were aware that she was probably the most thoughtful, well-mannered person of her day. I would tell my friends in those days that she never ceased to amaze and impress me. Before each conversation, she would say, "How are you Henry? Is everything going well? How is Roz and how are the children? Did Roz buy that new hat I told her about the other day? Was Marcia's report card better this month than it was the month before? I remember how upset you were about that." For at least five minutes, she inquired about aspects of my personal and business life; then we moved on to discuss her. Every Christmas there were gifts for us and the children. Easter Sunday, there were egg-rolling contests on her lawn. Thank-you notes rained in on us. "Darling," she would write, "how kind of you to tell me that you liked the new picture last night. Your opinion means so much to me." Another one: "Dearest, please forgive me for sitting you between Mabelle Webb and Babe Blum at last night's party. With all the young, pretty girls in the room how could I have done that to you? I will make it up to you one day. I promise, love, Joan."

When our children grew up, the Christmas gifts ceased, but the hand-written note on her personal stationery always arrived two weeks before December 25. "Darlings Roz and Henry," her letter would always start, then there would be some expressions of holiday sentiment, which included how much we meant to her, and how important our friendship was to her. She always concluded with "All my love to you and the children" and then "Joan," in strong, readily recognizable gold script. The letters continued for more than twenty years, even when she lived in New York and we rarely saw her.

There were probably hundreds of people on her letter-writing list. The fact was that good manners were sufficiently important to her to expend that enormous effort year after year. What does it all mean?

Her critics say that she never did anything altruistically, that everything was done for a purpose, everything was done for effect. Yet, forty years later, I am singing the praises of Joan Crawford. I don't care if she had ulterior motives. Did she believe that I would work harder for her if she showered good manners on me? She was right: I did. I'm just a human being who responds to kindness, graciousness, thoughtfulness, and good manners.

Is there someone you want to impress? Is there someone who can help you to become more successful? Is there someone whose cooperation you need, love you desire, respect you seek, admiration you yearn for? Take a tip from Joan Crawford.

The thank-you note, the telephone call to a friend expressing appreciation for something he did for you, a warm smile at the appropriate moment—all take little effort, but they are a giant step toward achieving success through psychorelations.

I always have an added respect for, and I remember in a favorable light, the employee who resigns from my company and writes me a note of appreciation for the considerate treatment received during his or her years with our company. I am impressed, too, with the man or woman who greets me with a hearty "Good morning," rather than the one who averts his eyes as I approach. In situations where I have any influence on the degree of success a person is to achieve in his business career, I, in fact, give greater consideration to the person who has good manners than the one who doesn't.

There are several excellent manuals on manners. If you are rusty, bone up. But, short of the formal Emily Post rules about which fork to use and how you introduce the congressman to the archbishop, here are some short cuts to thoughtfulness:

Rogers' Quick Guide to Thoughtfulness

1) Develop a memory for names and faces. Many people make the mistake of assuming this ability is a gift, saying, "So and so has

a knack for remembering people." It's not a gift, it's a skill, and an important one at that. Those who are good at it work hard. It's a major technique in the art of making people feel important and putting them at ease.

2) Keep a Rolodex; keep it updated. It's much easier to remember people's names if you have a chance to write them down. Add the names of wives, husbands, and children if you know them or learn them in subsequent meetings. Review these before meeting with people.

3) Keep a "special occasion" calendar. Do you know when your boss's birthday is? Keep a calendar or date book marked with these events. Every January, transcribe them from the old year to the new. Don't just mark the date, mark a date a week or so in advance to give yourself time to send a card or note, purchase a gift, or make plans for a lunch or dinner date.

4) Keep an inventory of cards and stationery for these occasions. Buy a bunch of birthday cards, congratulations cards, thank-you notes, get-well cards, and blank notes. Keep them at your desk near your calendar or date book. That way it's easy to drop a line or get off a card. There is no point in being aware of the boss's birthday if you don't get around to doing something about it.

5) Be prompt with thank-you's. Try to phone the next day if someone takes you to lunch or dinner. It's not only polite, it's a good way of cementing the contact you made and offers a good opportunity to review the topics discussed.

"OLD BLUE EYES" TEACHES THE ART OF DIPLOMACY

We all have a tendency to be blunt and candid in our intimate relationships with people, yet it is often the degree of sensitivity we display in those relationships that affects the degree of success we achieve in our lives.

I have been guilty of a lack of sensitivity on numerous occasions in my professional life, and in each instance, I realized after the fact that I had hurt myself and pushed my career back a step. I have learned from these mistakes and try now to avoid the brusque remarks that were once part of my nature.

Frank Sinatra fired me many years ago when I had, with a lack of sensitivity, been "too honest" in answering a question. Frank had asked me why I thought he had such a bad image with the press and the public, and I had blurted out one word, "You."

I hurt him. I wounded him. I offended him. Did I get a certain satisfaction out of telling off the king, taking "Old Blue Eyes" down a peg or two? Maybe I did. I now know that my negative, crude answer was unforgivable.

If I had it to do all over again it would be different. Based on what I have learned about psychorelations, today the dialogue would go like this:

Frank would say, "Henry, I have a lousy image. What's wrong and what do you think we can do about it?"

"Frank, let's start with the facts. You don't have a lousy image at all. You're the most admired and most respected singer-personality in the twentieth century. However, you're not perfect. No one is. For every million people who love you and respect you there may be twenty who don't like you and don't respect you.

"Over the years you've offended some people. Who hasn't? You've offended some press people. Who hasn't? Big deal. Did you ever read what the press used to say about Abraham Lincoln—about Franklin D. Roosevelt? You don't have a lousy image at all. You have a great image with 99 percent of the people and a lousy image with 1 percent. If you want to do something about that 1 percent, let's start there. We'll work out a plan that will get them on our side."

Had I conducted myself in this way, Sinatra would have undoubtedly been much more amenable to my suggestions. I would have handled a sensitive situation in a sensitive manner. I would have avoided hurting someone who did not deserve to be hurt, not by me at any rate, and I probably would still be representing Sinatra today.

I made a similar mistake on another occasion.

Bob, a major corporate executive, had been a client for a number of years. It had come as a shock to me to learn that, after five years' association, he was about to give a lucrative assignment to a new competitor. The shock was particularly traumatic because the competitor had worked for our public-relations firm for some ten years. I had introduced her to Bob. She had been working on his account under my supervision and had left our employ only a month before under what I considered to be less than ethical circumstances. Now I found that he was leaving us to go with her.

Although the split-up with my former colleague was something that should have remained between the two of us, I was so shocked at being told that Bob's next project was going to her that I voiced my grievance to him. I told him how, without advance warning, she and one of our other associates had sneaked into the office on a Saturday morning, had "stolen" company files, and spirited them out of the building. When I finally learned what had happened on Monday, she was safely ensconced in her new offices, and three of our clients had written me that they were leaving Rogers & Cowan for her organization. She had obviously been planning this for weeks and had performed her maneuver, in my mind, like a master criminal. Now, one of our most valued clients was telling me that, in effect, he accepted her behavior, was not critical of it, and was turning his account—at least part of it—over to her.

I could not understand his acceptance of her actions. How could an important executive at one of the nation's largest and most respected corporations condone what she had done to her employer—at a time when she was still on the employer's payroll?

I was angry, not at Bob particularly, but at the whole situation. "Are you saying then," I asked, "that you condone her dishonesty?" The words were no sooner out of my mouth than I knew I had committed an unpardonable sin, had made an error that would cost me dearly. A thunderous silence seemed to descend on the office.

Bob looked at me. Did I imagine it or had he blanched under my attack?

"No, Henry," he replied, "I'm not saying that at all. I'm just saying that I'm giving the next project to someone else. Our company policy is always to use more than one supplier, more than one service organization. When the next project comes along I'll consider Rogers & Cowan just as I always have in the past."

I started to say something in response but never got to it. Bob continued, "And now, Henry, I must ask you to leave. I am late for my next appointment." He stood up—a signal that the meeting was over. I left his office, closing the door quietly behind me. I sensed that I had wounded him and I would probably never do business with him again. I had touched a raw nerve, had figuratively slapped him in the face—and it was inexcusable.

I had broken one of my own rules. I had told the client the truth, but brutally, coldly, and insensitively. I had put him in a position from which he couldn't retreat. In one sentence I implicated him in her unscrupulous behavior. You cannot expect to continue to do business with someone you have wounded, or insulted. I paid a high price for breaking my own rule. He has never done business with our firm since that day.

Rogers' Rules for Diplomacy

1) If the other person is speaking softly, consider that he or she may be carrying a big stick.

2) If the other person is speaking loudly, consider that he or she may still be carrying a big stick.

3) Be tactful *always*. Total truth is for your priest or your psychiatrist.

4) Remember that every story has two sides; try looking at the other person's side before you speak.

5) Never alienate people for *any* reason. If you must criticize, do so gently, constructively.

SUGAR-COATING THE TRUTH

Is honesty always the best policy? I say "no." My own theory on
honesty is based on the contention that there are two types of lies
—the "black" lie that results in injury stemming from deception;
and the "white" lie that, as philosopher Mortimer J. Adler explains,
"consists of a harmless deception, or one that even may work to the
benefit of the person deceived."

I do not compromise my integrity if I don't tell my client
that I hated the movie he produced. Will the movie improve
any if I am completely forthright with him? Of course not. Nothing will be gained, although much could be lost if I succeed in
offending him. He would probably resent my bluntness and our relationship would never be the same. Eventually, I would lose the
client.

It *would* compromise my integrity if I told him that I loved his
production—that would be completely dishonest and I wouldn't do
it. There are ways to handle a delicate situation like this, to be
sensitive and still retain one's integrity. I might say, "There's a big
audience out there for a movie like this." This implies that I believe
the film can be financially successful. My personal taste has nothing
to do with the financial outcome of a motion picture. For example,
I was bored by the immensely profitable *Star Wars,* and thoroughly
enjoyed other productions that were financial disasters. With a
comment like "There's a big audience out there for a movie like
this," I am telling the truth. I could also say, "It's fascinating the
way you were able to get such sensitive performances out of the
actors," or "You've made a film that is beautifully directed and
superbly acted."

One evening I drove to Santa Barbara to see a sneak preview of
Green Mansions, a movie that starred Audrey Hepburn, directed
by her then-husband Mel Ferrer. The studio had asked Miss Hepburn not to attend this first public screening of the film, because
they wanted to test it before an impartial audience and make any
necessary changes before they regarded it as a completed produc-

tion, ready for her to see. Mel was in Paris on another assignment. Her agent, Kurt Frings, was in New York. She was depending on me, her long-time friend and public-relations representative, to give her an objective report. "Please call me from a phone booth right after the screening," she requested. "I'll be waiting for your call."

I hated the picture, and walked out of the theater into the street, pacing. "What do I do now?" I thought. "She's counting on this picture, more for Mel than for herself. Their marriage is rocky because her career is zooming and his is floundering. If the movie is successful, it could mean that they'd be able to make a go of their marriage. Am I the one to tell her that the picture is lousy? Besides, I know what happens to the messenger who brings bad news.

"I'm not going to lie and tell her that *Green Mansions* is wonderful. She'll see it herself and she'll never trust me again. I'll have to figure out how to handle it diplomatically."

I went to the phone booth and a moment later Audrey was on the other end of the line. "Well, what do you think?" "I think it needs a lot of work," I replied. There was a pause. "What do you mean?" "I mean that it's a beautiful film with magnificent visual qualities and you give an enchanting performance. The problem is that it's too long, the story line is confused, and the audience got restless a number of times. I don't think they related to a lot of it."

"Oh, I'm sorry." There was disappointment in her voice. "Do you think it can be fixed?" "I don't know," I said. "I'm not a filmmaker. The studio executives are in front of the theater right now arguing among themselves. I don't know how it will be resolved. It would be better if Kurt talked to them in the morning and figured out what changes they are going to make."

Another pause. I thought I heard a sob. "I wanted this so much for Mel," she said. "It means so much to him."

"Maybe they can fix it. Maybe my reaction wasn't typical. Maybe other audiences will react more favorably than this one did, who knows? Maybe it will be a big hit after all. You know there are a hundred case histories of bad sneak previews that turned out to be hits."

"Henry, you're a dear. Thank you for being so gentle with me. I knew what you've been trying to say, and if you were trying to cushion the blow, you did."

Rogers' Half-Dozen Handy Reactions to a Turkey

1) "Audrey, I think it needs a lot of work."
2) "Orson, that movie is simply incredible!"
3) "Roger, I don't believe it. I really don't believe it."
4) "Otto, a lot of people out there are going to love it."
5) "Francis, it looks like a million bucks!"
6) "Ingmar, you've done it again!"

IF THE GAME IS GOING BADLY, CALL FOR "TIME-OUT"

Often, it's a good idea to ask for time to make a decision or express an opinion. No one will criticize you if you say, "I'd like a little time to think it over. I'll get back to you later in the day." This is a particularly useful strategy if you're caught off guard and there's a possibility that a response not thoroughly considered could injure or offend.

In our business I find it advantageous on many occasions to say, "I'd like to think it over and I'll get back to you." I was very fortunate, for example, in not coming to an immediate decision the day that David Scott, our client at Ford Motor Company, assured me that there was no conflict of interest if we decided to represent the new DeLorean automobile—the DMC. Actually, we had represented John DeLorean before we represented Ford. We had worked for him for two years when it became apparent to both of us that our efforts were premature because the revolutionary car was so late in coming to the marketplace. We agreed that a break was in order, and a short time later we began our representation of Ford Motor

Company. A year later DeLorean telephoned from New York. "We're ready, Henry. I'd like you to go back to work for us." I was apprehensive. Would this conflict with our representation of Ford?

"I'm not sure we can do it," I replied. "We're representing Ford now, and I think we might have a conflict of interest."

"I wouldn't regard it that way," countered DeLorean. "We're planning to produce only 20,000 sports cars, and Ford isn't even in the sports-car business. It wouldn't bother me a bit."

I stalled. "I certainly appreciate your call, and I've always enjoyed working with you." (I had) "Give me a little time to think it through and I'll get back to you."

John was not offended. We had developed a close personal relationship over the years. I had been entertained by him and his wife, Christina Ferrare, in New York on numerous occasions, and we had entertained them when they were in Los Angeles.

I thought about it. There really was no conflict. We wouldn't represent General Motors or Chrysler, Toyota or Datsun while we represented Ford because they were obviously competitors. The DMC was different. With their limited production plans, it was like comparing a tiny boutique on Madison Avenue to Macy's or Bloomingdale's. Still, the situation was not clear cut. I was cautious. How would Ford regard it? I called David Scott and told him of my dilemma. What did he think?

"I'm not sure," was his answer. "Let me run it by Walter." (Walter Hayes was his boss.)

The next day David Scott called back. "Walter and I don't feel there is a conflict, and besides, we don't think we have a right to tell you how to handle your business."

I was elated. John DeLorean paid us a very substantial fee and the reinstatement of the DMC to our client list would make a sizeable impact on our earnings for that year.

There was a pause in the conversation. Then David said, "But, Henry, I think it's only fair for me to tell you that Walter is a bit uncomfortable about it. We might be getting back into sports cars one of these days, and then there *would* be a problem."

"What do I do now?" I asked myself. Stall for time, I decided. Think it through.

"Thanks for your confidence," I said to David. "I want to think about it some more. I'll get back to you and let you know what I've decided."

I began to think. The income was tempting, but the word "uncomfortable" bothered me. What did Walter mean—"uncomfortable"? Then I knew what I had to do. My relationship with Ford was too important for me to make them uncomfortable about their relationship with Rogers & Cowan for any reason. I called David Scott again and told him of my decision. I called John DeLorean. "I've decided there's a conflict with Ford. I appreciate your offer but I have to respectfully decline." DeLorean took it graciously and I wished him success on the then highly touted DMC.

About a year later when John DeLorean's photo appeared on the front page of almost every newspaper in the world, I phoned David Scott.

"David, I'm calling to thank you."

"For what?"

"For telling me that it would have made you uncomfortable if we represented the DMC."

"Don't thank me, Henry. You made your own decision."

"I know," I replied, "but if you hadn't used that buzz word, 'uncomfortable,' I would have made a new deal with DeLorean— and if I had—I could very easily had been in that motel room when he was busted by the FBI."

I could sense that David was smiling.

"I guess you're just lucky."

Lucky? I don't think so. I had called "time-out" when I wasn't sure of what my position should be. I didn't feel that I had to make an immediate decision, and by giving myself extra time I came to the right one.

LOOSE LIPS SINK SHIPS

During World War II, the government had millions of posters on display in public buildings, railway stations, bus depots, elevators, and restrooms, warning "Loose Lips Sink Ships." Today the dangers of gossip and innuendo are still with us. If you can't speak well of others, don't speak at all.

"She's having an affair with her boss." "I know that he's been padding his expense account." "She looks at me very peculiarly, so she must be a lesbian." "He doesn't deserve that salary increase." "I overheard the boss say that business has dropped off and he'll be forced to fire some people." "I hear that Jim has his hand in the till and that they're closing in on him."

This is the kind of gossip that is harmful to everyone. It can ruin a person's career, destroy the morale of a company, cause a rift between a boss and his employee, or irreparably damage one's reputation. What does it do to the purveyor of gossip? He loses his credibility, his respect, and his standing in the company.

Your friends may relish the gossip you're dishing out. They may be entranced with your tales of your colleagues' erotic experiences or even their personal foibles, but that moment you leave, they will turn on you. "I wouldn't trust him an inch," someone will say scornfully. "If he gossips that way about Samantha and Joe, tomorrow he'll be telling stories about me." "If he's disloyal to his boss, and gives us information that should remain confidential, how can I respect him as a human being?"

Again, put yourself in the other guy's shoes. Look at yourself through his eyes. What do you see? Someone who deserves to be well liked, admired, respected? No, not really. Rather someone who will be discarded, even scorned, the moment he can't think of another piece of gossip. If you are interested in psychorelations, stop gossiping and spreading news that you picked up inadvertently— stop hurting people for no reason. You're really hurting yourself. Do you want to do yourself some good? Start to say nice things about the other guy. You will find that you are earning new respect.

Even more important than gossip is the overt or inadvertent discussion of company news when you are outside the office. We know about industrial sabotage. There are companies who plant "spies" in the offices and factories of their competitors in order to get inside information on what is happening. It is also normal procedure for many large industrial companies to require their employees to wear name tags, and all visitors are required to wear identification badges. In fact, there are companies that forbid visitors to walk down the hallways unless they are accompanied by a company employee. Just recently, a security guard stopped me in a Texas Instruments hallway as I departed from the men's room. I was not accompanied by an employee. He escorted me back to the office I had been visiting.

I mention these ultrasensitive companies only to illustrate that an employee of *any* company has an obligation not to repeat what he hears in his office during the course of a day. Someone was fired. Someone was hired. Someone got a new position and someone just received a new contract. Joe is in trouble with the boss because he sent in his report two days after it was due. We just lost a client. We just signed a new contract. Someone says, "There's going to be a wage freeze because profits are down." Someone else reports that "earnings are up and everyone's going to get a bonus." Half the news is usually true and half of it untrue. Whether you are reporting good news or bad, true or untrue, you are doing yourself a disservice and you are doing someone else a disservice by reporting news that is not ready to be reported. Do yourself a favor. Keep it to yourself.

DON'T PUT THE OTHER GUY DOWN

I was walking down the hallway toward my office one day when I inadvertently overheard a conversation taking place behind a closed door. Someone was saying, "Joe [one of our associates] is really a louse. I'm telling you—he's evil. He manipulates people, he has no integrity, and I don't trust him for a minute." I recognized the voice. He was one of our up-and-coming young men, someone we were grooming for a top position in our company. He was talking about the person who had hired him, his mentor.

In one quick moment my faith in the young man vanished. In biting the hand that fed him he displayed both poor business judgment and a lack of loyalty. This young man's imprudent remark demonstrated his potential to be an in-house troublemaker. If he talked with such lack of discretion within the walls of our office, how could I trust him to speak well of Rogers & Cowan once he walked out the front door?

You are not expected to admire and respect everyone you work with. You would not be a normal human being if you did. But if you really want to protect your public image, remember that if you can't say something nice about someone, just *keep your mouth shut.*

I was interviewing a young man for a job one day and asked him why he was no longer with his former public-relations firm.

"Because my boss was a rat," he replied. "He treated me shabbily, didn't reimburse me for legitimate expenses, and reneged on the salary increase he had promised me."

You don't have to guess: I didn't hire him. He didn't know that his ex-employer was a friend of mine; I found it hard to believe that his remarks were true. More important, this applicant's comments made it clear that he lacked a sense of psychorelations, that he had no idea how to relate to me. He unsold himself with one comment; but he should have known what my reaction would be. "If he talks about his ex-boss that way," I thought, "someday he'll be saying the same things about me." I don't want a person who thinks in such negative terms about his employer to be a member of our organization.

But wait. Suppose that he had told the truth. What if his boss really *had* been a rat? Suppose he actually had left his previous job for the reasons he had stated? Should he have lied in order to make a favorable impression on me?

Yes! He hadn't come to my office to take a truth test. He had come to get a job, and he could easily have named any number of more tactful reasons—reasons that would not have offended me— why he was no longer associated with the other firm. A little white lie that wouldn't have hurt anyone, and might have resulted in my giving him the job.

WINNING THROUGH NEUTRALITY

Because I am concerned with the continued success of my business and because my public image is tied to it, I generally don't express my strong personal opinions about sensitive issues to a client, a prospective client, or a journalist.

What are sensitive issues? Politics, world affairs, sexual mores, Israeli/Arab relations, Apartheid, Ronald Reagan, deployment of nuclear missiles in Western Europe, and numerous others to which there are no ready and simple answers. Many of my readers may call this a "Pollyanna attitude." I don't agree. I am willing to discuss these subjects with my family, my friends, and even casual acquaintances because I enjoy participating in lively talk. I never expect to win anyone over to my point of view if they are on the opposite side; still, the debate is stimulating and it gets my juices going. But what is to be gained by getting into a heated discussion with a client who is pro-Apartheid if I am unequivocally opposed to the policies of the government of South Africa? Why should I risk offending a prospective client who is an anti-Reagan, anti-nuke, liberal Mondale supporter by extolling the virtues of the Ronald Reagan administration? How many Arab clients will be sympathetic to the public-relations representative who insists that Menachem Begin was right in settling the West Bank?

I won't risk breaking off an important relationship by getting into an argument that I can't possibly win. Am I going to convince anyone that he's wrong? No. He won't convince me either. Acrimonious discussions about nonbusiness subjects leave scars long after the shouting has died down.

When I really want to have a discussion on an important subject, I'll have it with my personal friends and family. In the business world, I keep my opinions to myself. Bear in mind that as you become more successful, the phrase "it's a small world" becomes truer and truer. People change companies in the same field; they get promoted just like you do. The person whose opinions you belittle today could be hired as your superior tomorrow. Life in business is a lot easier if you don't make enemies.

Rogers' Catechism for Businessmen and Women

- Would I ever say anything disparaging about a client?
  What? And bite the hand that feeds me?
- Would I ever say anything disparaging about an ex-client?
  No, he might be back as a client next week.
- Would I say anything disparaging about a competitor?
  No, because I know that I win greater respect by praising him.
- Would I say anything disparaging about an employee?
  No, because if I did, people would question my business judgment in hiring him in the first place.

3

It's show time: the job interview

DOES THE THOUGHT of being interviewed for a job frighten you? Do you get goose bumps just thinking about it? Do your hands get clammy when you envision yourself walking into the office of that formidable-looking man or woman who may decide your destiny? Can't you just see them sitting there, looking you over, waiting for the right moment to say, "Sorry, you're not right for the position"?

If these are your reactions, don't be ashamed. Most people react the same way you do. Audrey Hepburn once told me that she ran to the ladies' room and threw up before being interviewed for *Gigi*, her first important stage role. Charlton Heston relates that his knees shook when he applied for his first job on the Broadway stage.

Every professional actor who steps on a stage or before a camera is nervous about confronting the audience. And, if you have any sense or sensibility, you will be nervous too about your job interview. But, like a good actor, if you prepare for this performance properly, you will be rewarded with the interviewer's admiration, and possibly the job. So get ready to learn your lines, put on your costume, and strut your stuff.

PERSISTENCE PAYS: GETTING AN INTERVIEW

When producer Sherry Lansing was asked, "How does one get a job?", the woman who at the time was president of Twentieth Century-Fox films gave a one-word answer: "persistence." She then went on to explain how she got her first job. She had set her sights on one particular person she wanted to work for. She called him for an appointment. No reply from the secretary. She called again—and again—and again. She called seventeen times, and by then, her prospective employer was so weary of seeing the same message on his desk every day, "Sherry Lansing called," that he finally agreed to see her. He gave her the job and her career was launched.

Most people don't really work at getting a job as industriously as they should. They see or try to see a few people a day and feel that they have done all they can in that twenty-four-hour period. But job hunting is a full-time occupation. You must go about it in an organized fashion, knowing exactly what kind of job you are looking for, and where you are going to look for it.

The more time you spend at organized, logical job hunting, the better your chances for getting a job. The more interviews you request, the more you will get. The more you get, the better your chances of getting an offer. The more offers you receive, the better your chances of getting the job you want. Persistence counts!

Rogers' Pointers on Persistence

1) Decide who your prospective employers are. Call and ask for an interview during lunch or breakfast or after closing. Explain that you are working and consequently cannot meet during normal working hours. Keep calling and calling and calling until you get the appointment or are told that the prospective employer does not wish to see you.

2) Do your homework. Study your own situation and what job

alternatives there are. Decide what your next move upward should be if you are to continue on the road to success.

3) Don't be reluctant to keep pushing. The prospective employer is more interested in you while you are working than when he discovers you are out of a job.

Rona Was Persistent, Too: Make Yourself "Employable"

Rona Barrett, "Miss Rona" to millions of television viewers, attributes her success to the fact that I once chided her into losing twenty-five pounds and improving her diction by taking long, arduous lessons from a diction teacher. She was one of my daughter's closest friends in those days, and lived with us when she first moved from New York to Hollywood. When my daughter Marcia asked me if Rona could talk to me about her career, I agreed. She walked timidly into our bar/den one Saturday morning and talked to me about her ambition to be another Louella Parsons or Hedda Hopper and to eventually become a television commentator. As gently and as politely as I could, I told her that she had no chance.

"You have the talent," I told her, "but you don't have the 'extras.' You must present yourself so that people will want to look at you and listen to you." Then I gave her a list of specifics of what I thought she would have to do before she had even a chance for a successful career.

Years later Rona told me that after I lectured her she went up to her room and cried. Then her tears turned to anger. "I'll show him," she said to herself. "I'll show him that I can be successful." Rona did show me. In a few years, she managed to transform herself into the elegant, chic, well-spoken woman you see on your television screens.

You may react in other ways. If your present or prospective employer says "no," it may discourage you from ever trying to move ahead again—or it may inspire you to eventually become the president of another company.

Whatever the result of the job interview may be, sitting across the desk from your boss or prospective employer and trying to convince him that you're the person for the job is never easy. The result of that job interview depends entirely on you. It depends on the first impression you make when you walk in the door, and what you say and how you conduct yourself in the next ten or fifteen minutes. When you finally stand up and leave, the outcome is directly related to how well you have sold yourself.

JOB-HUNTING ETIQUETTE

You may ask yourself whether it's ethical to look for another job while you are on someone else's payroll.

Remember that you and your present boss have equal privileges. He may be dissatisfied with your performance and may already be looking for a replacement for you without your knowing it. You have the same right to seek out another job. No, it isn't unethical.

What will happen if your boss discovers that you're job hunting? Let's face it, you might get fired, so it's up to you whether you want to take that chance. Remember that you'll never get ahead in the world if you always play it safe. Yes, he may fire you, but he may also give you a raise if you promise to stop looking. And there is another alternative to contemplate. Your boss may be shocked into talking about your dissatisfaction. When you explain that you are anxious to better yourself, there is always the chance that he will offer you the better position you are looking for.

PREPARING FOR THE INTERVIEW: I'M HIRING YOU, NOT YOUR RESUME

The most preparation that employment advisers ever suggest is a resume. There are some companies that make a substantial profit by helping employment seekers write one up. But a resume is only a step—and probably not the *first* step—you must take in preparing for a job interview.

Yet, you will need a resume, because in some cases it will be demanded of you. I, for one, never read them. They tell me nothing. It doesn't matter to me where you went to school, whether you are married or unmarried, or whether you are twenty-three, thirty-three, or fifty-three. I want to see you in person and give you an opportunity to "sell me." However, I'm probably different from other employers. Experts in the employment field agree that a resume is often useful as a reminder for the employer.

Most job hunters send their resumes ahead. I don't believe in that approach. You should leave your resume behind as a reminder. My interest was piqued one day by a young lady who told me that she didn't have her resume with her, and that she would mail it to me that same day. Subsequently, I hired her. A number of months later she confided to me that after our interview she went home and tailored her resume to the specifics of what we had discussed. There was no irrelevant information for me to wade through. It was prepared specifically for my needs. Very clever.

Don't depend on a resume to get you a job. Dr. Franklin Murphy, chairman of the executive committee of the multi-billion-dollar Times-Mirror Corporation, summed it up. When, as my guest lecturer at UCLA one evening, he said, "When I interview a job applicant I am first interested in how he presents himself. How does he look; how is he dressed; what does he say; how does he answer my questions?" Dr. Murphy can't get the answers to those questions by reading a resume. But you will need one, so here are a few suggestions.

Rogers' Tips on Preparing a Resume

1) Be specific.
2) Don't tell me you want a career in communications. I don't know whether that means you want a job as a telephone lineman,

a computer software operator, or a public-relations specialist.
3) Make every line relevant. I really don't care from which high
school you graduated.
4) Hand-tailor your resume for the company you are visiting.
Who said you should have only one resume?
5) Make your prospective employer feel important. Type his
name on your resume:

Resume—JOHN HOPKINS
Prepared Exclusively for: HENRY C. ROGERS
CHAIRMAN—ROGERS & COWAN, INC.

6) Double-space the typing. It's easier to read.

DO YOUR HOMEWORK: BE PREPARED

My own experience in interviewing literally hundreds of people—
men, women, young, old, middle-aged—suggests that fewer than
one person in ten comes in properly prepared.

Millions of students spend hundreds of millions of hours cramming for final examinations. That preparation is important for them
to graduate, get a high school diploma or a college degree. But isn't
it equally important for them to spend an hour or two "cramming"
for a job interview?

The other day, the door of my office opened and my secretary
walked in with an attractive young man. "Mr. Rogers, this is John
Andrews. Mr. Fischer had asked you to see him about a position."

I stood up from my desk and said, "Good morning, John, take
that chair over there." I walked over to him, shook his weak,
clammy hand, and sat down on the couch facing him. "Our mutual
friend, Mr. Fischer, tells me that you're interested in getting into
the public-relations business."

"Yes, I am," came the response.

I waited for him to continue. He didn't. I picked up the conversation. "Why does it interest you?"

"Well, I guess I like people and I get along with people very well."

I groaned inwardly: "Oh, God," I said to myself, "another one of those. Why did Fischer stick me with this guy?" Well, I'd be polite, but I knew what was coming next. "Yes, of course," I said, "that's very important in any business or profession. What do you know about public relations?"

"Not very much," he admitted.

I tried to catch his eye, but I couldn't. He was looking at my left shoe. I went on. "How much is 'not very much'?"

There was a long pause. "Well, I guess I really don't know anything at all about it."

"Excuse me, young man," I said as politely as I could, "but how can you be interested in public relations as a career if you don't know anything about it? I suggest that before we discuss the subject further, you should do some homework.

"There are dozens of books on public relations in the public library. I suggest you read three or four of them. After you're finished, call my secretary and make another appointment. I'll be delighted to see you again. Next time, we can really talk about why you're interested in public relations."

I stood up, opened the door, and the young man left, dejectedly, still looking down at the floor. I never heard from him again.

Doesn't common sense dictate that John should have learned something about public relations before he came to see me? Shouldn't he have read at least one book, tracked down at least one article? Mightn't he have asked someone, "What is public relations?" before he asked me for an appointment?

Believe it or not, this young man is not an exception. I have had the same experience a hundred times with a hundred John Andrewses who were as equally unprepared. It is significant that not one of them ever came back to see me. The reason is obvious. Either they were never sufficiently interested in public relations to heed my advice and read a number of books on the subject, or they followed my suggestions and discovered that public relations was of no interest to them after all.

Let's go back and spot the mistakes John made in his interview with me.

1) He gave me a weak, clammy handshake. It should have been firm and dry—even if he had had to wipe his hand with a handkerchief the moment before he extended it to me.

2) His first answer was "Yes, I am." Then he stopped. He should have continued for a moment, and explained what he had to offer in the area of public relations.

3) He should have prepared a better answer than "I like people" when I asked him why public relations interested him. He could have said, "Public relations deals with communications, and that's a rapidly growing area that I know would intrigue me once I got into it." He could also have said, "I am a people-related person and I know that I can be more successful in a field that allows me to use my ability to relate to people rather than to feed software into a computer." He could have given me any one of a hundred answers, all better than the vague "I like people."

4) He lost me when he said he knew nothing about public relations. Obviously, he had not been sufficiently interested to learn something about it before he came to see me, or, worse yet, it had not occurred to him that it was even necessary.

5) He never looked at me. My left shoe, however, was of great interest to him.

6) He was completely unprepared to have a meeting with the head of a public-relations firm, who was meeting him as a favor to a mutual friend.

I have no quarrel with the young adult who has not decided whether he wishes to pursue public relations, advertising, archaeology or pharmacy; I talk regularly to young people who are looking for guidance. But it doesn't take excessive brain power to conclude that they should know something about a profession before they approach a job interview in a field that might become their life's work.

Besides knowing what to expect regarding the person who will be interviewing you, it is also quite useful to know what that person will be expecting from you. While some likes and dislikes may be idiosyncratic, there tend to be a number of qualities that employers agree make a generally favorable impression.

Dr. Franklin Murphy, at that same UCLA lecture referred to earlier, summarized succinctly what impresses him when he interviews a job applicant. "I start by asking the person to tell me about himself. The manner in which the question is answered gives me a clue as to whether the person has possibilities and if I should press further. I look first for credibility, and I'm usually quickly able to spot it or recognize the lack of it. If, for example, the person being interviewed has done any homework on me, he knows of my interest in art. If he expresses an interest in art, I can soon determine whether it is a genuine interest, or whether he just mentioned it in order to impress me.

"As we talk, the person presents an image of himself. I am interested in the way he looks. A neat body indicates a neat mind. I'm also quick to perceive how he expresses himself. So few people have the ability to use the English language properly that I impressed with the rare person who does. I look for the person whose verbal expression makes clear that he knows what he is going to say before he says it. The person who tries to organize what he's going to say while he is saying it invariably gets mixed up, and, when that happens, he usually loses the opportunity to present the image of himself that he hopes to convey."

William Fine, former chairman of Frances Denney, the cosmetics firm, and now a top executive at Dan River, in answer to my question, said about job applicants, "I observe their degree of security. When I majored in speech at Kenyon College, John Wilson Black, head of their speech department then, told me that when someone puts his hands or fingers close to his mouth while talking, it's a sign of helping the words out of his mouth—a sign that he is insecure. I've never forgotten that.

"I do like to receive a firm handshake—from a woman as well as a man—because it suggests confidence.

"I like people to look me in the eye while talking. I listen for humor. I want to hear realistic opinions and attitudes. I like people to tell me about a couple of times in their career when they weren't 'brilliant.' I look for competitiveness. One thing I don't appreciate is being told how unfair someone's last employer was. I always visualize my company or me getting that kind of playback next.

"And, finally, I like people who think they are lucky. They usually are."

Remember, your challenge as a job seeker is to sell yourself to prospective employers such as Dr. Murphy, Mr. Fine, and myself. How do you make a vivid, favorable impression?

You have a decided advantage over any other job applicants if you show me that:

- You can fit in with the other people in our organization. You are enthusiastic about the prospect of working for us and are equally enthusiastic about the specific position we have been discussing.
- You care about your personal appearance and understand the importance of making a favorable impression.
- You have the drive and ambition that makes for a successful employee.
- You have the basic skills that qualify you for the position.

Add up all of this, and you will stand out among all the others who are competing for the same job.

Rogers' Checklist for Job-Interview Preparedness

1) Make sure you *really* want the job. Or if you are seeing the interviewer on an exploratory basis, simply for career guidance, be sure you say so.

2) Do your homework on the industry that interests you by boning up on it at the local library. Identify trade journals and magazines in the field.

3) Do your homework on the company that interests you. Get information from friends or acquaintances; obtain the company brochure or annual report. Understand the position of the company within the industry.

4) Do your homework, if possible, on the person who has agreed to interview you.

5) Dress to make the best impression. Find out what kinds of clothes the other professionals wear and dress accordingly.

6) Prepare your sales approach. Be prepared to tell the interviewer why it is in his best interest to hire you.

7) Practice your lines. Let a friend interview you and give a critique.

8) Be thoughtful after your interview. Write a thank-you note after your interview, regardless of whether or not you were successful.

SELLING YOURSELF ON A JOB INTERVIEW

If the steps for job-interview preparedness have been followed, you should be ready for a hypothetical appointment to see me.

Pretend you are applying to Rogers & Cowan, and I will be interviewing you. You will have already done your homework on our company and on me, and you have prepared your argument as to why I should engage your services. However, you will probably discover that your interview may not go as smoothly as you planned. I might be on the telephone finishing up a call before I turn my attention to you. I might be in the middle of a conversation with my secretary.

This is an opportunity to size me up. Am I in a good or a bad mood? Do I seem to be at ease or do I seem to be rushed or distracted? Look around my office. Look at the furniture. Look at the paintings on the wall and the objets d'art on the coffee table. All this should give you a hint as to the type of person I am.

You will sell yourself to me if you say, "You seem to be very busy, Mr. Rogers. Maybe it would be better if I came back another time." I will immediately be impressed with your perception that you caught me at a bad time and that you are considerate enough to offer to make another appointment.

You will also sell yourself to me if, before we start our serious conversation, you comment on something that has caught your eye in my office. It might be my desk, or a photograph, a painting or an artifact. If the *Wall Street Journal* is on my desk, you might comment on what happened in the stock market yesterday. If there is a diploma displayed on the wall, you can compare it with your own.

If, for example, you tell me that you read my book, *Walking the Tightrope,* and learned something about public relations from it, I'll have an added interest in you.

I am a human being, too, and am as susceptible to compliments as anyone else. If you are bright enough to perceive my interests, and find a way to include the subject in our conversation, I'll be impressed.

Sit up straight and speak in a firm voice. Your mother told you this a hundred times, but you never paid attention to her. I am immediately distressed by the young person who slouches down in his chair, and is not sufficiently aware of the importance of his own appearance to sit erect and to address me in a clear, strong voice.

I have already told you to dress for the occasion. I'll repeat it. Try to determine in advance how you can make a favorable first impression by what you are wearing. Most of the men in our Beverly Hills office don't wear ties. Open-neck shirts, sweaters, and sports jackets are the order of the day. I am one of the few who dresses quite formally, however, and if you were to come in to see me wearing a proper suit, shirt, and tie, I would be impressed that you had anticipated my personal preference and thought the interview sufficiently important to dress appropriately.

As for women, the dress code is equally flexible. I judge the intelligence of a woman, to a certain extent at least, by the manner in which she dresses for a job interview. I love to look at sexy women, but not in my office. A shirtmaker dress is always appropriate as is a suit with a blouse. A loose sweater with well-fitting slacks is a proper combination. If a woman walks into my office for a job interview with a plunging neckline, a tight sweater, a miniskirt, or pants so tight that her buttocks are prominent, she has no chance of getting a job with me no matter how talented she may be. Her lack of sound business judgment outweighs her talent. I believe most male employers agree with me.

Marilyn Bender, a reporter for the *New York Times,* once stated that a major obstacle to success for a woman is the problem of dressing appropriately. She said that most business women looked "sloppy," but in my opinion the problem is that many women have a lack of style and a tendency to underdress or overdress. My own advice to business women is that they should dress as if they were already executives. If you're a secretary, or even still in the mailroom, and if you're looking upward, it is important that you look, as Michael Korda stated in his book *Success,* "as if you will fit in with those above you, not those at your level." Be on time. In granting you an interview, I have opened the door to my office to you. Give me the courtesy of promptness. You don't know how precise I am. Maybe every minute of my day counts. I might be the kind of person who expects that a four o'clock appointment takes place at exactly four, not five minutes after four. To be sure, arrive at your appointment five or ten minutes before the scheduled time.

Display confidence. It is important that you walk into that meeting at least with the appearance of self-assurance, convinced that you are well qualified for the job. Are you sure you want this job? Can you anticipate the questions that will be asked of you, and do you have the answers?

Describe how you can make a contribution to my business. What are you going to do for me? It may sound presumptuous to you, but I will be impressed if you tell me you are confident that, with proper training, you can enhance my company's success. This holds true whether you are applying for a job as a mailroom clerk or as vice-president. Then give me some good reasons. Figure out for yourself what those reasons are. If you have confidence in yourself, you can make a good case for yourself. Tell me what you're going to do for me. Don't ask me what I'm going to do for you.

Be enthusiastic about the prospect of working for our organization. Having done your homework, you will know what distinguishes us from other companies, and you should cite your reasons for wanting to become associated with us. If we are among the leaders in the field, don't be reluctant to stress that. Impress me with the fact that you hope one day to be a leader and that one way to attain such a goal is to work for people who are already recognized as such. Don't flatter me. I'll see through that, but if you show me an inspired zeal and fervor in your presentation, I'll be impressed.

Practice active communication. Look directly at me. Speak to *me*, not the wall in back of me. You cannot sell yourself to me if you don't look at me, because you would be depriving me of your reactions. I'll be asking you questions. Listen to them carefully. You also have a better chance of selling yourself if I know that you are really listening. When I ask a question, give me more than a yes or no answer, but keep your answers short and precise. Stick to the point. Don't go off on tangents; don't ramble on about irrelevancies.

Read the newspaper and watch the TV news that morning. In addition to your qualifications, your experience, and your schooling, I may be interested in your general knowledge and awareness. I may assess that awareness by asking you what you thought of the president's speech, or, depending on the job you are applying for, about an item that appeared that day in the business, entertainment, sports, or real-estate pages.

If you can follow that plan of attack, come prepared, and wow me with psychorelations—*you've got the job!*

Rogers' Plan of Attack for Interviews

1) Be prepared.

2) Arrive ahead of time for your appointment, knowing what you want to say.

3) Walk in with a confident air and give me a firm, dry handshake.

4) Reject my offer of a cigarette or coffee. And don't chew gum.

5) Sit up straight and speak with a firm voice.

6) Tell me you have a resume but don't offer it to me until you are ready to leave.

7) Tell me why you are qualified for the job you're seeking.

8) Let me know that you've done your homework before visiting me.

9) Tell me what you are going to do for me. Speak to me in terms of my own interests.

10) Speak enthusiastically about the prospect of joining my firm.

11) Give me the impression that you are a worldly person with a variety of interests.

12) Practice active communication—look at me, and listen to me.

HOW TO "UNSELL" YOURSELF

In addition to the importance of preparation and positive presentation, the job hunter should be aware of a few simple pitfalls that are guaranteed to "unsell" almost any potential employer.

Don't falsify your background. Don't try to tell me about experiences you haven't really had. You will be unmasked and rejected.

I'll ask you another question or two and I'll eventually find you out, at which point any enthusiasm I might have been feeling over your application would shrink. I'll think much better of you if you give it to me straight. Even if you get away with lying to me and you get the job, it will come out one day and then I'll find an excuse to fire you. Level with me.

Don't tell me your life story unless I ask for specific details. I'm not really interested in where you came from and where you went to high school. Just tell me why you are qualified and how you are going to help me improve my business. If employers are interested in such details, they will ask.

Don't ask me to read your resume. If I want to read it, I'll ask you for it. When I agreed to see you, it was because I was interested in talking with you in person. Your personality—not your resume —will make the impression on me, good or bad.

Don't ask me if I mind if you smoke. This isn't a social gathering. You should want me to concentrate on you, not your cigarette.

Don't worry about being nervous. Everyone gets nervous on a job interview. You can relieve a little of your anxiety by remembering that your prospective boss gets nervous at times, too, and he will, consequently, understand if you get flustered.

Don't ask me questions until I give you an opening. Many interviewees, eager to demonstrate their interests and knowledge, zealously proceed to interrogate the interviewer and, in so doing, end up unselling themselves. The employer interviews the applicant. The applicant does not interview the employer. So don't ask me how many employees we have or what our vacation policy is. When I am sufficiently impressed with you and begin to think about hiring you, I will invite your questions.

Going on a job interview can be a difficult experience, but remember that nearly everyone has gone through it at one point in his life. If you are just starting out, it is your first important opportunity to sell yourself. Your first job interview may turn out to be a disaster, but don't get discouraged. Think about everything you did wrong. Remember all the mistakes you made. Write them down.

Look at them. Study them. You will find that the next time around you will make a much better impression.

GETTING TOP DOLLAR

What I am about to tell you will cost me and other employers dearly, for most employees settle for too little money in their initial negotiations. There are a few simple secrets to negotiating for top dollar.

We must start with the premise that your responsibility is, of course, to get as high a salary as possible within reason. My responsibility, as chairman of our company, is to maximize our profits, and one way of accomplishing that is to keep our costs—including your salary—down.

The most effective interview strategy for you is not to bring up the subject of money. If I introduce it before I've given you an indication that I'm interested in hiring you, don't give me an answer. Tell me that there is little point in our discussing salary until I've decided that I'm definitely interested in hiring you.

Once the employer has committed himself, even tentatively, to hiring you, then you have the advantage in salary negotiations.

Initially, you must name an amount higher than you expect to receive before the interviewer names a figure that he is willing to pay. If you mentioned $25,000 a year (even though you only expect $20,000), you've given me a ball-park figure from which we can start to negotiate. Make sure that the figure you mention is one that you can justify, and that it is consistent with the upper rates for the kind of work for which you are applying.

I might say to you that the position has never paid more than $20,000. Now comes your opportunity to sell me. Explain to me that maybe it never paid more than $20,000 before because the people who held the job previously weren't worth more than that, and then go on to explain why you are. We are now in the midst of a negotiation. The longer you can keep me in this discussion, the better chance you have of my paying you the amount you've asked for.

Roberta Greene, one of Rogers & Cowan's top executives, surprised me in our first salary-negotiation discussion by rejecting our substantial offer and requesting an additional $100 per week.

She said later, "I guess that was nervy of me, but I did have an advantage. I had a good job, and I decided that if I was to work for Rogers & Cowan, it should be in a position rather than just a job. I decided before I walked in what salary I wanted, and your offer was $100 a week less than I had planned. When you made me your offer, I knew that if I accepted it I would weaken my relationship with you. But even more important than that, I would weaken my relationship with myself.

"I decided that if I were you, I would hire me, and that's why I felt that I had to hold out for the extra $100 a week." Roberta was right. I was impressed with her approach and hired her on her terms.

Most salaries are negotiable. If you don't speak up in your own self-interest and try to impress me with your worth, then I'm not going to think you're worth very much.

When you try to convince me that I should pay you $25,000, keep your argument on a business level. Tell me of your accomplishments and why you are convinced that you are worth $25,000. Don't tell me how much money you *need*. That is not my concern.

There will come a moment when I ask you how much you were earning in your last job. This is a standard negotiating ploy for employers. Tell the truth, but don't fall into the trap of negotiating with me on the basis of that salary. If you were receiving less money, say so, but explain to me the difference between this job and the other. Tell me I should pay you what you are worth to me, not what you were worth to someone else.

Rarely will a potential employer be upset if you negotiate aggressively for your salary. He is *always* trying to hire you for less than you are worth, and if he really wants you he will pay your price— or at least make a counteroffer. If you settle for less than the salary you've suggested, there will also be the implication that your employer "owes" the difference to you when you are negotiating an increase six months hence.

Not being afraid to ask for money is a sign of strength. The person who does it well is regarded as a good business person.

Rogers' Rules for Getting Top Dollar

1) Know the financial parameters of the job you are seeking.

2) Don't bring up the subject of money. Wait for the interviewer to do that.

3) If he asks you what salary you expect before he indicates his interest, stall him. Tell him that until he decides that you are right for his organization, salary is not an issue.

4) Once interest is indicated and he begins to discuss salary, ask for top dollar.

5) When you negotiate, keep your discussions on a business level. Your prospective employer at this point is not interested in your personal needs.

6) Don't sell yourself too cheaply. If the offer is below your needs and expectations, ask politely for time to reconsider. Then, when you are not under pressure, realistically evaluate the offer in the context of other job possibilities.

4

Success and the office game

Most of you reading this book work for someone else. You have a boss; in fact, you probably have several. This chapter is a boss's eye view of the office game and how to play it—what you as an employee can do to show the company you have "the right stuff."

CORPORATE HIERARCHY AND THE OFFICE GAME

There is a hierarchy in every business, every government agency, every educational institution. From the mom-and-pop grocery store to the conglomerate with many thousands of employees, the pecking order is there. It's a little like the army. The man on the bottom reports to someone a step above him on the organization chart, who in turn reports to someone higher up. If you're looking at a large company from the top down you will first see the chairman/chief executive officer. Under him is the president/chief operating officer, and then, in gradually descending order, an executive vice-president, a number of senior vice-presidents, vice-presidents, assistant vice-presidents, general managers, assistant managers, and down the line until you get to the janitor and garage attendant.

Each of these institutions is a hierarchy where someone reports to someone else who is a rung up on the corporate ladder. Because a substantial number of career-minded people want to move up that ladder, you can readily understand the existence of the phenomenon called "the office game." It involves the interrelationship between people on different levels of the hierarchy. It determines who sets policy and who sees that the policy is carried out, who gets promoted and who gets passed over, who decides that the air conditioning is set at sixty-eight or seventy-nine degrees, who uses the executive bathroom and who uses the public restroom, who has reserved parking space, and who must fend for himself.

There are those who perceive the office game as distasteful and want no part of it. If that person is ambitious, he will soon discover his ambitions are thwarted. The ambitious person learns quickly that he must become a player in the office game, and that there are certain unwritten rules that must be followed. Granted, some unique mavericks go their own way, and through drive, personality, ability, and chutzpah, ignore these unwritten rules and still make it to the top, but they are exceptions. It's time that the unwritten rules were spelled out.

Rogers' Rules for Winning the Office Game

1) Know the power structure—both formal and informal.
2) Make yourself known.
3) Honk your own horn.
4) Be a team player.
5) Don't always play by the rules.
6) Make corporate end runs—ever so carefully.
7) Seek out responsibility.
8) Be an early bird.

9) Leave your personal problems at home.

10) Run faster than anyone else.

Know the Power Structure

When you first join an organization, study the power structure. Who is important, who isn't, and who is in a position to help you move ahead.

I see many young people who sit down at their assigned desk and never look up until they leave the company's employ or are moved into a new position. If your immediate superior doesn't personally introduce you to everyone in the organization (it depends on the size of the organization, of course), then make it your own responsibility. Introduce yourself to the person at the next desk and in the next office. Stop people as you are walking down the hall, tell them your name, and ask them for theirs. Find out whom they work for, and what they do.

Never have lunch alone. That half hour or hour is your opportunity to find out how the office operates, what makes it tick, who the principal players are, and how they relate to each other. You will need that information if you are to succeed at office politics. Understand that there is a formal power structure, as represented by the organization chart, and an informal power structure—the one that really works. At least go through the motions of reading the corporate policy manual. In it you will probably find an "official" organization chart, together with "official" job descriptions for everyone.

You will probably be given a 400-page looseleaf notebook that no one has read lately, since it was compiled by a long-forgotten management consultant firm twenty years ago. It will tell you that "everything you want to know about how the business is run is contained in these pages." It just isn't true. What is indicated on the printed page, and what actually happens in a company, are often completely different.

One day an associate walked into my office. He wasn't sure how many weeks of severance pay he should give to a departing employee. "You don't have to ask me that," I told him. "It's all spelled out in the company policy manual." "Policy manual?" he asked. "I never knew we had one." I was shocked.

My associate had been with us for three years. He didn't know we had a company policy manual. I investigated. How could such a thing happen? I discovered that the person whose obligation it was to have a meeting with each new employee had forgotten that explaining the company manual was one of her obligations. We assumed that everyone who joined our firm was completely briefed on all our rules and procedures but they weren't. To my horror, I learned that unless one specifically asked, they had no information on medical insurance, holidays, bonuses, life insurance, withholding tax deductions, severance pay, education and vacation policies. The situation has since been straightened out, but I'm certain that it also exists in many companies—particularly small ones.

The way the business is run is better discovered if you sit down with a group of secretaries in the company cafeteria while they are munching on their tuna fish sandwiches, or learned from two assistant managers who stop at the corner bar for a drink before they go home for dinner. In fact, the office cafeteria and the local bar are two great places to begin to learn how the power structure *really* works.

Make a point to learn who's who and who does what. Be aware of "ringers"—people whose job titles are less than commensurate with the power they wield. Many a secretary has her boss's ear on important decisions. If the kid in the mailroom is the president's nephew, you can be sure he won't be in the mailroom for long.

Also be on the lookout for "dead wood," people who have been kicked upstairs with impressive titles and nothing important to do. Currying favor with these folks, exalted though their titles may be, won't get you anywhere.

Once you have learned the workings of the power structure, use it to your advantage. Use your psychorelations skills to let the people who matter know you're there.

Make Yourself Known

You must become more than a name on the organization chart, for you can't make a favorable impression until the company becomes aware of your presence.

A cheery good morning is the first step, and look the other person right smack in the eye when you're saying it. There is a young lady in our office who has never said good morning to me. Of course, I've never said good morning to her because she always averts her eyes when she see me coming down the hall and invariably ducks into someone's office before she gets close to me. One day I'll stop her in the hallway, give her my biggest, cheeriest good morning, and see what happens.

There are other ways of making yourself known. You can arrange to go up or down the elevator with the person you would like to cultivate. You might pop your head into his office and say, "I was just going to get myself a cup of coffee, would you like me to get one for you?" Send him a memo about something you feel will interest him. You might attach a clipping from the morning paper he may have missed. Stop him in the hall and ask him for some advice on a new restaurant that recently opened in the neighborhood.

All of this is applicable to impressing one person. But if you want to impress a group, a department, a division, or the whole company, join the company softball team, write an article for the company newspaper, partake in community activities, especially those that are encouraged by company management. Invite some of your colleagues to join you in a TGIF drink.

Honk Your Own Horn

The oft-quoted adage "God helps those who help themselves" goes hand in hand with that principle of psychorelations that states you must promote yourself. No one else is going to do it for you.

In television, radio, and indeed in all the media, someone is always trying to sell you something. Why? Because a manufacturer, a distributor, a retailer is trying to convince you to buy his product rather than his competitor's.

The analogy applies to you. You too must be sold to someone— your immediate superior, the person at the top of the hierarchy, your clients. You don't have an advertising agency or a public-relations firm to carry your message for you. There is no one to extol your virtues, no one to sing of your accomplishments except yourself. It's not easy to do and still retain the respect of your coworkers and management. You don't want to appear flamboyant and self-serving.

I'm a boss, but I have a hundred bosses: each client of Rogers & Cowan. I had better impress each one—or else! How do I impress them? By communicating with them, by letting them know what we are doing for them, by sending them activity reports, by meeting with them regularly. What is the point of working industriously and devotedly for clients if they don't know what we're doing? Getting the job done is not enough. I also have to tell them about it and impress them with how well we have done it.

I had been thinking about John, an employee, for a couple of days. I had not been conscious of him for quite some time and I wondered whether he was performing up to par. I had not seen him, had not read any reports from him, and had not been aware of any recent reports he had sent to clients who were his responsibility. I left my office and walked down the hallway to see Janice, his immediate superior.

"I've been thinking about John," I said. "What's he been doing lately?" There was a pause. A quizzical look came over her face. She took out a cigarette, lit it, turned to me, and replied, "I don't know. I've been so jammed up the past few weeks that I haven't given him the supervision I should. I must confess that I've lost track of what he's been doing." I stood up, and started to move toward the door. "I'd appreciate it if you'd check up on him," I said quietly. "Thanks for reminding me," she concluded, and I could sense the concern in her voice.

An hour later she walked into my office. I stood up. "Would you like a Coke, or coffee, or tea?" I asked. "No thanks. I came in to tell you about John. I blame myself for not watching him more closely." She was shaking her head in wonderment. "I just don't understand him. He's doing a fine job. The three clients he's responsible for are in good shape. He has an NBC network news segment, a piece in the *Wall Street Journal*, a *Los Angeles Times* interview, and a spot on the "Merv Griffin Show" all coming up in the next two weeks."

"That's great," I said with great relief. "Why don't you understand him?"

"Because he not only didn't tell me what he was doing, but he didn't tell you, and I'm ashamed to say, he hasn't even reported to the clients. In fact, he hit me up for a raise."

"What did you say?"

"I turned him down. I told him that he was doing a great job for his clients, but that was only half of his responsibility. I explained to him, and this, incidentally, is probably the twelfth time I've told him, that equally important, he must *impress* the client as he must impress us. I just can't seem to get through to him."

"What are you going to do about the raise?"

"I told him that if in the next thirty days he learns to communicate what he's doing to us and the clients that I would recommend a salary increase for him. If that doesn't make him understand, and motivate him, I won't know what to do."

John did learn finally to impress his bosses and his clients by constant communication and he is now moving ahead rapidly at Rogers & Cowan. It probably would never have happened if I had not one day asked, "What is he doing?" But that's what a boss is for.

At a staff meeting in our New York office a few months ago, I was gently expressing dissatisfaction with the recent performances of a number of our associates. They weren't accepting very graciously what I felt to be constructive criticism. Each of them told me what they had accomplished in recent months, and I was impressed. "I didn't know that," I said time and again. I decided that my criticism was unjustified and I apologized.

Kathie Berlin, president of our New York Entertainment Division, had been sitting quietly next to me at our conference-room table, smiling at the replies given to me by the young men and women who reported to her. In effect, my criticism of them was criticism of her, and now her performance as an executive was being vindicated.

Suddenly a cloud passed over her face. During a lull in the conversation, she stepped in. "Just a minute, all of you," she said to her staff. "We've made a mistake. Now I know where we've gone wrong. We have all forgotten that Henry Rogers and Warren Cowan are our most important clients. We've been so busy impressing ourselves and our clients, we've forgotten that bosses have to be impressed too. How do we ever expect to get salary increases, and year-end bonuses, if the people we work for don't know what we're doing?" She turned to me and said, "Henry, watch and see what happens from this day on."

Our New York associates devised their own system to sell themselves. Every week we receive from our New York office a batch of newspaper and magazine clippings. The name of the person responsible is attached to each clipping. The bosses are impressed.

There was a time when I mistakenly believed that public-relations people should be anonymous. They should place their clients under the spotlight and remain in the shadows themselves. Over the years I changed my thinking. I decided that if I cannot perform a creditable public-relations job on myself, my clients may begin to wonder if I am capable of doing it for them.

Walking the Tightrope, the Private Confessions of a Public Relations Man, was published a few years ago; I promoted it heavily. I sent copies to hundreds of clients, friends, acquaintances, and media representatives. I booked myself on network, syndicated and local television and radio programs, arranged for newspapers and magazines to interview me, made personal appearances in department and bookstores, and set up a college lecture tour for myself. Having a book published is an accomplishment in itself, but I was not reluctant to tell the world what I had done.

What should you do to promote yourself? Primarily communicate: communicate effectively with everyone on every level. But you will see other opportunities analogous to those I have suggested as you analyze the structure of your own organization. For some businesses, a high profile in community action and charity work is an important way to promote yourself in the corporate picture. In other businesses, a good volley on the tennis court or a steady putt on the greens may be the ticket to being better known. For the expert on psychorelations, every move must count toward your goal, and management must see all of your accomplishments as contributing to corporate success.

Be a Team Player
Success requires that you develop a reputation for being a team player. Very few corporations have room for prima donnas. Although you, of course, may view the prosperity of the corporation as a means toward your own end (personal success), you and the company share a common path.

How do you become a team player? It's really very simple. These are the ingredients. First, play your position—do your job. Be sensitive in dealing with your associates, being careful not to step on anyone's toes. Be cooperative—pinch-hit when there's a crunch. Offer to help your associates, even when the work to be done is "menial." Every boss has probably helped staple reports together and run the copying machine. Next, be a volunteer—don't wait for your superior to give you added responsibilities. If you see something that needs doing, do it.

Share the glory—give credit where it's due, especially to someone whose contribution has not been sufficiently recognized. Be a cheerleader—let your boss know you're a loyal member of the team. Make recommendations and suggestions in areas where you are not directly involved in order to serve "the best interests of the company" (and your best interests as well). Take corporate "good news" personally—let others know you are delighted about new clients, new contracts, improved sales figures.

Although none of these is very hard to do, each one establishes you as a "member in good standing" of the team. Being recognized as a team player is often more important than displaying brilliant talent. Conversely, even the most innovative individual is eventually replaced if he or she doesn't participate as part of the team.

Several years ago I was meeting with the president of Jantzen Sportswear in Portland, Oregon. We were discussing one of his marketing executives with whom Rogers & Cowan had worked closely in recent years, but whom I had not seen on this particular visit to corporate headquarters. "Richard isn't with us any longer," I was told. I was surprised. In the few years of my association with Jantzen as the company's public-relations representative, Richard's influence had been apparent in every area of the company's marketing efforts. I had heard in the trade that he was destined to become the president of the company. "What happened?" I asked.

"Richard is a very talented marketing man," came the reply, "but here at Jantzen we don't have room for individual geniuses. He wasn't a team player, and although we recognized his contributions to the company, we finally decided to let him go because he rocked the boat in too many areas."

Here is a perfect case history of a talented man being unaware of psychorelations. He got the job done, but as his boss said, he rocked too many boats in the process. He must have offended so many people his company was forced to weigh his obvious assets against his inability to play on the team. Perhaps they made the right decision, because Richard is long gone and the company is more successful than ever. There really is no indispensable man or woman.

Let's look at what it takes to be a team player. First, realize that being a team player doesn't mean that you have to be the same as everyone else; it doesn't mean that you have to be a robot or automaton. It does mean that you have to work within a certain framework, and that even though you are working primarily for your own success, you must at least give the impression you're working as a member of this team. If Richard had been aware of that, he might now be president of Jantzen.

Your ambition to be the captain does not eliminate you from the team. To the contrary, it will spotlight you, and focus attention on your accomplishments. Give the impression that you're always thinking about the team—never hurt your chances of succeeding by giving even a hint that your real interest is self-interest.

Without deviating from your own thrust and goals, it is important that you always give credit to the team—that will win you the respect essential to your success.

I once asked Dr. Franklin Murphy to what factors he attributed his success. He said, "The people around me have made me successful. I would never have been able to accomplish anything on my own. I have always sought out people who I felt were talented, who had self-discipline. I then tried to develop their affection and loyalty. I recruited them, motivated them, and, when we were able to achieve something, I shared the credit with them. You rarely read my name in the paper. The other executives in our company have the high visibility."

Dr. Murphy not only shared the credit with his associates, but, consciously or unconsciously, he enhanced his image when he made that statement. He is a team player.

Whenever anyone asks me the secret of my success, I answer "Warren Cowan." This is neither false modesty on my part nor an overabundance of humility. I genuinely believe it's true. I'm sure I would have done well without a partner, but I know that I would never have achieved the level of success Rogers & Cowan enjoys without Warren standing next to me for many years. I am happy to share the glory with my partner, and my image remains at a high level, because I don't seek the solo spotlight for myself.

Deep down inside you may feel that you did it all by yourself. You may be convinced that no one helped you, that you climbed up all by yourself. It might even be true (though personally, I doubt it), but don't tell anyone.

There was a delightful example of sharing the glory at the Academy Awards many years ago. The late Dmitri Tiomkin, one of

Hollywood's most distinguished composer-conductors, was awarded his Oscar one memorable night, and immediately thanked Beethoven, Brahms, Bach, Shostakovich, Rimski-Korsakov, Ravel, Mendelssohn, Strauss (both Richard and Johann), Handel, Bizet, Stravinsky, and Rachmaninoff. He went on for what seemed like ten minutes, naming every conceivable composer from whom he had ever lifted a chord or a movement. He won not only the laughs he expected, but a standing ovation as well. The audience, appreciating both his self-deprecating humor as well as his accomplishments, understood he was admitting that others had contributed to the success he was enjoying that night.

The hero of the football game knows he is expected to mention the accurate passes thrown by the quarterback. The no-hit pitcher always gives credit to the infielders and outfielders who back him up. At Rogers & Cowan, there is a lot of sharing the glory. The day after we stage any event—it could be a press conference, a parade, a cocktail reception honoring a client, a luncheon at which our client is the principal speaker—an interoffice memo goes out from the account supervisor to each person who helped him, with copies to management. Two purposes are served. The account supervisor shows himself as an effective executive sharing the glory with his associates and each of these associates is pleased because his contribution is recognized by management.

Being flexible is another aspect of team play. For example, walking down the hallway of our office one day I stopped to pick up a scrap of paper that had been carelessly dropped on the floor. "Why did you do that?" asked an associate. "Someone else would have picked it up. After all, you're the founder of the company, the chairman of the board. You shouldn't be picking up pieces of paper from the floor."

"Maybe someone else would have picked it up," I replied. "Maybe not. It might have stayed there until the janitor saw it tonight. Some of our people think it's undignified to pick up a piece of paper from the floor. I don't. I do it in my own home. Why wouldn't I do it in my office?"

There are a lot of us who think it's beneath our dignity to take on a menial task. Did you ever notice what happens at a staff meeting when the room is short a few chairs? Everyone waits to see who will fetch them, and invariably one of the top executives makes the first move. He gets up, because he's not worried about status or dignity. He knows that he's talented and well respected for his accomplishments.

The person who is willing to do a menial task without being asked shows the qualities that it takes to move up the corporate ladder. Rogers & Cowan is small enough so that management sees and knows what everyone is doing. We notice who stoops down to pick up a piece of paper from the floor, and I use that only as an example of how we quickly spot who the team players are—those who care.

In a larger company, the same thing happens. Everyone reports to someone, and there, too, the person who shows team spirit wins the respect of his superior.

As an employer, I really don't care what your inner motivation is. I really don't care whether you are looking out for number one or looking out for Rogers & Cowan. I won't try to analyze your motives, because as an employer I know how important team play is to our operation. The person who wins my respect is Bill who says, "Boss, I know we're having a tough time solving the problem of this particular client. He's Joe's responsibility, not mine, but why don't we have a staff meeting and put our heads together for a couple of hours. Something constructive is bound to come out."

I immediately accept Bill's suggestion. I should have thought of it myself. We have the meeting, and as Bill predicted, something constructive does come out of it. It's not important who eventually conceives the idea that solves the problem. Bill instigated the meeting. In my mind he gets the credit because he sparked the team play.

I don't necessarily look for volunteers to take on someone else's responsibility. After all, everyone is kept fully occupied handling those chores that have been assigned to him. I notice three different reactions to a request for help.

"I just can't handle it," says the first. "I'm up to my neck with priorities as it is." (As far as we are both concerned the issue is closed.)

Then there is the person who agrees to take on the added task but does it grudgingly. "Of course I'll do it for you, boss, but jeez, I'll have to stay up all night to get it done. You and I both know that I'm a workhorse, so just keep piling it on me and I'll manage to get it done somehow." (I'm sorry I asked him.)

Then there is the third person. He/she responds, "Just give it to me and I'll handle it." (There's no further conversation or explanation or comment. I find this is the person who is busier than anyone else, handles a bigger load than anyone else, but is essentially a team player and knows that in his/her hands it will be handled quicker and more efficiently than if I had asked another associate to take it on.)

If you're working on your psychorelations program, and realize that being a team player will help, decide for yourself who among these three you want to be.

Don't Always Play by the Rules

There are times when rules can and should be bent—sometimes broken—without causing a backlash or damaging consequences. Remember that rules are established for the good of the company. If you can figure out a way to circumvent policy for your own best interests while further benefitting your employer, you will have taken one more step to advance your career.

A dear friend, the late Harold Mirisch, a leading movie mogul of his day, kept a plaque on his desk that read, "What is to the best interests of United Artists is not necessarily to the best interests of the Mirisch Company." The Mirisch Company was a successful independent motion picture production firm whose films were financed and distributed by United Artists. Harold's interest was to turn out motion pictures that were financially successful, and if they were, it would benefit both himself and his distributors, so he made his own decisions as to what was good for both. He was right most of the time, so there were no complaints. Of course, you are probably not in as strong a position as Harold, so it is important not to broadcast that you're a rule breaker.

Michael Korda, in his best-seller *Success*, writes that "the fastest way to succeed is to look as though you are playing by the rules but quietly playing by your own." There is, of course, a certain gamble involved. If you're a winner, you won't be criticized. Your boss will close his eyes and look the other way. If you lose, if your rule breaking results in financial loss or embarrassment to your company, you might find yourself looking for another job. Remember, the road to success is filled with potholes, soft shoulders, and detours, and you must decide for yourself whether or not to take the gamble.

We have always had a policy at Rogers & Cowan that all employees travel in coach or economy class when we fly on company business. This policy saves us many thousands of dollars each year. At one point we discovered that one of our top executives had been traveling first class. He just hadn't told anyone about it, and his unauthorized expenditures for plane tickets had eluded the attention of our accounting department.

We confronted him with his malfeasance. He laughed. "I was wondering how long it would take you to catch on. In fact, I've kept a record of the results of my first-class travel in the past year." He took a notebook out of his pocket and read us eight entries. He recited the difference in cost of coach travel versus first class on each of his eight trips between Los Angeles and New York. Then he pointed out whom he'd met and talked with on each flight, and concluded by explaining that the contacts he had established resulted in his bringing to the company four new high-paying clients.

"Now," he concluded, beaming at us, "I have come well prepared for the meeting. Here is my personal check for the difference between coach and first-class fare. Take it." With a smile on his face, knowing that he had played his strongest hand, he placed the check on the desk in front of us. We laughed too. I took the check and tore it up without looking at it. "The meeting's over," I said. Our esteemed associate continues to fly first class and we close our eyes to this breach of company policy. Rules are made to be broken, by the right person at the right time.

Make Corporate End Runs

Going over your boss's head is both challenging and dangerous. Before you decide whether or not to make the big step, you must first determine how closely your immediate boss plays by company rules and how sensitive he is. Will he resent you? Will he be out to get you when he discovers what you have done? There are no easy answers. You must size up the situation and realize the chance you are taking.

Remember that it might cost you your job. But that is unlikely. Unless your boss is a completely unreasonable person, you may at worst wind up with a mild rebuke. Your client is taking off on what you are certain is a wrong direction. You want to advise him to change course but you don't feel your relationship with him is solid enough for you to speak up. Your immediate superior is not taking any action because he's probably scared too. A journalist is giving you a hard time. Again, you're not getting any help from the person whose responsibility it is to help you solve your problem. Another associate seems to be undercutting your position in the company and you don't know what to do about it. One solution is to seek advice from a person higher up in the organization. This very often happens in our office.

Sally asks to see me. She works in our television division and reports to Alice, who in turn reports to Don, who heads up the department. Sally walks in, apprehensive and frightened. Is she doing the right thing in bringing her problem to me? She has thought about it for weeks, she confides, and her mother has convinced her to bite the bullet. She is ambitious, and wants to move up in our organization, but Alice is stifling her. She is given little more than menial chores to perform and she knows she can handle responsibility if she is given the opportunity. On four different occasions she has asked Alice to give her more to do, but Alice never does. What shall she do? Shall she go over Alice's head and take the problem directly to Don? "No," I reply, "don't go to Don yet." I explain to her that the way to take on more responsibility is to seize it before anyone knows that you've done so. I ask her what added responsibilities she would like to take on. She tells me. "What are you waiting for? Alice is probably not giving you more to do because she doesn't know what you can or can't do. You know what you want to do. Do it, and after you've done it, show Alice the results. I'm sure she won't be angry with you. She'll probably admire your ambition."

"What do I do if Alice gets angry?" Sally asks timidly.

"That's the chance you have to take. If she gets angry, you're faced with a dilemma. That's when you go over her head to Don. Then it becomes his problem and I'm sure he'll handle it. Remember, there's always the chance you'll get fired, but if I were you I would take the risk."

"Shall I tell anyone I talked with you?"

"I don't think that would be wise. People might resent it."

A month later I saw Alice in the hallway. "How is everything going in your department?" I asked.

"Just fine."

"How is Sally doing?"

"Don and I are so pleased with Sally. She's shown a lot of initiative that we didn't know she had. She's becoming a valued member of the department."

Every situation doesn't turn out as satisfactorily as the Sally story. Going over your boss's head takes a lot of thinking. Ponder your alternatives. Weigh the consequences. There are risks involved but in most cases I believe they are worth taking.

Seek Out Responsibility

The person who plays the office game best is the one who sees a need that is not being filled. No one else has spotted it. Without announcing his intentions, he steps in and takes it on as a new responsibility. He does this a number of times. He has taken advantage of every opportunity that presents itself, and gradually his job has become more important.

At some point his new responsibilities become apparent. Either he announces it himself very casually one day or management suddenly becomes aware of it. (This is where honking your own horn comes into play.) At that moment if an increase in salary and a more prestigious title aren't offered him, he is in a particularly strong position to ask for them.

What is the difference between our friend, let's call him Raymond, who has maneuvered himself into a more important position on the organization chart and his associates who have been tending to their own jobs in routine fashion, unaware of what has happened right under their noses? Raymond is different, and is better at using psychorelations because he knows what his associates don't—that anyone can do more and take on greater responsibility. Everyone else says they don't have time to take on any more than they are now handling. Raymond knows this isn't so.

Raymond can accomplish more in a day than anyone else because he has learned not to fritter away his time as many of his associates do. He has watched them and knows that many work five hours out of an eight-hour day. He knows that their days go something like this:

9:15   Go to the coffee machine and chat for a while.
9:30   Read the newspapers. After all, public-relations
        professionals must keep up with what is happening
        in the world.
10:00   Call a friend to make a lunch date.
10:15   Look at the desk and start to work on the first piece
        of paper that catches the eye.
10:30   An associate drops in to ask a question, and there is
        an ensuing discussion as to the relative merits of the
        Rams and the Raiders. Five minutes are spent in
        amenities before any business telephone conversation
        gets underway.

11:00   A trip to the copying machine and more chitchat.

11:30   A trip to the men's room (or ladies').

11:45   Another trip to the coffee machine.

12:00   Time-out for lunch.

In contrast, Raymond's day goes something like this:

6:00   Up and out for one hour of jogging.

7:00   "Today," "Good Morning America," or "CBS Morning News" while dressing.

7:30   Read the papers during breakfast.

8:00   Arrive at the office at eight, not nine.

Organize his work load so that he knows exactly what he hopes to accomplish before the day is over.

Get his associates in and out of his office quickly. He impatiently cuts off chitchat.

Limit his telephone conversations to two minutes.

Ask the switchboard operator to hold his telephone calls while dictating.

Plan office meetings with a cut-off time. No open-ended meetings.

Never work according to the clock. Remain at his desk until his allocated work load for the day is completed. He may leave at seven but he also may leave at five.

Make numerous breakfast and cocktail appointments so that he can meet with people during nonoffice hours.

That is how Raymond conducts his day and that is why he can take on more responsibility than anyone else.

Paul Bloch started in our television department as a gofer and in a few years worked his way up to being a very capable account executive. When we became involved in the contemporary music scene, we moved him over to the music division because he related well to the individual artists and groups we represented. Paul gradually took a leadership role, assuming more and more responsibility. We decided that it was to the company's advantage as well as his to name him president of the Music Division.

But Paul had not yet arrived at the top of the mountain. He was just beginning to climb. Without our realizing it, he became involved with motion picture and television personalities, and began to bring them into his division.

There was still more. He pushed himself into the motion picture industry. Production companies asked him to handle publicity for their movies, so motion pictures were also added to the Music Division. On his own he decided we should have a sports division and moved into that area too.

With his involvement in so many different areas, it was no longer logical for Paul just to be president of the Music Division, so he now has moved up to executive vice-president of Rogers & Cowan, with such clients as Sylvester Stallone, James Caan, Dudley Moore, Paul McCartney, and David Bowie.

Where does Paul go next? He has been spending more and more time in my office recently and I notice he has been looking covetously at my chair. That's okay with me. Paul can go as far as he wants because he is one of the few who learned quickly that in order to be successful, you must seize responsibility without being asked.

Be an Early Bird

Be the first to arrive in the office in the morning. It is an important step in impressing your boss—and everyone else. Besides making a favorable impression, that extra hour will make you more productive, and added productivity is another factor that will contribute to your success. I have always come in early myself. Many years ago I explained to my wife why I arose before dawn every morning. "I assume that my competitors and I have equal talent. Isn't it logical, then, that I'll become more successful than they if I start working two or three hours before they do every morning?"

I get a feeling of well-being and security when I walk into my office at seven-thirty in the morning. Three women in our accounting department have already started their bookkeeping chores. Paul is slouched in his chair, making his third telephone call to his associates in our New York office. Carla is pounding on a typewriter. Don walks in and with a grin on his face, knowing that he is one-upping me, says, "Where have you been all morning? I'd like to talk to you for a few minutes."

I am impressed. I know these people really care. They have found that if they get in an hour or two earlier than anyone else, they can get a lot more accomplished than if they work the normal nine-to-six weekday. Early birds impress me because, based on my own experiences, I know they have time to get their day organized and get more work done. They work more effectively and more proficiently because there are no disconcerting, jangling telephones. They don't feel pressure if they take an extra half hour for lunch or leave a half hour earlier, and they have time to do all the extra reading that should be done but can never possibly get done during the course of the normal working day.

Leave Your Personal Problems at Home

"Allan is crisis prone." That's what I said to an associate after one of our young executives had limped painfully and dramatically out of my office. He had just taken fifteen minutes to explain how he had sprained his ankle when the steps leading down to his cellar had collapsed under him that morning.

"You're just being kind to him," replied my associate. "To me he's become a dreadful bore, and I don't have the patience to listen to him anymore. This is the eighth consecutive day that he's had us all in tears, telling us about one of his hour-by-hour catastrophes. I feel sorry for him but why, *why*, do we have to listen to his laments every single day? Maybe we should ask him instead to post a memo on the bulletin board every morning. He could title it, 'Allan's Catastrophe-of-the-Day Report.'"

"Very funny," I said, "but I guess it is time for us to do something about him. I admit his stories become trying after a while."

"That's the understatement of the year. I'm sure everyone in the office would be grateful if you could get him to leave his personal problems at home."

I dropped in to see Allan in his office later that day. As gently as I could under the circumstances, I told him that we all sympathized with his problems, that we all carried certain problems in our head when we arrived at the office in the morning, but that we tried not to burden our associates with them. We were running a business, and we just couldn't take the time to listen to his nonstop personal problems.

Allan didn't understand. "But all of you are my friends. Who else can I tell my troubles to?"

I was getting nowhere. I felt sorry for him, but I had to weigh our own sanity against his hurt feelings. I finally left his office, feeling disappointed, irritated—frustrated.

A few weeks later Allan resigned without an explanation. He must have been deeply hurt. He must have felt that we didn't care enough about him to listen to him. He was wrong; we did care, but only up to a point. He had asked us to go beyond that point. He expected us to serve as his mother, his father, and his psychiatrist, which was too much of a burden for us to carry because we still had our own jobs to handle. I don't know where Allan is today, or whether he is better or worse off than when he was with us. Sadly, I envision him sitting in some far-off place, still telling his personal horror stories to a group of impatient listeners. Allan couldn't change, and evidently didn't want to change his behavior of asking his business associates to act as his psychiatrist.

Of course, if you *really* have a problem, don't just lean on your fellow workers, *do* something about it. Marital problems, a death or illness in the family—these serious problems demand attention.

If personal difficulties are affecting your job performance, get counseling; take a leave of absence if necessary. You can lose a lot more than the office game if these situations are not resolved.

Run Faster Than Anyone Else

Late one night many years ago I was walking down Second Avenue in New York with David Susskind. David was then the producer of a television series, "The Dupont Show of the Week." We had been engaged by the Dupont Company to handle publicity for the series, and it was to our mutual advantage that we work closely together. We were talking about various publicity problems that had arisen on that particular week's show. David was giving me a critique of our performance so far when he suddenly stopped and looked at me. "Henry," he said, "you've really got it made. You have a lock on the television publicity business in New York. You represent more than half of the advertiser/sponsors in the business. But watch out for the warning signs. Your competitors are barking at your heels and you'll have to keep running faster and faster to keep ahead of them."

I have remembered Susskind's sound advice. I must admit that I haven't followed it twenty-four hours a day over the years, but I've noticed that when I slowed down, the competitors did catch up with us, and when I accelerated my efforts, we moved out ahead of them once more.

Running faster than anyone else is one of the most important factors of the office game. I see it around me every day. The people who come in earlier in the morning, work harder, practice psychorelations, impressing their bosses and their colleagues, move ahead faster. They seldom have to ask for an increase in salary, because they get one before they expect it. They get bigger bonuses at the end of the year, and they are offered perks some of their slower-running associates never enjoy.

Everyone is able to run fast, but everyone doesn't No one can force you to try to run faster than the person in the next office. That is a decision you must make for yourself.

There was one person who ran faster than we did whom I recall fondly. Many years ago we had a competitor named Arthur Jacobs. He infuriated us. We always prided ourselves on being swift-footed, but even though there were two of us and only one of him, he ran faster than we did. We were already the leading public-relations firm in Hollywood and represented most of the top stars in the industry, but how did such luminaries as Marilyn Monroe, Rex Harrison, Gene Kelly, and yes, Ronald Reagan during his acting days, elude us and become clients of Arthur Jacobs? We studied him and discovered the reason.

Arthur had no personal life at all. He worked seven days and seven nights a week. We had wives and children who took up a lot of our time, but Arthur was a bachelor and had no such distractions. His clients were his wives and children. He would fly to London to get a new client and return to Hollywood the following day. Two days later he was in New York and then back again to the West Coast. We finally admitted to ourselves that Arthur ran faster than we did, so we had no other recourse than to ask him to become our partner, which he did. A year later, we found that we were incompatible—by mutual agreement, we broke up the partnership and the firm became Rogers & Cowan again.

Shortly after, Arthur, who always had movie production ambitions, sold us his business and became one of Hollywood's most successful producers. Eventually he became our client. Arthur passed away a number of years ago. We miss him but we have always been grateful that there haven't been any other competitors who ran as fast as he did.

Learning to play the game skillfully requires keen powers of observation. Look around you—where are the centers of power and who controls them? Whom must you impress in order to move up in the organization? What person or persons can take you out of your present job and place you in another—at a higher salary? If you're having trouble trying to figure out where the power lies, take my advice: go with the money.

A company remains in business because of its ability to generate profits. Can you pinpoint the person or those persons who are responsible for profitability? In a business such as ours, it is the person who brings in and services the most important, the highest-paying clients. These are the individuals to set your sights on, the people you must impress. If you know that you are good at your job, and know that by now you should be higher up in the organization than you are, it is time to use your psychorelations skills. This is the time to show the obvious profit makers just how valuable you are.

5

Emotions and psychorelations

IF YOU ARE actively playing the office game, you will be increasingly involved in important decisions about your company's future. You will also become more involved with other rising stars in the business, whose ideas may not always coincide with yours. The tendency in such situations is to take the office game *personally*, to make every office decision a win-lose situation for yourself. An office full of people behaving this way can generate a lot of heat, most of it unpleasant, some of it career threatening.

Many a promising executive has been shot down by an inability to handle emotions such as anger and embarrassment, and emotional situations resulting from criticism and complaints. Psychorelations provides a number of tools to help you cope with emotions that get out of hand—both yours and those of others. This chapter discusses these issues and shows you how to make your emotions work for you on the road to success.

CRITICISM

Curiously enough, one of the most dangerous emotional areas is criticism. I say curiously, because an effective executive must offer criticism all day long, every day, to everyone in his or her organization in order to spur improvements. The cumulative effect of these criticisms will either be more effective employees who understand the needs of the organization or a group of people burning with resentment that builds up comment by comment. Psychorelations will make the difference.

Before you act, first determine your objective in criticizing someone. What separates criticism from complaint is simply your objective: to inspire improvement. If you want improvement, you must find ways to inspire change by dealing positively and constructively.

You must stop, look, and listen for the clue, the right words, that will turn on rather than turn off the offender. Let's consider a switchboard operator who has been slow to answer the telephone. You want the switchboard operator to answer promptly. Yelling at her is not the answer. Neither is firing her. The next person might be worse. In fact, this switchboard operator is quite good. On a scale of one to ten, you would rate her as an eight. How do you get her to function as a nine? Here are some tips:

- "That man who called me this morning commented on your pleasant voice, but did complain about waiting for you to answer the telephone."

- "You really have a tough job juggling all these calls. I don't know how you do it. That's why I don't get too upset when it occasionally takes you so long to answer the telephone. Can I do anything to help you speed things up a bit?"

- "The boss was telling me the other day how proud he is of the organization when he calls in from the outside and you answer the phone on the first ring."

. "My wife told me last night what a joy it is to hear your voice on the telephone. She said that most telephone operators are so rude but that you're one of the few exceptions. I agreed with her, of course, but I wonder if you could figure out a way to answer the phone a little faster."

If criticism is preceded by or tempered with a note of praise, it can serve as a constructive rather than a destructive vehicle and you will have a better chance to achieve your objective.

Use your psychorelations skills—sugar-coat the truth, be kind but direct in your approach. Imagine yourself in the other person's place.

Rogers' Rules for Offering Criticism

1) Before launching into criticism: stop, look, and listen.

2) Criticism must always have an objective.

3) Criticism should turn someone on, not turn him off. Negative criticism will always elicit a negative response.

4) Precede criticism with a note of praise.

YOU CAN DISH IT OUT, BUT CAN YOU TAKE IT?

It's easy to criticize but how do you react when the criticism is directed at you. Do you get angry? Do you sulk? Do you make excuses? Do you rationalize, or do you just tune out and ignore what is being said? Or, do you accept the criticism graciously and thank your critic for caring enough to tell you?

There are a thousand reactions to criticism. No one can say that you are right or wrong in the way you behave. But we are about to play in a new ball game—a game that will determine whether or not you will become a more successful person. Everything you do, every reaction you display in a given situation, is now directed to psychorelations, that quality that is about to help you become a *success*.

We will now develop a program that gives you the opportunity to make a favorable impression each time criticism is directed at you, and making favorable impressions on the right people is what psychorelations is all about. Let's forget whether the criticism is justified or not; let's forget whether your critic is right or wrong. Your objective, whether the critic is your boss, your spouse, your fellow worker, or a friend, is to enhance your image, and make your critic become an admirer rather than a detractor.

Your boss has just criticized a piece of work you have turned in. You think it's quite good. Is it more important for you to score points for yourself or score points with him? I would handle it like this:

"You're right. I agree with you. I've given it my best shot but I just can't get it to sing like it should. Can you spend a little time with me, and show me where I've gone wrong?"

He is bound to help you, and he will admire your attitude because you have set him up as the ultimate authority in the company.

We all have a tendency to react emotionally to criticism, and that is where we all make our big mistake. With image-improvement foremost in mind, you must strive to listen to criticism with an objective ear. Can you learn something from it? Is your critic right? Your first reaction is to put up your fists and start swinging, but what good will that do you? The key is to come out of it looking better than you did the moment the criticism was first directed to you.

The other day I received a telephone call from a movie studio executive criticizing our performance on a project we were handling for him. My first impulse, as yours would have probably been, was to counter with an angry retort. But I really didn't know whether he was right or wrong so I followed my normal procedure in such a situation. "You may well be right, but I want to think about it before I reply. I'll call you back in the morning." I did think about it, and decided that we had a very strong position that refuted his contention. I didn't call. Instead, because my critic had quoted two of his associates as agreeing with him, I sent over a polite letter by special messenger the next morning with copies to the associates. I heard nothing more and the business relationship continues. This simple situation could have resulted in an angry confrontation. Instead, through the use of psychorelations skills, it was handled in the diplomatic style expected of public-relations professionals.

Your reaction should be based on the premise that your critic is right and you are wrong. Whether that is the actual situation or not is beside the point. You are playing in a game where point scoring is all-important, and the number of points you score is dependent on the response your reaction elicits. The answers I have given you are guaranteed to bring you the favorable responses you are seeking.

Rogers' Rule for Accepting Criticism

"You're right and thank you for caring enough to tell me. What can I do to improve?"

THE CONSTANT COMPLAINER

Are you a complainer? You are apt to give me the immediate answer: "Who, me? Of course not!" Think about it for a minute, though. Just between us, don't you complain to your fellow workers a bit more than is justified? Don't you complain about your boss's bad temper or that you are underpaid, or that no one appreciates you? Do you complain about the weather, taxes, interest rates, and the bad telephone service in your office?

You might reply: "Why shouldn't I complain? I have legitimate complaints. Why shouldn't my fellow workers share them with me?"

You're right. I agree with you. You have a perfect right to complain, but then forget about psychorelations. You pave the road to success by developing favorable relationships with the people you work with. Complaining will ruin those relationships, not enhance them.

The constant complainer has image problems. People shy away from him. They have a tendency to avoid his company.

I had the satisfaction of watching a young man's image improve several years ago; his chances for success today are unlimited because I forced him one day to take a hard look at himself. I had become concerned about his reputation as a constant complainer, and, because I felt he had an enormous potential in our organization, I decided to talk with him about it.

"I'm talking to you because I don't want you to blow it. You're a very talented man, and you have everything it takes to become a success, but you might just miss because you've been turning people off. You never stop complaining. You never take the time to say a cordial word to anyone. You can't. You're too busy criticizing and complaining about everyone's performance.

"Just keep an open mind about what I'm saying. Let me tell you some of the things I myself have heard you say in the past few days. You scolded your secretary because she didn't correct a small typo in one of your letters, and you made such a point of it that she was almost crying when she left your office. In the strategy meeting we had this morning, you complained to Susan that her report was twenty-four hours late and then barked when your coffee was cold. You stopped in my office last night before you went home to complain about the mechanic who didn't fix your car properly, that you had to go out with a client for dinner, that the cleaner left a spot on your suit, and that a reporter from the *Times* misquoted another client."

I paused. "But all those things happened," he said. "Don't I have a right to complain?"

"You have a right to be upset, but you're missing the point. We're the image experts. We tell our clients how to conduct themselves so that they can create a favorable image for themselves. Let's follow our own advice. Of course, you have a right to complain, but you don't see the price you're paying for that right. Don't you realize that you're blowing your own image? You're not noticing that people are beginning to dislike you, because you're not looking at yourself through the eyes of the other person. If so many things are upsetting your life, why aren't you doing something more constructive than complaining? Stop complaining so much and maybe you'll wind up taking over my job."

"I know you're speaking in my best interests," he replied, "but it's hard for me to accept that I'm that insensitive to the impression I make. Give me a little time to think it through." (He showed good sense here by calling time-out to think about what I had said.)

I changed the subject and we went on to discuss a client's problem that had arisen that morning. A few days later, I walked into the constant complainer's office. He had just finished signing a number of letters. His secretary was standing at his desk, about to leave. He said pleasantly, "I noticed a little typo on page two of that last letter. Will you correct it, please?" His secretary smiled. "Of course. I'm sorry I didn't catch it." "Don't worry about it. We all make mistakes."

I had been standing there and had overheard the interchange. The former constant complainer looked at me and smiled. "I thought about what you said the other day. You were right. I'm a new man. You watch—everyone's going to love me. My image is going to get better than yours. You had better get your desk polished. I expect to be sitting behind it soon."

I laughed out loud. "Whenever you're ready, let me know." If you are really interested in improving your office image, stop complaining. Then whom are you entitled to complain to? You can't continue to keep everything bottled up inside. Take the complaints home to your wife, your husband, your best friend, but remember that your image at home is important, too.

Then what should you do? Stop, look, listen, and think. Is your complaint trivial? Does the weather ever get any better because you complain about it? Does your boss have fewer temper tantrums? Do interest rates come down faster? Complaining about trivia, which most of us do, is a self-indulgence you can't afford. Your psychorelations program will not allow it.

Once you have stopped, looked, listened, and thought about it,

and decided that you have a legitimate problem—not a complaint
—that warrants discussion, then you should bring it home. Ask your
spouse to discuss it with you and help you find a solution.

What's the difference between a complaint and a problem?

Complaint: "Oh my God, I have another splitting
                headache." (Groan.)
Problem: "I have that same splitting headache again.
                What do you think I should do about it?"

Complaint: "Jesus, my boss started ranting and raving again
                today."
Problem: "I wonder what I can do to stop my boss from
                ranting and raving."

Complaint: "Why oh why oh *why* can't I get anyone to do
                something right—just once!"
Problem: Do you feel that I have a problem in
                communicating with people? I just can't get
                them to do anything right."

Do you see the difference? When you complain, you are expressing your disapproval to the world, and expect everyone to listen to
your diatribe, sympathize with you, and lovingly pat your hand,
saying "Don't worry, everything's going to be all right." We used
to call that being a crybaby.

In contrast, when you present your complaint as a problem, you
are asking for help and guidance from someone who loves you, and
the loving understanding you seek, you'll usually find—without
impairing your image.

Rogers' Comments on Complaints

1) *Don't.* Never complain
2) If it's something that's fixable, fix it, or set the wheels in
motion to improve the situation.

3) Don't sympathize with the complainers. Avoid the whiners in the office.

4) Find constructive ways to express your dissatisfaction.

5) If you slip into a complaint, stop. Think of your image. Repair the damage.

6) If it's a legitimate complaint, approach it as a problem, and ask your mate to help you solve it.

WHEN THE COMPLAINTS ARE DIRECTED AT YOU

As an employer, complaints are directed at me constantly. A client is unhappy. A client hasn't paid his bill in ninety days. An associate offended a journalist. A journalist offended an associate. The air conditioning broke down. The telephones are out. Payroll taxes weren't paid in time. The New York office doesn't understand the problems the Beverly Hills office faces. London didn't answer our telex. That new client hasn't sent in a signed contract yet. It's hot. It's cold. It's raining. It's snowing. I get all the complaints. What do I do about them?

1) I listen. (I make certain that the complainer knows I care and am willing to hear him out.)

2) If the complaint is trivial, I try to point out as gently as possible how unimportant it is, and try to convince the person that the subject is not worthy of discussion. Sometimes it works. Sometimes it doesn't, but I've done my best.

3) If the complaint is legitimate, I approach it as a problem and set the wheels in motion to solve it. I try to point the complainer in the right direction for him to solve the problem himself. At times we solve it together. Occasionally I handle it myself but try to avoid that for I feel it is my obligation to help my associates solve problems through their own efforts.

HANDLING EMBARRASSMENT

In your relationships with people you must learn to handle embarrassing situations with aplomb. It's not easy but it is a skill you must acquire, for it is important for you to spare your associates discomfort because of an embarrassment you caused. We all find ourselves in embarrassing predicaments. Your public image—how you are perceived by your coworkers—depends on how you handle them. Do you run for cover, leaving everyone uncomfortable, or do you handle difficult situations adroitly and confidently so that no one is upset?

If you focus on the other person's feelings rather than your own, you will find that those awful moments are easier to handle, and your relationship with that person will be enhanced.

I have had many embarrassing experiences in my life but none had a more profound influence than the one I am about to relate. In fact, it changed the entire course of my life and helped make Rogers & Cowan into what it is today.

It was back in 1953. The late Taft Schreiber and Sonny Werblin, top executives at MCA, had set up a meeting for me at the offices of American Tobacco Company in New York. I was to make a publicity presentation to represent a long-forgotten television series titled, "Biff Baker, USA." When I was told that attending the presentation would be Paul Hahn, president of American Tobacco, and Ben Duffy, president of its advertising agency, Batten, Barton, Durstin, and Osborne, I broke into a sweat. Paul Hahn! Ben Duffy! Greats in the world of big business. This was one of my first appearances in the Madison Avenue majors, and I knew I was going to stutter. I was about to make a damn fool out of myself. What could I do about it? Nothing, Goddamn it! I told myself to forget the stuttering and prepare the plan.

When it was finally written, I decided to incorporate it into a visual presentation. We prepared two-feet-by-four-feet cards, with large type, highlighting the proposal's major points. I planned to read the headlines printed on each card, and then expound on the subject from the written presentation I held in my hands.

The presentation was completed and sent off to New York. I followed. Panic time. The fear was back. I started to sweat again. Why was I doing this? Why didn't I just remain in Hollywood with my comfortable business where by this time I could handle my stuttering problem with comparative ease. Who needed all the agony? At that moment I got angry with myself. I had to bear the agony. I had to conquer my fear, even if I did make an idiot of myself.

Why did stuttering remain after all these years such an inexplicable problem? For some unknown reason, I could get through meetings with movie stars and movie executives without the anguish I was experiencing now. I obviously had a hang-up about meeting with leaders in the world of Big Business. Somewhere deep in my psyche I was saying, "What right does a punk kid from Irvington, New Jersey, have to make a presentation to the president of American Tobacco Company?" Was I that insecure? Yes!

The plane arrived in New York. An hour later I checked into the Madison Hotel. Exhausted, I went right to bed but I couldn't sleep. I tossed, turned, tossed, turned. Too hot. Too cold. The covers went up to my chin, then were tossed aside. I envisioned Mr. Hahn and Mr. Duffy laughing as I stuttered my way through the presentation. I finally came to a decision. To hell with it. I wasn't going through with it.

I decided to call the next morning and say that I had suddenly taken ill—with pneumonia, or pleurisy. I was so sick that my doctor had advised me to return to Los Angeles immediately and check right into a hospital. I would apologize for the unseen turn of events. It must have been 4:00 A.M. when I finally fell asleep. Then the alarm clock went off. It was eight o'clock. I crawled out of bed and staggered to the bathroom. What a ghastly sight. I was a pale green color. I dragged myself into the shower. The water was hot. I tried to soap myself, but I couldn't—I didn't have the strength.

"What for?" I kept asking myself. "Why am I doing this to

myself? Screw that goddamned mountain that I wanted to climb. It's not important. It's not worth it. I want to get the hell out of here. Who needs television? Why can't I just stay in Beverly Hills and live the good lush life?" No, I was stuck. I had to go through with it.

I dressed, gulped down a cup of coffee, and shuffled around the corner to the MCA offices at 598 Madison Avenue. Schreiber and Werblin were waiting for me.

We taxied to the American Tobacco offices on lower Broadway. In the reception room I felt as if I were in the Victorian era. Nothing seemed to have changed since the turn of the century. The receptionist had probably been there as long as the furniture. I was pointed in the direction of the boardroom where I was to make my presentation.

I opened the door, and looked around. It was a scene out of *The Hucksters* or *Executive Suite*. I was in a huge paneled boardroom. In the middle of the room was a fifty-foot-long walnut table. Around the table were thirty-six cushioned chairs. In front of each chair was a yellow lined pad, a sharpened pencil, and a water glass. Neatly placed from one end of the table to the other were eight cut-crystal water pitchers. On the walls were oil paintings of distinguished, stern-looking gentlemen who must have been the presidents and chairmen of American Tobacco Company from years past. At the end of the room where I was standing was my easel with the Rogers & Cowan presentation cards placed neatly on it. An office boy, as planned, had arrived before I had and had done his job well.

I took all of this in in a moment. Nope. I just couldn't do it. It was too awesome, too overpowering. I could not possibly stand up there and give a presentation to all those people who would be occupying those chairs in just a few minutes' time. The fear of stuttering surged up in my guts. I felt nauseous. Droplets of sweat slipped down the sides of my body from my armpits. "Okay, that's it," I told myself. "I'm getting out of here right now. I'll tell the receptionist I suddenly took ill. Let someone else read the presentation." I moved toward the door, but at that moment it opened. An army of dark-suited, white-shirted gentlemen walked in. I was intro-duced to each of them, who shook my hand and then walked to his appointed place at the table. It all seemed to be planned with militarylike precision. They seemed to be clicking their heels as they shook my limp, wet hand, and then goose-stepped to their chairs. I was going mad. How could I get out of this? I couldn't.

Finally, someone said, "Henry, meet Mr. Ben Duffy, president of BBD & O, and Mr. Paul Hahn, president of American Tobacco Company."

I hastily wiped my hand on my trousers and gave them each a handshake. As I shook Mr. Hahn's hand, I experienced for the first time in my life a sensation that I had heard and read about a thousand times. My knees actually shook. I felt my whole body tremble.

Thirty-four gentlemen stood behind their chairs. I stood in front of the easel. Mr. Hahn and Mr. Duffy walked briskly to the far end of the boardroom. Mr. Hahn sat down at the head of the table; Mr. Duffy sat at his right. The other men slipped quietly into their chairs. I was the only one left standing in the room.

Mr. Hahn cleared his throat as a sign that he was calling the meeting to order. He looked at me. "You may begin, Mr. Rogers."

"Th-h-h-h-hank you, M-m-m-m-mister Hahn," I replied. Every-one turned their eyes to me. They waited.

"G-g-g-g-gentlemen!" Getting out that one word had taken my breath away. I gasped for air. My hands were wet as I gripped the written presentation I would refer to if I could ever get started. Now I felt the sweat dripping from the inside of my thighs. I took a deep breath.

"Gentlemen," I said it again. This time it came out smoothly. "I want to thank you for giving me this opportunity to tell you about Rogers & Cowan and what we hope to accomplish through our publicity and promotion efforts on 'Biff Baker, USA.' "

I had gotten through the first sentence. I stepped to the side of the easel and read the first three headlines. Then I got stuck on a word. I couldn't go any further. I felt my face flush. My lips tightened up. My throat constricted. At first the word wouldn't come out, then suddenly it burst forth.

I looked around. I wanted to run. I looked for the smirks I expected to see on their faces. I listened for the snickers I was certain were there. But there were no smirks. There were no snickers. They just sat there. They were waiting for me to get started again. "Maybe they know what I'm going through," I thought. "Maybe they're not bad guys after all. Maybe each one of them has had to make a presentation like this at one time. Maybe they were frightened too. Except that they don't stutter. I do."

I stumbled through the presentation. It must have taken an hour instead of the half hour it should have. To me, it seemed like twelve hours. For a few minutes I would talk fluently, then I would get stuck on a word. It seemed an interminable length of time until I could get the word out. I got embarrassed. I wanted to tell everyone that I was sorry to put them through this ordeal. But it wasn't an ordeal for them. They seemed to be listening intently. It was just an ordeal for me.

Finally it was all over.

"Thank you, Mr. Rogers," said Paul Hahn. "Do any of you gentlemen have any questions for Mr. Rogers?" There was silence.

"Well," he said, "then that winds it up. We can all get back to work now."

I stood there. I was a failure. I had had the perfect opportunity to break into the big time and I had blown it. I was just plain stupid to have let that stuttering get the best of me.

Everyone stood up and began to leave. Taft and Sonny stood beside me saying goodbye to everyone as they left. I tried to keep a smile on my face to hide my mortification. Finally, Mr. Hahn approached. He extended his hand and shook my still-clammy one.

"Nice presentation, Mr. Rogers. Congratulations on a job well done."

I couldn't believe it. A good job? A job well done? He was just being kind. It was a catastrophe.

A few weeks later, there was a telephone call from Taft Schreiber.

BBD & O and American Tobacco Company had decided to engage Rogers & Cowan to handle publicity for "Biff Baker, USA." We had made the breakthrough. We were handling a television series for a national advertiser. We were into a new phase of our business.

The phone call did more than get Rogers & Cowan into the television business. It got me over my fear of stuttering. If I had been turned down by American Tobacco, I would have felt I had failed because of my speech, not because of the content of the presentation. It would have inhibited me for the rest of my life.

This agonizing experience taught me two important lessons about handling embarrassment:

The person with the handicap is much more sensitive to it than the people around him. *Everyone has a handicap.* It might be shyness, or bitten fingernails, a scarred face, fat legs, skinny legs, large breasts, flat chest, bald head, club foot, or even a speech defect, and because of that everyone has empathy for and understanding of your problem. I expected everyone in that boardroom to laugh derisively at my stuttering. They didn't but I was aware that it made them uncomfortable. That taught me another lesson.

Talk about your embarrassment.   Don't try to cover it up. In my case, I now talk about my stuttering. If I had to do that American Tobacco Company presentation over again, I would have stopped the first time my stuttering became apparent. I would have said, "Excuse me, gentlemen, I have a speech problem and this presentation may take a little longer than you had anticipated, so if you will bear with me, I'll try to get through it." I would have grinned and chuckled at my own misfortune, and the tension in the room would have dissipated. Everyone would have smiled and relaxed; by making light of my problem, I would have gained added respect. I know this to be true, because even now, when I occasionally get stuck on a word, I make light of it and my audience smiles along with me.

We never know when we will be confronted with an embarrassing experience, nor can we conceive what will happen under what circumstances. I certainly could never have foreseen what happened to me one day at Fred MacMurray's home. Long before he became the star of "My Three Sons" and other television series, Fred was one of Hollywood's most sought-after motion picture stars. And he was one of my most important clients. In the early 1950s, I had interested *Look* magazine in doing a layout on Fred and he had asked me to drop by the house to discuss it with him.

On this particular day I arrived at the MacMurray home precisely at five-thirty. The door was opened immediately by the six-foot-four, black-haired actor. "Hi, Henry, come on in," he said in a warm, welcoming voice. Fred's red-and-black plaid wool shirt, khaki work pants, and thick-soled shoes didn't fit the formal atmosphere of his home. The highly polished wood-floored foyer led into a lushly carpeted living room, replete with richly textured curtains and drapes, magnificent breakfronts, pull-up chairs, and end tables of highly polished oak, walnut, and mahogany. Fred was dressed for a ranch, not for this tastefully furnished living room.

"I just drove in from Healdsburg," he explained. "I went up to look at those heifers I bought last week." Fred was a cattle rancher and spent many of his nonworking days at his ranch east of San Francisco, some four hundred miles away.

"Lillian will be down in a minute. Come on into the den and we'll have a drink."

As he prepared Cokes for both of us, Mrs. MacMurray joined us. Since passed away, Lillian MacMurray was one of the most beautiful women I had ever known. Tall, slim, with black, glistening hair, erect carriage, and an engaging smile, she was the epitome of Eastern chic. I always thought her formal elegance and Fred's taste for fishing, hunting, and raising cattle were incompatible, but it was readily apparent that they shared a great love and mutual respect for each other's interests. Lillian greeted me warmly and then the three of us sat down to discuss the upcoming layout in *Look.* The editors wished to have their photographer cover the MacMurrays both at their home and the ranch, and my clients readily agreed.

When the meeting was over, Fred and Lillian walked me to the door. We were standing in the foyer saying our goodbyes when I suddenly became aware of an odd sensation in my mouth. Something had gone wrong. I felt movement where movement should not have been. As I parted my lips, I felt a sudden draft between my front teeth. I began to panic. What was happening? These sensations lasted only a second or two. Fred had just extended his hand to shake mine and send me on my way when a pivot tooth, which had been in place for twenty years, suddenly dropped and clattered onto the highly polished oak floor. That first bounce sounded like a rifle shot. The three of us stood there in momentary shock, listening to the unexpected noise and watching that suddenly freed tooth click, clack, bounce, and roll across the seemingly endless expanse of hardwood floor, until it finally landed safely and softly on the carpeting in the adjoining living room.

I clapped my hand across my lips. I didn't want them to see the gaping hole in my mouth.

I had already learned from other disconcerting moments that people became embarrassed only if I did and that their discomfiture generally equaled mine. I had discovered that if I could laugh at myself, my audience could laugh, too. Even though I was mortified, I knew that if I appeared to be the MacMurrays would also be mortified, and I didn't want that. I wanted to spare them, so I made certain they noted I was grinning beneath my whitening knuckles. At that point they started to laugh, too.

I sprinted across the foyer into the living room, retrieved the elusive porcelain, and clapped it back where it belonged. With my forefinger holding the tooth in place, I mumbled, "So long, Fred. I'll talk to you tomorrow."

"Not before you go to the dentist," he yelled as I drove off.

It could have been a dreadfully awkward situation, but it wasn't. We were all able to laugh about it, but only because I initiated the laughter. I was able to hide my discomfiture behind a veil of laughter and in so doing put the MacMurrays at ease.

In my future dealings with Fred, the memory of this incident actually became an advantage (although at the time I saw my tooth skittering across the waxed oaken floor I never would have thought so). Because we had come through an embarrassing situation and

were able to laugh about it, we shared a secret camaraderie—
something that belonged only to us—the Brotherhood of the Loose
Tooth.

Maybe I learned to handle embarrassment early in life because
I seemed to have a continuing series of embarrassing experiences
right at the outset of my career. It was back in my office boy days,
probably before my twenty-first birthday, that an incident occurred
that is still vivid in my memory. Today I laugh about it. When it
happened, I could see nothing amusing about it. In fact, it was
horrendous. Grace Kingsley had invited me to escort her to a party
on New Year's night at the home of Leon Errol, a prominent screen
comedian at the time. Mrs. Kingsley told me that I would meet
some of Hollywood's great character actors. I remember her men-
tioning such names as Edgar Kennedy, Ralph Morgan, Frank Morgan, Eric Blore—people you've probably never heard of, but I was
thrilled at the opportunity to meet them. I dressed appropriately,
I thought, for the occasion. I arrived at my host's home a fashionable half hour late. He opened the door himself, looked at me from
head to toe, said "Good evening," and motioned for me to come
in.

I was shocked when I saw him. "He must be eccentric," I
thought. He was dressed in an old, torn sweater, khaki pants, no
socks, and straw sandals. A corn-cob pipe was clamped between his
teeth. I shrugged my shoulders, thinking that maybe I had come to
a costume party. Knowing that *I* was dressed properly for a Hollywood New Year's night party, I confidently strolled into the living
room.

Everyone else was dressed the way my host was—in jeans, cor-
duroys, sweaters, leather jackets, sneakers, even ski boots. I was
standing there—*in white tie and tails, a silver-topped walking stick
in one hand and a collapsible top hat in the other!* Remnants of my
Eastern university days! In a matter of interminable seconds, it
dawned on me: I had mistakenly dressed for New Year's *Eve!*

What can I say? How can I explain to you the horror of the
moment? I had not only demonstrated ignorance, but I had done

so before a large group of people (not one of whom apparently shared my ignorance), and these were people I had hoped to impress. I was chagrined, apologized to Mrs. Kingsley, arranged for one of the guests to drive her home and left the party, certain everyone was glad to see me leave. I not only embarrassed myself but the other guests were embarrassed for me and discomfited by my discomfiture. That night, when I went to bed, I was certain that my budding Hollywood career was over. Why hadn't Mrs. Kingsley told me that I was improperly dressed? She never told me and I was too embarrassed to ask.

I mentally replayed the scene a number of times over the next several days, reliving the misery of the situation and, for the sake of my sanity, analyzing my reaction to it. I remembered that when I had arrived at the party, the host—who, from the way he looked at me, had clearly noted my unusual attire—did not seem the least bit perturbed. It was after I had entered the house and had seen just how out of place I was, that the situation deteriorated. My confidence melted, and this made the other guests uncomfortable. Had I made light of my gaffe, I now reasoned to myself, the rest of the party-goers might have remained relaxed. I decided to test my hypothesis.

One night, at a party with some friends, I tried out my new-found insight. They were all attentive as I started to tell them about that catastrophic New Year's night. I explained almost gleefully that I hadn't known the proper attire for the occasion. I told them how I had wanted to *die!* I told them that the other guests were so taken aback by my silver-topped walking stick and top hat that *they* wanted to die, too. "And as I ran from the house," I concluded, "praying to God that He strike me dead at that moment, I imagined that I heard a round of applause and loud cheers coming from the house—because I had had sense enough to get the hell out of there."

I had established an air of confidence. My audience screamed with laughter. I laughed too. A week before I had told this story, bemoaning my embarrassment, and those I told, embarrassed themselves, walked out on me so that I could cry alone. Tonight I told the same story, only this time as a young man so secure that he could laugh over his own blunder, and now the world was laughing *with* me. I had learned a priceless lesson.

The person who can handle mishaps with a sense of humor always commands my respect because I know how rare this ability is.

Have you ever thought about what you would do if you were caught with your pants down? I was caught literally one evening in just that position, and I've wondered a hundred times since then whether I could once more practice what I preach about handling embarrassment if it ever happened again.

We were invited by our friends Bonita and Jack Wrather to be their guests at the premiere of their "Lone Ranger" movie, which was to be held at the Kennedy Center in Washington, D.C. Jack, who was a member of President Reagan's "kitchen cabinet," which advised and counseled the president during the transition period, had close relations with the administration, and was assured of a big turnout of government celebrities for the opening night. He and Bonita wanted their Los Angeles friends to share in the festivities and had reserved the entire first-class section of a DC-9 for the trip to Washington. Western attire was the order of the evening and for weeks prior to the event, other invitees were busy searching the shops for the newest in chic cowboy or Indian clothes. Not me. I decided that some blue jeans borrowed from my son, a plaid shirt, a leather-fringed jacket, and western riding boots were good enough.

On the evening of the premiere, when it came time to dress in our room at the Madison Hotel, I confidently took son Ron's blue jeans out of the closet and started to slip them on. I pulled and jerked, writhed, wriggled, squirmed and twisted until I got them up over my buttocks. That done, all I had to do was zip up the fly. I pulled in my stomach. And confidently pulled up on the zipper. Nothing happened. I looked down and finally saw what I should have known days before. Ron's waistline is at least four inches narrower than mine. It was impossible for me to get into his jeans. Roz watched my contortions with amusement. "Why don't you do it the way the kids do?"

"What do you mean? The way the kids do what?"

"They way they zip up their jeans. The only way they can get into those skin-tight pants they wear is to put them on while they're lying on the floor."

"I'm not about to revert to teenage habits at this stage of my life," I thought. "That's ridiculous!"

"Don't be stubborn," chided my patient wife. "Get down on the floor, hold in your stomach, and they'll zip up easily."

Grunting with resentment over this indignity, I crawled onto the floor, did as directed, and sure enough, the zipper did its stuff.

I jumped up very pleased with myself, and then bent over in agony, grabbing my crotch. "Ouch!" I screamed. "I can't stand it."

The jeans had fastened themselves around my private parts so tightly that I was gasping for breath. I twisted and turned until they loosened sufficiently to allow me to walk—slowly and carefully, of course.

Roz roared at my contortions. "Very funny," I growled. "I hope you never have to go through this."

"Serves you right," she replied, unsympathetically. "Someday you'll actually go out and buy yourself a pair of jeans. I'm sick of hearing you boast that you've never owned any."

"Oh, shut up," I replied with feigned anger. Of course, I knew she was right and the sight of me on the floor deserved a laugh.

We joined our fellow guests in the lobby and a few minutes later we arrived at the Kennedy Center. After dinner and canapes, we all strolled into the theater to see the movie. Fifteen minutes into the film came the horrible realization that I had to go to the toilet. I was in the middle of the row, and had to crawl over all the guests to get to the men's room, whispering "Excuse me" to each person on whose toes I stepped. I finally arrived on the aisle, and hurried to the men's room where I performed the essential ritual. Then a horrible thought surfaced. How was I going to get these damn blue jeans back on? I knew there was only one way. I had to get down on the tile floor, pull in my stomach, and pull up the zipper. I started to ease myself down to the floor, and then stopped, raising myself to my full height again.

There I was standing in the men's room of the Kennedy Center in our nation's capital, in my undershorts with my jeans around my knees, perplexed as I had never been in my life. If I got down on the floor and went through the same contortions to get the jeans zipped up again, what would be the reaction be if someone walked in and saw me? What if it was Jack Wrather, or Mike Deaver, Ed Meese, or Jim Baker of the White House staff, or the president himself?

That did it. I had to hurry. I dropped quickly to the floor with a thud and started the wriggling process all over again. An expletive popped out of my mouth—or was it my crotch? The zipper was stuck. I twisted, pulled, inhaled, sucked in my stomach. At that precise moment, I experienced an agony I will remember all of my life. The door opened. Two Washington "cowboys," suited up in their most elaborate dude-ranch-style clothes, walked in, the high heels on their Texas boots sending reverberations through the tile-floored men's room. They didn't see me for what was only a fraction of a second, but in that time span, I closed my eyes and envisioned the page-one headline in the *Washington Post* the following morning—"SECRET SERVICE DISCOVERS MAN PLAYING WITH HIS PRIVATE PARTS IN MEN'S ROOM OF KENNEDY CENTER."

I opened my eyes. It was better to call attention to myself than to be discovered. "Hey, fellas," I called out. They stopped talking and looked down at the floor. They didn't laugh. They looked concerned. "Wh-wh-what's wrong?" they both said, almost in unison. I could understand that, seeing me lying on the floor in a contorted position with a horrified expression on my face (because of their sudden appearance), they thought I was hurt—had had a heart attack, had slipped and broken a leg. "I must take control of the situation," I thought. I had to turn the most embarrassing situation I had ever experienced into a laugh. "Nothing's wrong," I countered now with a big grin. "I just can't get this f—in' zipper to work. It's stuck." "What the hell are you doing on the floor?" one of them asked. By now all three of us were laughing. "I'm wearing my son's jeans. They're too tight. My wife says that the only way to get them on is to lie on the floor, pull in your stomach, and zip them up, but she didn't tell me what to do if the zipper got stuck. I may be here all night."

By this time my two new "friends" were doubled up, hysterical at my plight. The zipper finally got unstuck; I pulled in my stomach and pulled it up into proper position. "Let's help you." They both grabbed an arm and in an instant I was on my feet. We were still laughing. Simultaneously we each took handkerchiefs out of our pockets to dry our tears.

"Thanks," I said with a rueful smile as I began to step gingerly into the lobby. "Next time get a pair of jeans that fit," one called out. "You're so right. I will, I will," I replied as the door closed behind me. I could still hear them laughing as I walked away.

I had been caught with my pants down but managed to avert an experience of total embarrassment, by handling it with humor, humility, and poise.

Rogers' Rules for Fearlessly Facing Embarrassing Situations

1) Above all, *laugh.* Your sense of humor about yourself and your predicament is the key to making others feel comfortable about your discomfiture. It demonstrates your self-control, poise, and self-confidence.

2) Set your own ego aside—always think of how the other person feels.

3) Don't dwell on the situation. Laugh about it, make the best of it, and proceed as normally as possible.

4) Create the secret camaraderie that comes from a shared embarrassment; don't pretend the incident never happened.

DEALING WITH ANGER

Your psychorelations program will be adversely or positively affected by how you deal with anger. Exploding can damage your career because it can alienate you from the people you need as allies. Suppressing your anger, keeping the volcano capped is destructive to you, physically as well as psychologically. But there are ways to deal with anger that are constructive rather than destructive. If you can learn to manage your anger creatively, you can eliminate much of the pain you now associate with this normal human emotion, and simultaneously enhance your relationships with the people in your life.

It took me many years before I learned that anger is a normal human emotion, and should not be repressed. For much of my adult life I thought of anger as something to be avoided or covered up because I felt that any display of it, in my business particularly, was simply not proper.

I was afraid to feel anger and was afraid to express my feelings. Any emotional display, I reasoned, constituted inappropriate public behavior that would be detrimental to my career.

As a result of these feelings, I grew up in an unreal, inhibited emotional climate. I wore a mask for many years and it became such a permanent part of my personality that it was impossible to distinguish between the masked me and the unmasked me. I finally became aware that this cover-up caused me intense anxiety and almost complete emotional paralysis.

For many years I was a cool and quiet man, and very proud of myself for it. I kept a calm appearance but inside my gut there was always turmoil. I loved and hated, liked and disliked, felt anger and elation, frustration and joy, tenderness and harshness, but never showed it, even to myself. The notion had been implanted in my head that staying cool was the best and the only way to lead one's life and that was my adopted style. Did my mother once say to me,

"Nice boys don't show their feelings"? She may have. I don't remember.

If I never got angry, everyone would like me and my public image would continue to improve, I reasoned. A display of anger would deflate my public image and was a threat to being loved and admired. I never scolded my children, for example, in fear that they wouldn't love me.

I must not get angry, I felt, because anger indicated that I really cared about a particular situation. Showing that you care is emotional and there is no room for emotion in the public-relations world. If I stayed cool, I would be loved by everyone. Because I was cool, I tried always to stay in complete control, and any display of anger was an indication of loss of control—something inexcusable.

When occasionally I blew my top, I was upset and confused, and chastised myself for what I felt at the time was inexcusable behavior.

One day I flared up at Bill, one of my associates. In sheer frustration I slammed a heavy paperweight down on my desk. His mouth dropped. He couldn't believe that I had lost my cool. It had never happened before. He retreated hastily from my office. I brooded over the incident for weeks. I had shown emotion. I had shown anger. Inexcusable for me—the cool cat. I sent him three different notes of apology.

Another day it was even worse. I was talking to a client on the telephone. He was unreasonable. He kept nagging and nagging at me. He raised his voice, higher and higher. I sat quietly listening to him. I was steaming. I was dying to say, "Go f—k yourself" and then hang up. But I didn't. I remained apparently detached. I just kept saying "Yes, Jeff," "Of course, Jeff." I wouldn't allow myself to let go. I wouldn't let him know that I was burning inside. The conversation was over. I smiled. I was very proud of myself. I had shown no emotion. But I was furious with myself, not because I hadn't told him off, but because he had gotten to me. My anger toward him turned inward. I could feel myself boiling inside.

Was something wrong with me? Maybe being so controlled

wasn't such a good idea after all. Could I have been wrong when I had said to myself a thousand times, "Keep smiling even though you feel like screaming"?

I decided that I needed help from an expert. I went to a psychologist and told him about my problem dealing with anger.

After three sessions, my philosophy took a 180-degree change in direction. The evening he told me that there was no need for me to see him again, I wrote down the following points expressing my new and current belief about anger:

1) Anger is a normal human emotion and should not be repressed.

2) I had always repressed my anger because I wanted to be loved.

3) I know now that it is easier to win love by expressed anger than repressed hostility.

4) I always worked hard at not being angry, and did not realize that although I could put anger down, I couldn't put it out.

5) I always avoided small confrontations so as to avoid one big confrontation, and when I finally exploded, my anger was directed at a "safe" person (wife, child, employee).

6) Occasional expressions of anger help improve communication and understanding between myself and others.

7) Occasional expressions of anger also improve my public image.

8) Expressing anger reduces my anger.

9) An outburst of anger does not require an apology.

10) Getting angry is not synonymous with losing control.

11) An acceptance of anger as a normal human emotion is not an excuse for tirades and temper tantrums.

THE RIGHTS AND WRONGS IN EXPRESSING ANGER

Once I discovered that there is no shame in anger, I began to study how members of our firm, and other people with whom I dealt in the world of business, handled it.

Adam, for example, gets mad at one or several of his colleagues day in and day out, usually because of some trivial nonsense. The cumulative effect of his anger is totally negative. He is like the boy who always cried wolf. People pay little attention to him, and his public image leaves much to be desired. No one takes him seriously because in their eyes he is an angry fool. His anger is not just counterproductive to what he wants to achieve, but to his own credibility. The key people in his life anticipate his angry outbursts and actually entertain themselves by mocking them behind his back.

In contrast, Samantha knows how to express her anger in a manner that enhances her public image. She and Adam share equal pressures as account executives, but Samantha knows that constant outbursts of anger will achieve nothing in getting the day-to-day work done. She could get just as angry as Adam about those annoying matters that provoke his tirades but she brushes them off as inconsequential. Instead, she looks for constructive ways to solve the minor frustrations that arise in every office. She is much more effective in her relationships with her associates than Adam is, and I predict that five years from now she will have achieved more success than he.

But Samantha is a human being, too, and there are times when she gets angry and shows it. When she has worked hard on a proposal for a client, and two of her colleagues have not done their share of preparing for an important meeting, she erupts. Those at fault know she has a right to get angry and they don't resent her outburst. Her associates respect her occasional displays of anger because they are always justified.

While Adam's and Samantha's ways of handling anger represent the more common methods, there are other ways that complicate the problem.

George's anger is genuine. And he becomes so violently angry so often that he intimidates those around him. He is different from the boy who cried wolf because he takes on a fearsome appearance. His face flushes, his fists clench, and his voice rises to such an uncontrollable pitch that he appears to be on the verge of exploding. Rather than be subjected to his wrath, people have a tendency to snap to attention when he raises an eyebrow. He gets things done, and his accomplishments are prodigious, but he rules with fear, and I often think, "Who would want to spend an evening with him?" George is a law unto himself.

Frances is difficult to read. I have watched her keep her cool, seemingly without an emotion in her soul, under circumstances that would have provoked logical and justifiable outbursts of anger in most of us. I suspect she is like I used to be—a cool cat who is ashamed to show her natural emotions. It wouldn't surprise me to hear she goes to the ladies' room and throws up after a confrontation. She won't let anyone know that she is probably seething inside, and I fear she will get an ulcer one day. People like this need to *learn to blow up*—at the right time, of course, and with proper control and justification.

The timing of your expressions of anger is one of the factors that will elicit respect, contempt, or even humor from the people at whom it is directed. Getting angry won't hurt your image. To the contrary, a show of anger can actually win you respect—*if* it is expressed with justification at the right time and the right place. However, choosing the right time takes control.

Do you want to let off steam? Do it when the other fellow is alone in his office and doesn't seem to be harassed by a lot of other problems. You want him to listen to what you have to say with as few distractions as possible. Also, pick a time that is advantageous for you. Try and do it at the end of the day, so that you can go home and have a martini to ease the tension that automatically builds up during such explosions. Don't carry it around with you all day.

Timing assumes a proper choice of location, and circumstances. When a boss yells at an employee in the presence of others, he embarrasses everyone and loses respect. Two people yelling at each other within earshot of other members of the staff will find that they both have slipped in the esteem of their colleagues. Losing your temper in public is bad timing. Expressing anger should be a private matter, not a public affair. If you're angry with one of your associates, raise your voice and tell him off if you must, but do it behind closed doors and soundproof walls. If you suspect that you will be seen or overheard, take him for a walk in the park, or go out for coffee.

As I have tried to improve my own method of dealing with anger, and watched how others deal with it, I have come to certain conclusions that may help you cope with this problem.

Anger can create chaos in your life. Violent crimes, rape, and murder result from uncontrolled rage. Lives and careers are ruined by anger. My cousin, author Budd Schulberg, who has been writing a screenplay based on the life of Woody Hayes, the renowned Ohio State football coach, told me recently that Hayes's whole career was punctuated by violent outbursts of temper. His anger was uncontrollable. He constantly struck out at people physically in fits of anger. In fact, he was fired by Ohio State after a twenty-eight-year career for assaulting a player.

Because anger is a normal human emotion, you cannot eliminate it from your life, but you can certainly harness it. It's not easy but you can master your own anger, and you can learn to make constructive use of it.

In the early part of this book, we dealt with self-image and public image. Both play important roles in learning to deal with anger. In self-image, I have found that the better I feel about myself, the more effectively I can deal with my anger. In public image, the more effectively I am able to deal with anger, the better the impression I make on the people around me.

The first rule I set for myself when I learned to deal with anger was:

Don't Explode

Explosion is a natural reaction for so many of us. Someone attacks us, and we automatically strike back without thinking of the consequences. Someone insults us, slights us, treats us shabbily, and *pow!* we start swinging.

Again, I repeat that it is not easy to break long-established behavior patterns, but even if you have been exploding all your life, it is possible to break this destructive habit.

What do you substitute for an explosion, an outburst? It will take tremendous self-control but you can do it. Instead of exploding:

Think

Yes, think. Count to ten, and think. Think about how you are going to handle this situation. What do you hope to accomplish by expressing your anger? What is your objective? You are too mature, too intelligent to blow off steam just for the hell of it. Take some time to develop a strategy. Stay in control. This won't dissolve the anger. It shouldn't. But your anger should be expressed so that it doesn't hurt you or others.

Neil Clark Warren, formerly dean of the graduate school of psychology at Fuller Theological Seminary and founding partner of Associated Psychological Services in Pasadena, California, in his most recent book, *Make Anger Your Ally* (Doubleday, $13.95), writes: "My own experience has led me to devise a three-thought process:

1. Why am I angry? Focus on hurt, frustration, and fear.
2. What do I want from this encounter?
3. How can I get what I want? What is an effective strategy?"

Once you have developed a strategy, you must follow through and express your anger in a controlled manner. Learning to deal effectively with anger means that you are in control of your life.

Handled properly, the expression of anger can be an asset rather than a liability.

There are some experts in psychorelations who can express anger effectively without raising their voices—certainly an admirable trait if you can do it—with perfect control, and a few short words. The person on the other side of the desk becomes putty in their hands. A master of this technique is Lew Wasserman, chairman and chief executive officer of MCA, a billion-dollar entertainment and publishing empire. One day, many years ago, I was the person on the other side of his desk.

I was holding a meeting with the late Taft Schreiber, a business associate of Lew's, who, in an aside, told me, "Lew is mad as hell at you. He thinks you're handling that situation very badly. You ought to see him and straighten it out." I thanked Taft for the advice, and we continued our discussion along other lines.

As I was driving back to the office, I realized how disturbed I was. I had known Lew for many years. We enjoyed both a personal and business relationship. MCA was in the process of converting from a theatrical agency to a television production company, and he had asked us to handle the public-relations programs for a number of the television series it was producing. Why would he be angry with me? What had I done or not done? If there was something wrong, why didn't he call me and tell me? I began to get angry with him—a natural reaction for most of us. The moment we hear that someone is angry with us, we rear up like wounded horses and start kicking in self-defense.

I walked into my office and asked my secretary to call Mr. Wasserman's secretary to make an appointment. Twenty minutes later the call came back. Mr. Wasserman could see me at five o'clock that afternoon. From two-thirty to four-forty-five I stewed and stewed, my resentment rising to a fever pitch. I left my office and walked quickly to the MCA offices, arriving precisely at five o'clock.

"You can go right in, Mr. Rogers," said his secretary. "Mr. Wasserman is expecting you."

I stormed into his office. He stood up from his immaculate, paper-free, eighteenth-century desk and smiled.

"I hear you're mad as hell at me," I said angrily, ignoring his smile. I was itching for a knockdown, drag-out confrontation.

"Sit down, Henry," Lew said quietly. I did. He sat down too.

"I'm not mad as hell at you at all," he continued, still with a smile on his face. "I'm not even angry with you. I'm very disappointed in you, but I'm not mad at you."

Suddenly, the whole atmosphere changed. I took a deep breath and then let it out. I looked at him. He looked at me, still smiling. I had been itching for an argument, but you can't very well argue when there's nothing to argue about. My mind began to race. "He's disappointed in me. I let him down. I must have done something to make him lose his confidence in me. I've failed him."

"You're disappointed in me?" I queried timidly.

Lew went on, explaining the specifics. He was right. What I had done was not commendable, although I had not been aware of it until that moment. Ten minutes later I left Lew's office, knowing that I would never make that mistake again. Despite having received a slap on the wrist—albeit a constructive one—I left liking and respecting Lew Wasserman even more than I had when I walked in, and that's what psychorelations is all about.

"I'm disappointed in you." What an apt expression! It says so much. It so affects the person to whom it is said. It says, "I like you, I have a high opinion of you, I respect you, I want to continue to be your friend, but you let me down, so we have to talk it out calmly and intelligently and then you have to do something positive if you want to restore my faith in you." That is what that expression meant to me when it was uttered by Lew Wasserman. Think about what he accomplished when he said, "I'm disappointed in you." He rid himself of his anger and resentment without exploding, he let me know what he thought of me, and he strengthened my image of him, all at the same time. A rare accomplishment, and I am proud we have remained friends over the years.

I expect that you will get angry at times. There's nothing wrong with an occasional show of temper. Begin to think, however, about what kind of impression you make on people when you do get incensed. Make sure that your outbreaks are not damaging your public image. Remember, too, that there are times you will be more effective by controlling your emotions and saying, "I'm not angry with you—but I'm terribly disappointed in you."

Rogers' Advice on What To Do When You're "Mad as Hell and Not Going To Take It Anymore"

1) Don't explode.

2) Buy time—think it through.

3) Decide why you are angry, what you want from this encounter, and how you can get what you want.

4) Develop a strategy to express your anger based on your answers to these questions.

5) Follow through.

6) It is best not to get angry with superiors or clients.

7) If you can, keep your cool. Save your anger for when it really matters.

8) Direct your anger where it belongs. Don't take it out on "safe" targets—a spouse, a child, a subordinate.

9) Keep your anger focused; don't let it degenerate into wholesale name calling. Be angry about what happened, not angry at who did it.

10) Above all, be sure you have your facts straight. There's nothing worse than getting angry at the wrong person, or about something that did not happen the way you thought it did.

6

When things go wrong

IN PREVIOUS CHAPTERS I have advised you to accept responsibility, indeed, to seek it out. What happens when disaster strikes—when things go wrong? What happens is that those most skilled in the use of psychorelations are able to make the best of a bad situation, minimizing losses or even turning a problem into a new opportunity. How do you respond when the going gets tough? This is the proving ground for many on the road to success—your superiors will judge you on your ability to handle difficult and tricky situations.

TAKING THE BLAME

In the business world, Murphy's Law ("When anything *can* go wrong, it *will* go wrong") operates continuously. All of my life, I have had to listen to people making excuses for disasters. And nothing that goes wrong is ever their fault. Can you imagine how often a business executive has heard these excuses?

"Don't blame me. Joe was supposed to do that."
"My alarm clock didn't go off."
"The statements are late because the computer shut down."
"The secretary made an error."
"I never got the message."
"The messenger never showed up."
"We checked the sound equipment just before you started to speak, and it was working."
"The copy machine broke down."
"I didn't know there wasn't film in the camera."

I've heard them all. Excuses, however, are cover-ups at best. They are never solutions. The unfortunate consequence is that when there is a cover-up, the problem doesn't just disappear. It usually festers and grows out of proportion until it explodes, causing a major upheaval.

In most cases, people blame someone else. If that is your normal inclination and you want to improve your image within your organization, then it's time to assume a new posture. Open up the problem to public view and take the blame—even when you aren't responsible for the problem.

It is usually fear of punishment or humiliation that prevents a person from taking responsibility for something that has gone wrong. Yet, if you look around carefully, you will find that the person who assumes the blame is the person who is often the most liked, most respected, and most admired. No one punishes him, no one humiliates him. He is trusted because he has the self-confidence and self-assurance to say, "It's my fault."

Why should you take the blame even when the problem may not be your responsibility? Because each time you say, "It's my fault," you put yourself in a leadership position, you win added admiration and respect. You set yourself apart from everyone else, because you are, in effect, saying to your associates, your boss, your clients, or your customers, in a very gentle way, without offending them or putting them down, "I have sufficient confidence in myself to take the onus off someone else, and eventually I shall be recognized as a distinctive person who is moving forward decisively and aggressively."

By the way, this applies to your personal life as well. Millions of marital problems could be averted if the husband or the wife would just say, "I'm sorry, darling, it's my fault." It is impossible to estimate how many pending divorces might disappear from the court dockets if one of the claimants would have the courage and the humility to say, "I admit that I'm to blame for our troubles. Let's get back together, and I'll try harder this time to make our marriage work." But it rarely happens that way. Pride, arrogance, and poor psychorelations prevent most people from solving their marital problems—simply by taking the blame.

"It's my fault. I'll take the blame."

Have you ever noticed that when you say that, all the tension leaves the room? Suddenly a situation that was beginning to develop into a major conflict disappears. The other person is suddenly disarmed. There is no longer a point of contention between the two of you. You have taken the other party off the hook. The moment you place the load on your own shoulders, the problem is resolved.

There are different types of situations where taking the blame is appropriate. There are the times when the only response to discovering you've made a major goof is to come forward spontaneously to face the music. At other times, you may have made an unwitting error that comes to your attention only when someone confronts you with it. But there are plenty of problems that are caused by someone else; and still others for which no one is really at fault. In *all* of these situations, coming forward to take the blame can serve your public image well.

On rare occasions someone walks into my office and says, "I messed up a situation. Will you help me straighten it out?" I look at that person with added respect. It took courage for him to tell me a problem exists that I should know about, and that he is responsible for it.

For example, Elizabeth came in one day, her face pale. She was smoking furiously, obviously in an agitated state. I had never seen her like this. "Sit down," I said. "Would you like some coffee?" She shook her head vigorously. "No, no thanks, I'm just so upset. I don't even know how to tell you what I did."

She had inadvertently put herself, our organization, and an important client in an embarrassing position. She had given United Press International incorrect information on the client that he felt was damaging to his business. He had asked us to demand a retraction from UPI, but it was difficult to demand one on information we had given them in good faith.

For anyone not familiar with the public-relations business and with the world of journalism, this may not sound like an earth-shaking tragedy, but I knew it was a serious problem that had to be dealt with. In my book *Walking the Tightrope*, published in 1980 by William Morrow & Co., I explained the title. I told the reader that in the public relations business we always walk on a tightrope. We have the client on one side, and the media on the other. If we offend the client and he discharges us, we have taken the first step toward bankruptcy. Simultaneously, we must retain the respect, confidence and good will of the media, for without their cooperation, we cannot properly represent our clients. Hence her dilemma and consternation.

"Stop fretting," I said, "we'll figure out a way to handle it."

I tried to console her, and, finally, when she began to calm down, I started to question her. She opened up and finally explained how she had gotten herself into such a mess. There was no immediate solution to the problem, but I knew that a number of diplomatic telephone calls could begin to smooth over the ruffled feathers of the other parties involved in the imbroglio.

"I feel terrible about this," she said.

"I don't," I replied. "I'm very pleased—at least about the long-range implications."

She looked up. "I don't understand."

"You learned something today that I've been trying to get through to you for years. You have a tendency to sweep your problems under the rug; you avoid discussing them. You never seem prepared to admit that you are human and make mistakes. Worse, you avoid taking the blame for anything that happens. I'm not upset with you. You made a mistake that any one of us could have made, but this time you didn't hide it. You came in and told me the whole story, and together we figured out how to handle it. Who knows what kind of repercussions we would have faced if you hadn't? I'm not at all upset. I'm grateful to you."

As she stood up and started to open the door, I looked at her and smiled. "Next time I mess up I'll tell you, and you can help me straighten it out. Okay?" This time *she* smiled. "Okay, you've got a deal." I was left thinking that it was probably the first time she had smiled all day.

ALWAYS TAKE THE BLAME

I mentioned earlier that you could improve your public image by taking the blame in *all* situations. You are probably skeptical, wondering how it could possibly be in your interests to do so when the problem at hand is not your fault.

Victor Kiam, president of Remington Products, is a name you should recognize. He's the man in the television commercial whose wife bought him a Remington electric razor for Christmas and he liked it so much that he bought the company. Victor has been a friend and a client for many years. We first met when he was sales manager for a division of International Latex Corporation. That is when we established our friend/client relationship. A number of years later he became president of Benrus Corporation and once more hired us to represent his company. One day Victor called with a complaint.

"Damn it, Henry," he said, "your people have really screwed things up this time. I asked them to handle a project for me and not one thing has gone right with it since they started." I had to think quickly. I didn't know anything about the project he was referring to, and I could do nothing to appease him until I learned the facts.

"Excuse me, Victor. I can't speak with you intelligently until I get briefed on my end. Let me speak with Richard about it and I'll get right back to you."

"Okay," he grumbled.

Richard gave me a rundown on what had taken place. Our public-relations plan had gone wrong because Victor's associates had second-guessed us and had worked counter to the agreed-upon program. It was clear that we were right and the client was wrong. I stood up.

"What are you going to do?" Richard asked.

"I don't know."

"Are you going to tell him off?"

"Of course not," I replied firmly.

"Why not? You admit that we're right and he's wrong."

"That has nothing to do with successfully resolving the problem. This is a case of client relations. It's a case of retaining our integrity and overcoming a client's dissatisfaction at the same time. Telling him he's wrong won't accomplish that at all."

In the seconds it took to walk back to my office and get Victor on the telephone, I had decided what to do.

"I just got all the facts, Victor, and you're absolutely right. We really handled this situation badly."

"Well, I'm glad you admit it," he said, and I noticed that his voice was a little more pleasant than it had been minutes before.

"I'd like to talk this over with you. Let's have a drink and kick it around. Can you meet me at about five-thirty?"

"Sure," he replied, "I'll meet you at the Oak Bar at the Plaza."

At five-thirty-five we ordered our drinks.

Victor, looking very pleased with himself, smiled and said, "So your people admitted that they screwed up."

"You're so right. I'm glad you called. How else can I find out what's going wrong in my office unless a client like you calls up and complains? When I checked it out, I found that the situation was even worse than you had painted it."

Victor took another sip of his drink. "Really? What don't I know?"

My moment had come. "Well, you really should know that we're only 98 percent responsible for the mistake."

"Who's responsible for the other 2 percent?" he asked warily.

"Your people. We were on the right track and everything was going smoothly until your people, Jim and Ed specifically, started to second-guess us. But it was *our fault*. We let them get away with it. We should have stood up to them and insisted that we continue with the plan as it had been laid out. If I had known about it, I would have called you."

"Why, those idiots, why didn't they stay out of it? I'm really going to tell them off in the morning." Now Victor was getting angry all over again, though this time, fortunately, not at us.

"Don't do that," I advised. "Your company has had a good relationship with Rogers & Cowan for a long time. Jim and Ed are our day-to-day contacts. If you blame them, they're going to take it out on us, and that won't do either of us any good. Just forget about it. They were probably doing what they thought was right. Next time we'll insist that it be done our way."

The crisis was over. The client had been in the wrong, but I took the blame. And the company benefited because I did.

Always take the blame. There are even situations where no one is at fault, but where it still pays to take the blame.

For example, recently I had a meeting with another client. Jim Roberts, an investment banker, was complaining in a not-unpleasant manner that we were not accomplishing enough for him. (Incidentally, please don't get the impression that we represent only dissatisfied clients. I deal with problem situations in this book because my experiences with them better illustrate business difficulties on the road to success.) This situation I handled in a different manner.

"You're embarrassed about bringing up your dissatisfaction," I said to our unhappy client. "We're friends, and you don't want our personal relationship to be impaired. You thought it was your problem. Well, it isn't at all. It's our problem, and I'm about to turn it into a nonproblem. You're expecting me to convince you that we should continue to represent you, but I'm not going to. We haven't been able to accomplish anything meaningful for you. It's not because we haven't tried. We have, but our efforts have been fruitless. The media just haven't responded to our approaches. We've done our best, and we can't do any better. Maybe someone else can. I'm going to tear up our contract, even though it doesn't expire for another six months. In fact, I'll help you find another public-relations firm that might be able to do a better job."

Jim was dumbfounded. He looked at me in disbelief.

"I can't believe it. You mean that you won't try to convince me that you've been doing a good job?"

"No, I won't. I'm like a lawyer. I'll take your case, but I won't guarantee winning it. I'm like a doctor. I'll give you the benefit of all my experience, but I won't guarantee curing you. Unfortunately, there are always some clients whose public-relations problems we can't solve, and I'm sorry that you're one of them."

"You've really surprised me," Jim said. "Your frankness is very rare in the business world."

"Maybe you're right, but don't forget that this isn't just altruism. I'm a businessman. I could have insisted that you live up to the terms of our agreement, but, if I had, you might have bad-mouthed us all over town. When I agreed to tear up our contract, I knew that I had earned your good will, and, someday, when someone asks you about Rogers & Cowan, you may even speak well of us."

Three months later an important new client walked into our office. He had come to us upon the recommendation of Jim, my friend and ex-client.

You can see how much can be gained by taking the blame.

Rogers' Hints on Taking the Blame

1) *Always take the blame.*   Consider taking the blame as an extension of taking responsibility.

2) Take the blame even when you are not directly responsible. It puts you in a leadership position and enhances your image.

3) Use taking the blame as a way of defusing potentially explosive situations.

WE HAVE A PROBLEM

Try this exercise:

Say to the young man who sits next to you in the office, "I have a problem." He will probably yawn and continue to clip his fingernails.

Walk into your boss's office and announce, "I have a problem I would like to discuss it with you." She will probably look up from her desk and say, "See me later in the day. I'm busy now."

Inform your wife after dinner tonight, "I have a problem." She'll probably reply, "Wait until I finish reading the newspaper."

Then, wait a few days and try a variation.

Tell the same young man who sits next to you in the office, "*We* have a problem." He will probably sit up, drop his clipper, and eagerly ask, "Oh, what is it?"

Your boss will ask you to sit down and tell her about your collective problem, and your wife will let the newspaper wait until you tell her about the problem you share.

No matter how much you care about someone, it is impossible to respond with the same interest to "I have a problem" as to "*We* have a problem." The moment *we* enters the conversation, you have touched a sensitive nerve in the other person. Suddenly you are talking about him or her—not just you. Suddenly the problem affects you both.

When you say, "*We* have a problem," you are relating to others in terms of their own interests. You will find that when you do this, they will be more likely to listen to you and understand you. They will be more sympathetic and ready to help you solve your problem because you will have made it their problem, too.

One day, I received a letter that, on the face of it, clearly looked like *my* problem. "Dear Henry," it began, "I have been very dissatisfied with your services in recent months, and I wish to discontinue our relationship as of December 31." It was a letter of discharge from Peter Fearon, President of Kronenbourg, USA. I must admit that we deserved it.

The account supervisor we had assigned to work on Kronenbourg couldn't relate to the French-born marketing director who was the day-by-day client we dealt with. He was accustomed to French marketing methods; my associate was rigid in his American way of thinking, and there was no rapport between them. Another account supervisor then took over and exceeded the budget we had quoted for a promotion at Bloomingdale's. Finally, a press conference we had set up did not get the results both we and the client had anticipated. The public-relations business never operates smoothly but I could never recall so many mishaps as those that befell us as we attempted to launch Kronenbourg beer in the United States.

I thought the situation was irreparable, but I decided to try to persuade Peter to change his mind. It was a challenge in psychorelations. The first good sign came when I called and asked him to have lunch with me. He agreed. If he was willing to meet, he was willing to talk. Had he been adamant about severing his relationship with us, he would have refused my invitation. At least I had a chance.

"It's really remarkable," I said after we had ordered our lunch the following day, "how an organization like ours, successful as we've been for so many years, can make so many mistakes on behalf of one client in so short a time."

I could sense that Peter was relaxing. I was making it easy for him to get his complaints off his chest.

He started on Jack, who had been our account executive. Not

only had Jack made a number of mistakes, but his behavior toward Peter's associates was questionable.

"But you have to understand that Jack hasn't been the only culprit in this messy business," I said.

Peter seemed surprised. "Really! Who else?"

"Me."

"Why you?"

"I should have spotted the first mistake and stepped in. If I had done that, all the problems we're talking about now could have been avoided."

"Oh, come on now, Henry," Peter protested. "You can't be on top of every client in your organization. You can't know what's going on all the time. Your business is far too big for that."

"That would be a bum excuse, and I won't use it. Between Warren Cowan and myself, we're supposed to know what is going on with every client. I'm more responsible for what's happened than Jack is. I'm the one who goofed."

Peter was my guest. He couldn't very well criticize me personally at that point, but I was taking all the blame, and I felt that he might now be reconsidering his decision. Toward the end of lunch, I felt the time had come for me to take my best shot. How do you get a client to rehire you after he has discharged you for doing a bad job?

"Pete," I said, "*we* have a problem."

"What's that?"

"How do you know that the next public-relations firm you hire won't mess things up even worse than we did? You spent hundreds of hours indoctrinating us in your business. Now you'll have to start all over again with another office. They might perform better than we have, but maybe they won't. Then where will you be? Will you then start up again for the third time?"

"Well, there's something in what you say," he countered. "What do you suggest?"

"Here's my suggestion. Give us another chance. Rescind the discharge letter—temporarily. Give us a week to work out a new plan. We've learned a tremendous amount about your business in recent months, but we never developed a strategy that worked. I'll be personally involved, and this time you and I will agree on what the strategy should be. Then I'll bring in a new team to work on your account. I'll stay on top of the activity, and once a month you and I will have lunch, go over everything that is happening, and, if we spot any problems, we'll catch them before they become serious."

"That sounds logical to me, Henry. The idea of starting up with a new firm doesn't appeal to me at all. I'm willing to give it another try."

About six weeks later, I received a letter from Peter saying that he had been quick to complain and that he now wanted to tell me how pleased he was with the services he was receiving from Rogers & Cowan.

Peter remained a client for a number of years, but he would not have if I had not used my best psychorelations techniques on him. I acknowledged that our company was at fault for his dissatisfaction and that I, in particular, was taking the blame. That was one point I established. The other was that it was just as much his problem as it was mine. I approached it as something we both had to solve together.

Rogers' Hints on Presenting a Problem

1) Although you take the blame alone, *share* problems with others. "*We*" have a problem. Others will take a personal interest in it. Even if they recognize that it is more your problem than theirs, they will be flattered that you brought it to them for discussion.

2) Remember that timing is important in presenting problems. "We" won't feel like discussing our problem unless "we" have the time to do so. Choose the time and the place to discuss the problem carefully.

3) If the problem is serious, choose a nonoffice situation, such as lunch or cocktails out. The atmosphere is pleasant, and other business distractions are minimized.

LOSING THE BATTLE TO WIN THE WAR

Just as taking the blame is an indication that you have a healthy, mature ego, so is your acceptance that winning every battle every day of your life is counterproductive. Let's study this statement, for essentially it's what psychorelations is all about. Have you ever tried to carefully evaluate what you actually gained when you won a battle and supposedly forfeited when you lost? If you ever did, you would be shocked to discover that many times the losses were wins and the wins, losses.

Over the years you can remember winning many arguments you've had with your business associates, your friends, and your family. You stepped on toes and gave other people's egos a series of blows. Don't wince. We have all done that. In each case you won a victory of some sort, but what did you win? Too often, all you won was short-term satisfaction, ego gratification. "I showed that SOB," you said to yourself, and then went on about your business ready to step on the next person's toes as soon as a similar situation arose.

Conversely, what have you lost? What do any of us lose when we insist on winning every battle? I believe very strongly that relentless insistence on victory brings us closer and closer to losing the war, the war we are all waging, to become successful. If success is your target, start to think long range. Forget the satisfaction you get from winning a minor skirmish, and begin to focus on your long-range objective—*building a favorable public image.*

In the public-relations business, we quickly learn that building and retaining positive relationships with our clients, the media, and our associates is essential to success. We know that winning an argument can hinder rather than help those relationships. If I must disagree, it is imperative that I get my point across without putting down a client or making him suffer the humiliation of defeat.

What do I gain if I prove my client wrong? Nothing. Oh, for a moment, I may feel smug and superior, but in fact I have lost. My client doesn't want to be told that I am more intelligent or have better judgment than he has.

What do I gain if I win an argument with one of my associates? Nothing. Usually, all I will have earned is his resentment. He will be annoyed with me for besting him in what he regards as a battle of wills. Our relationship will be damaged, and my business will suffer as a result.

I do not suggest that you always knuckle under. I don't recommend that you compromise your self-respect. I just want you to think long range rather than short range. Size up every situation as it arises. When you get into a discussion with someone, consider the consequences. Is it important in the overall scheme to retain his respect? If so, choose your words wisely and remember that you have a long-term goal—success. Sometimes it is even appropriate for you to deliberately make a point of losing an unimportant battle.

A number of years ago, for example, two of my associates were in combat over an issue they apparently both considered vital, but which, in reality, was comparatively unimportant when viewed within the context of their careers and our total business.

The issue was the administration of our New York office. The Beverly Hills office, which is corporate headquarters, is charged with supervising the New York operation, but there was disagreement as to what constituted supervision. It was logical for the Beverly Hills office to guide and counsel New York-based personnel on how Beverly Hills-based clients should be handled, but New York had its own long list of clients to represent. How could Beverly Hills supervise work on clients who were 3,000 miles away? If we were to build a solid New York organization we had to give them their head, allow them to take on greater responsibility without supervision. Their argument was spilling over to others in our organization, and I could see that our normally smooth-running firm was now divided into two camps. I decided to step in and try to settle the argument. I selected the person I thought was most flexible as my target.

I asked her to have lunch with me one day.

"Jennifer," I said, "you can't win that argument. I advise you to back off."

Her lips tensed, she puffed furiously on a cigarette. "I'll be damned if I will. I'm right, he's wrong, and I have to fight for what I believe in."

"I agree that you're right."

"You do?"

I could see her soften up perceptibly.

"Of course I do," I continued. "But there's no way to prove it, and where is it leading you? You've lost sight of your priorities."

"Priorities? Priorities? What do priorities have to do with it?"

"Everything. The number-one priority in your life is your daughter and your husband. If you're irritable in the office because of this situation, as you are, it's only logical that you're taking it home with you. I'll bet your family isn't too happy with you these days."

Jennifer smiled ruefully. "You're right. I've become a bitch at home."

"Your number-two priority is your success as a businesswoman." I was speaking carefully and softly because I knew I was stepping into sensitive territory. "You've worked hard to get where you are now. You're very ambitious and you want to go even further than you already have. This silly argument can prevent you from getting there. If you finally win, you still lose because the guy you're battling with is your immediate superior on our organization chart. If you force him to back down, he'll always resent you, which means you've probably cut yourself off from further growth in our company. If you back down now, he'll feel as though he's won a great battle."

Jennifer took my advice and backed off. She took the long view that the argument was deterring her from her goal. As a result, she is much more successful in our firm than she was when her feud was at its height, and one reason why is that her opponent still thinks he won the argument. In fact, he is her most devoted champion.

Assess the way you've been conducting your life. Are you intent on winning short-term battles? Do you ever say to yourself, "Well, I certainly put him in his place?" You probably learned the importance of winning battles as a kid on the playground, and it's been a part of your psyche ever since. That is why it is so difficult to change your thinking. Don't infer from my sermonizing that I was born with this wisdom. I paid high prices to acquire it.

For weeks, I had been planning a dinner party. The guest list was comprised of personal friends, clients, and a number of out-of-town press. One of my associates came into my office a few days before the event. He sat down and said, "I just got a call from Charlie. He's back in town unexpectedly and asked what was going on in the social season. I told him I'd check around and let him know. I was just thinking that he'd probably love to be invited to your party."

I thought for a moment and then made a decision. "I'd rather not. I know he's a very important client. But let's face it. He's a boor. I just don't think he would fit in with the other guests."

My associate bristled. He stood up and began to pace the floor. "Damn it, Henry," he said angrily. "It doesn't matter that he's a boor or whether he fits in or not. You said yourself that he's an important client. You've invited some of his friends, and he'll be hurt when he discovers he hasn't been invited."

"Christ," I replied petulantly (I must admit). "Don't I have the right to determine my own guest list when I host a personal party in my home?"

"It's not a personal party," he retorted heatedly. "Once you invite one client and one press person, it becomes a business event."

He was right, but I wouldn't relent. My associate stood up and glared at me. "You just don't understand," he muttered, as he stormed out of my office.

That night I began to think about the confrontation. "What a damn fool you are," I berated myself. "What difference does it make if Charlie comes to your party? The party will proceed smoothly. What does it matter if he is comfortable with the other guests or not? Is it really important that some of your other guests aren't comfortable with him? He won't make or break the party. Don't you realize that you're offending one of your key business associates by satisfying your silly ego—your ego that demands that you and only you determine who gets on your guest list? You always tell your people to watch their priorities. Here's a case where your own priorities are all screwed up."

The next morning I walked into my associate's office. "Do you remember the argument we had yesterday about Charlie?"

"Yes," he snapped angrily. "I remember it very well."

"Well, I thought it over last night, and I decided I was wrong. I've just added his name to the guest list."

He smiled and, looking up from his desk, nodded appreciatively and said thanks. I would have lost a lot if I had won this battle and persisted in keeping Charlie off my list. If I had not backed off from my original stubborn and unwarranted position, the dissension caused by the confrontation would have permeated the whole office. It was just another case of losing the battle and winning the war.

"YOU'RE WRONG—NO, I'M RIGHT"

"I know nothing except the fact of my ignorance." If this axiom was good enough for Socrates, whose wisdom has survived for 2,400 years, then it is good enough for me. There are very few things in life of which I am really sure, and, consequently, I am reluctant to tell anyone he's wrong. It may turn out he's right, and where does that leave me? Not in a very enviable position.

Besides, such polarized argument or debate is a waste of time. It took me many years of agonizing business and personal experiences to discover that telling a person he is wrong is useless. No matter how convincing I am, when the discussion is over he still will not agree with me.

If I use a psychorelations approach, and talk it out, trying to convince him of my position, and allowing him to try to convince me of his, we will usually arrive at an understanding that satisfies us both. This is another example of losing the battle and winning the war.

If I am pro-abortion, can I ever convince an anti-abortionist that

I am right in my beliefs? I am better off discussing another subject with him. If I am a Palestinian can I ever convince a Zionist that I have a right to return to the land I consider my home? If I am interested in having a conversation with him, I had better find something else to talk about rather than waste my voice, my time, and my energy on a no-win situation for both of us. If I am pro-Reagan, is there any point in discussing Reaganomics with a liberal Democrat? Will we ever get beyond the point of "You're wrong" —"No, I'm right," "No, you're not." What is ever accomplished?

One day, in a meeting with one of my associates, I said, "Paul, I may be wrong, but there could be a better way to develop this campaign on Paul McCartney."

Paul bristled. "I'm on the right track, and I'm sure of it."

"I'm not arguing with you. I admitted I may be wrong. In fact, you're probably right, but I wish you would explain the strategy to me so that I can understand it."

Paul was not on guard any longer. He was no longer defensive. I had asked him to become the teacher, with me as the student. He patiently started to explain the approach he was using with the client. Suddenly, he stopped. His mistake was becoming apparent to him.

"I guess I might have to change this a bit. What do you think?"

"I'm not sure," I replied. "Let's explore it a little further." We did. The words "right" and "wrong" were never mentioned again. Two businessmen discussed a public-relations strategy, without a show of temper, ego, or emotion. We finally decided what the strategy should be—not by my making an arbitrary decision, but through the process of give and take.

Paul left my office that day feeling good about himself, feeling good about me, and realizing that the client was about to be better served than if the original plan had been executed. If I had opened our conversation by saying, "Paul, you're wrong," a useless argument would have ensued, which could only have brought results detrimental to the client and to our relationship.

Why try to prove to anyone that he is wrong? If you believe in the importance of your public image and accept my premise that life is fuller, richer, and more rewarding if people think well of you, then most arguments based on right and wrong can be easily avoided. If you want to argue, then realize that your opponent will still remain firmly convinced that he is right and you are wrong; understand that if you force your viewpoint on him, he'll resent you because you made him feel inferior and inadequate.

Rogers' Rules for the Strategic Retreat

1) Avoid heated nonbusiness discussions of highly controversial, emotionally charged topics. Keep your opinions on abortion, the Middle East, etc., out of your daily business life.

2) Never trample over someone else's opinion, even if it is (in *your* opinion) incredibly stupid. Resist the temptation to humiliate him by showing him how thoroughly wrong he is. Save your ego gratification for something positive.

3) Don't respond in kind when someone tries to run roughshod over your opinions. How did you let yourself get roped into discussing a volatile subject anyway? Diplomatically change the subject or otherwise find a way to call for time-out.

4) Know when to give in. "The customer is always right" may sound trite, but saying "You're right" or "I may be wrong" enables you to take the emotional heat off of a conversation so that the discussion can proceed toward a solution. Then you're *both* right!

7

Communicating your way to success

"COMMUNICATION" is the buzzword of the eighties. Today, we employ and enjoy the most sophisticated means of communication the world has ever known. Eighteen million homes in the United States are wired for cable television; satellites are already beaming billions of messages to us. In a few more years, shopping, banking, and even ordering a baby-sitter through our television set will become commonplace. The electronic communications revolution is upon us. Personal communication, or psychorelations, is obscured in this barrage of mass communication. Yet personal communication is the single most effective tool you can use to play the politics of success. From your first interview to your retirement party, personal communication is the key to success.

In psychorelations, each person sends and receives messages to and from other people every day of his life. His skill is dependent entirely on how proficiently he *communicates*. Your ability to communicate effectively will always be essential to your success. What value are your talents, your abilities, your charm, your personality, unless you are able to bring them to the attention of those people who can help you become successful? Effective communication with business colleagues will help you make the favorable impression that is the major objective of our psychorelations program, because it is that favorable impression that is the key to your success.

THE FIRST IMPRESSION

The first step in communication comes with the first meeting. Let's review what happened the first day you worked at your present job. In the first few moments that your presence became known, many people looked at you and sized you up. Without even being aware of it, you made your first communication—you conveyed your first impression. How did you look? Frightened and apprehensive—or confident? How were you dressed? Were you in conformity with the others, or did your appearance cause you to stand out like the proverbial sore thumb? Were you wearing jeans and a T-shirt while everyone else wore gray flannel Brooks Brothers suits with button-down-collar shirts? Were you wearing an elegant black dress with pearls, thinking that it was appropriate for the occasion, only to find that the other women were wearing preppy tweeds? Had you not thought about how you should look that first day or were you shrewd enough to anticipate the proper attire for the occasion?

If you hadn't thought about it before, start thinking about it now, for your personal appearance communicates a message about you, favorable or unfavorable, every moment of every day. Are you dressed properly? Are you neat and clean? Is your carriage erect, stomach pulled in, and shoulders thrown back? Are you smiling as you make your entrance or are you scowling? All of these elements determine your first communication with your associates every morning.

Think back to your first day in the office. Can you objectively look at yourself, and analyze what first impression you made on those who are important to you in the organization? Do you believe that you made a favorable or an unfavorable impression? If unfavorable, is there anything you can do to change the minus to a plus? What impression are you making today through your personal appearance and personal demeanor? Do your employers approve of the way you dress? Do they approve of your appearance and the expression on your face as you walk down the hallway or over to the watercooler? If succeeding through psychorelations has now become important to you, then you must consider seriously what your boss and your associates think about the way you present yourself.

Rogers' Rules for Making a Favorable First Impression

1) Try to anticipate the normal dress code for your particular company, and wear the appropriate clothes.

2) Be pleasant. No one likes a grouch.

3) Be clean—hair, fingernails, clothes, shoes.

4) Don't chew gum in the office.

5) Speak softly but forcefully. Timidity has no place in your life.

6) Stand erect, sit erect. An office is not a place for slouching.

7) Look everyone in the eye. Don't skulk to avoid notice.

8) A cheery "good morning" or "good afternoon" will win a like response.

9) Be positive—not negative

10) Give the impression of having great energy—even if you have a hangover.

VERBAL COMMUNICATION

Your next step in communication begins with the first words you utter, and from that moment until the end of every day your ability to communicate favorably—on a one-to-one basis, in a group, or on the telephone—depends almost entirely on your conversation. Your communication, good or bad, will be dependent on your ability to speak—to speak so that you capture attention, cause people to listen to you, and express clearly what you are saying.

The first key to verbal communication is to ascertain in advance who your audience is. Then you must adjust your speaking style to him or her and what he or she represents. You cannot communicate effectively with your boss, your spouse, your children, and your business associates if you use the same words and the same style of speaking with each of them. You may give a speech to a group of corporate executives and receive a standing ovation. Give the same speech at a labor union convention and it will probably have a lukewarm response. Know to whom you are speaking, and adjust your speech style accordingly.

It is only logical that we are impressed with a person who speaks to us in terms of our interests. If you hope to communicate through speaking, then remember to steer the conversation toward topics that interest your listener and speak to him in language that he will comprehend.

When I speak with David Mahoney, former chairman and chief executive officer of Norton Simon, I steer the conversation around to the television commercials he did for Avis Rent-A-Cars. If I am at a dinner party with John Coleman, I talk to him about the improved service at the Ritz Carlton Hotels in New York and Washington, which he owns. Sonny Werblin and I talk about the operation of New York's Madison Square Garden. I compliment Ed Ruscha on the retrospective of his paintings at the Los Angeles County Museum of Art. If any one of these gentlemen then want to turn the conversation around to me and my interests, I acquiesce, but I always make it a practice to steer the talk in their direction first.

Whether you are talking to your boss in his office, or to an auditorium filled with 200 people, the key to successful communication is the same: Know your audience; adjust your speaking style to them. Then speak to them on subjects that interest them.

How can you possibly know the interests of someone you never met before? Easy. What is her profession? Is she a designer, an architect, or is she with an advertising agency? Once you know that, it should be comparatively simple to get the conversation going, because you have a clue about that person's primary area of interest. If you happen to have lunch with your boss, and you get the impression he wants a break from the usual business talk, you should know where to steer the conversation. If you have been at all perceptive, you already know a lot about him. You know that he is interested in baseball or football, or his golf game, or art, music, or even his grandchildren. If you steer the conversation in one of these directions, he will quickly recognize your efforts to make him feel comfortable by addressing his interests. If you have misjudged his intention and you discover that he really wants to talk business, no harm has been done. He will soon stop talking about his grandchildren, and bring up the subject he originally planned to discuss with you.

I do my homework when I'm about to meet with someone I've never known before. Recently I lunched with a gentleman named James Marlas, president of Mickleberry Corporation. He had been buying up advertising agencies for ten years, and only a few months before had purchased Cunningham & Walsh, one of the largest agencies in the world. He was now interested in buying our company. I felt it was important that I know something about him before our meeting. I visited the *New York Times* the day before, read up on him in their files, and when we met face to face for the first time, I was already briefed on his background and his accomplishments in the business world. The two hours we spent together were comfortable, and the conversation was easy and enjoyable because I knew what to discuss with the man who sat on the other side of the table. He was impressed sufficiently with Rogers & Cowan to make an offer to buy our company before lunch was over. We rejected his proposal because the price was not intriguing to us, but the point is that the meeting was pleasant and productive because the homework had been done.

When you are speaking before a group, it is essential (either through research or previous experience) to know who they are and what subjects interest them. This requires your having done your homework in advance. Try to obtain a variety of opinions on who will comprise that audience and what their interests are. Even when you think you have done your research thoroughly, you still might run into problems. I have many times.

I was scheduled to be a guest speaker at a booksellers' convention dinner when my first book, *Walking the Tightrope*, was published. Never having addressed such a group before, I was concerned about the subject of my talk. I asked the manager of a Beverly Hills bookstore for some advice. He said, "These people mostly run mom-and-pop operations; I'm sure they would be interested if you gave them some tips about how public-relations and promotion techniques can help them improve their business." I took my friend's advice, prepared my talk carefully, and was convinced I would receive nothing short of a standing ovation.

What a surprise I received! My audience didn't listen at all to my prepared address. They laughed among themselves, oblivious to what I was saying. They never even realized when I finished; they just kept conversing as they had before. The president and the program chairman, who had invited me, were the only two who applauded, and not very enthusiastically at that.

I was naturally disappointed, and was curious about why I had not made a better impression. What had happened? Why had I failed? I asked a number of acquaintances who had been in the audience. One local bookseller, whom I knew well, summed it up.

"You blew it, Henry," he said. "These people are out for an evening of fun. They don't want you to tell them how to improve their operations. They're looking for laughs. They were expecting you to tell them funny stories about their favorite movie stars, and, if you had thrown in their bedroom habits, that would have been even better."

My mistake was that I didn't know my audience. I had accepted one person's opinion, and, while his advice was well intentioned, he had been wrong. I should have done more research. From then on, I knew better.

It took time but at long last I discovered how to talk to an audience in terms of its own interests, and in terms of its own aspirations and expectations. When I do, the response is always favorable.

If you are talking to your boss, the subject should be about his business problems, or his golf game, or the dinner party given by his beautiful wife—not about your broken leg, nor your inefficient secretary, nor your hangover. The fact is that he is more interested in himself than he is in you, and if you want to impress him, talk about him.

There are times, of course, when your best course of action is to say nothing, to listen intently, and to at least give the impression that you understand what is being said. I was reminded of this one day when I accompanied Danny Kaye to Washington, D.C., where he was scheduled to conduct the National Symphony Orchestra.

Danny had been invited to have lunch that afternoon at the Supreme Court, and he asked me to join him. By then I had been privileged to spend time in the company of not only the world's most important actors, actresses, and business executives, but with presidents, princes, princesses, an empress, and a number of prime ministers as well. The Supreme Court, however, I regarded as the ultimate elite.

I knew that the Supreme Court was in session, so I decided to bone up on the cases under consideration. I picked up current copies of *Time, Newsweek, U.S. News and World Report, The Nation,* and *The New Republic,* and by lunch I had a fair idea of what the court was reviewing.

Chief Justice Earl Warren had extended the invitation, and had told Danny that he would invite a number of his colleagues to join us. At twelve-thirty we walked up the steps of the Supreme Court building, and I felt as excited as a teenager going to his first dance. I looked at the frieze on the front of the building, on which is carved the legend EQUAL JUSTICE UNDER THE LAW, and I was reminded that despite incessant criticism of our federal government, the Supreme Court is still sacrosanct.

It was an exhilarating experience, mounting those marble steps, realizing that I was about to enter the most historic and the most famous hall of justice in the world, a site where the most important judicial decisions in our nation's history had been and were continuing to be made. We opened the enormous bronze door and entered the imposing marble foyer. We were announced by the receptionist, and in a few minutes were in the august, paneled chambers of the chief justice of the Supreme Court of the United States of America.

The chief justice was a striking-looking gentleman: tall, heavy-set, with a shock of thick white hair, a ruddy complexion, and rimless glasses that partially hid his sparkling, luminous blue eyes. He had taken off his official judicial robes, and was wearing a navy suit, white shirt, and dark patterned tie. A broad smile lit up his face. He was obviously pleased to see his old friend Danny.

"I won't ask you to sit down," he said. "Lunch is ready and we're all hungry, so let's go to the dining room. They're waiting for us."

I didn't know who "they" were, but I would soon find out. We left the chief justice's chambers and walked down a series of marble corridors to a formal dining room where the justices have lunch every day when the court is in session. Waiting for us, and I recognized each one of them from photographs that have appeared for so many years in newspapers and magazines, were Associate Justices Potter Stewart, Byron S. White, Thurgood Marshall, William J. Brennan, and the late William O. Douglas. They had all shed their black robes, and each was dressed in a conservative dark-colored suit and white shirt, befitting a Supreme Court justice.

I was momentarily awe-struck by the group, but the chief justice introduced me around and each judge extended a warm hand of greeting. We sat down, Danny between Warren and White, me between Brennan and Stewart.

I sipped my tomato juice and waited for the expected words of wisdom to start flying around the room. This is what I had been anticipating all morning. The greatest legal brains in our country, perhaps in the entire world, were about to dispense their erudite thoughts, their intellectual insights to these "commoners" from

Hollywood. I expected solemnity and ritualistic dignity. But instead I found myself in a warm, congenial, spirited gathering.

Justice White opened the conversation. "Well, Danny, you must be pretty proud of your Dodger team this year." "I sure am," replied Danny cheerily. "Walter has put together the best bunch of ball players in the league and I'm ready to bet that we'll win the pennant." "Oh, I don't know," chimed in Justice Brennan, "I think that the Padres may have some thoughts about that."

I didn't believe it. The greatest legal brains in the country were spending their lunch hour chatting about baseball! This was not the time for me to show my ignorance by trying to join in. I know little about baseball, so I was better off keeping quiet and making no impression at all.

At one point, Justice Stewart turned to me and said, "We haven't heard from you, Mr. Rogers. Do you think Sandy Koufax is a better pitcher than Don Drysdale?"

"I can't answer that," I replied. "I have to confess I'm not a baseball fan. If Danny had alerted me as to what the conversation was going to be at lunch today, I would have studied the sports pages this morning instead of boning up on some of the cases you have on your docket. I thought I'd make my mark by asking you some questions about some of the cases you are now considering."

Justice Stewart laughed. "You'll have to save those questions for another day. You see, we usually discuss baseball at lunch during this time of the year. It relaxes us and prepares us for the afternoon deliberations."

He returned to the conversation and I was left to listen to baseball talk through dessert and coffee. I knew when to remain quiet.

Rogers' Tips on Talking

1) Think *before* you speak. I can't emphasize this point enough. In psychorelations, it isn't how much you say, but *what* you say, *how* you say it, and *when* you say it. When in doubt, say nothing.

2) Know your target audience. Speak accordingly. Think not

only about the *content* of your speech, but also about the *quality* of it. Don't speak softly to a large gathering, or loudly to a small group.

3) In a one-on-one conversation, allow some time for small talk. You put the other person at ease and make him or her feel important by asking about their nonbusiness interests.

4) When addressing a group, be sensitive to the individuals in the group. Do not address a group as "gentlemen" if there are also women present. Saying "gentlemen—and ladies," with the "ladies" added as an afterthought, only makes it worse.

5) *Look* at your audience, whether it's one person or one thousand. For a large gathering, single out individuals to look at and speak to them personally.

6) Speak slowly and distinctly, if you can. If you find yourself getting nervous (I'm an expert on this!), call for time-out. Take a deep breath, perhaps a drink of water or coffee, smile, and proceed.

WHAT'S THE POINT?

Many of us never realize that before you start a conversation, before you make a point, you should determine the objective of what you are about to say. Do you want to convince someone of something? Do you wish to relate an anecdote? What reaction do you hope to elicit from your listeners? Do you want them to laugh or cry? Do you want someone to take some action based on what you say?

Very few of us think through in advance what we hope will come out of an impending conversation, what action we anticipate will be generated, and what we want to accomplish. That may well be the reason why we have such a problem getting our points across. If we don't have a specific goal in mind, there is a better than even chance that we also don't know exactly what we want to say.

If you believe you are not communicating because you are never sure what you want to say, consider this personalized communications program: First, determine your objective. Do you want a salary increase, do you want to solve a problem that perplexes you, do you want approval for a new idea, do you need help on a sticky situation? Once you have decided what you hope to accomplish through the impending conversation, clarify in your own mind what you want to say. You may even want to write down the major points you wish to make, in proper order, and then read them aloud so that you can satisfy yourself that they are clear, succinct, and persuasive.

Communication is a two-way process. You may be about to send out a message, but it will not have been communicated unless the other person receives it. Do you believe that the subject matter will grab the other person's attention? Is it a subject he understands? Is it something that interests him, something he can relate to? Decide all of this before you start to talk. What you say is important. *How* you say it is just as important. The only time you communicate with words alone is when you write a letter. Your voice utters more than just words. It also denotes enthusiasm, ennui, concern, elation, gloom, anger, contentment, authority, and much more. So decide in advance *how* you are going to say it.

Take the positive approach whenever you speak. Psychologist Dr. Herbert H. Clark tells us that it takes the average person almost twice as long to understand a sentence that uses a negative approach than it does to understand a positive sentence. So, if you want a salary increase you should not say, "Is there any reason why I can't get a raise?" Your boss will find plenty of reasons. Instead you should say, "I believe I should get a salary increase because ———." If you give a number of solid, justifiable reasons, your boss will find it difficult to refuse you.

If you want approval for a new idea, don't start by criticizing the old methods currently in use. The other person will immediately find reasons to disagree with you. In contrast, when you begin by outlining your new idea—and the other person agrees with its advantages—the old plans can be discarded with comparatively little argument.

The positive approach will help you achieve your objectives. As

Michael Korda says, "Negative statements not only interrupt the flow of your remarks, they antagonize and depress your listeners. Remember: nobody is interested in what you can't do, don't know, or won't agree to. Emphasize the positive, and let the negative points make themselves known unobtrusively, if at all."

Rogers' Pointers on Scoring Points

1) Have an objective when you speak. Do not blather.

2) Do not interrupt others when they are speaking, except to ask a point of clarification. A business conversation is communication, not a power struggle.

3) If you are in a group meeting that has lost its focus, do speak up—gently—to try to restore a sense of direction to the discussion. The ability to keep a business meeting on track is a skill that will help you immeasurably. Others will notice and respect you for not wasting their time.

4) Accentuate the positive whenever you speak. If you have good news and bad news, give the good news first. If you can, tie the bad news to something positive. "Although we did not realize our anticipated sales last quarter, our projected earnings for this fiscal year will still be 12.4 percent over last year."

TIMING

Timing is another all-important factor. If you are planning to communicate your ideas to the other person, you must make certain that he is listening to you, not just hearing, but listening, with both ears and both eyes. Make direct eye contact with him immediately and try to discern his state of mind before you speak.

Is he agitated? Is he harassed? Does he appear to have a hundred other matters on his mind? If so, postpone your conversation for another time. Make an excuse to get out of his office. If you are not sure of his mood and decide to chance it, keep monitoring your eye contact with him, and that will tell you whether or not your timing is right.

Watch your listener carefully as you speak, and you will soon determine whether you are truly communicating or whether you are being tuned out. If he is restless, if he looks at his watch, if he asks you irrelevant questions or makes unrelated statements, you will know that you have been tuned out, and you had better schedule your conversation for another time, probably another day.

Ignore the temptation to confront him about his inattentiveness. Remember that you're playing in a political game and your disclosing that you have caught him *not* listening will be perceived as an accusation and make him defensive. Just forget about it for now. Make up an excuse to break off the conversation. At some point later—it could range from hours to weeks—when you feel that the timing is right, start the conversation again, and don't even refer to your first time around. The chances are good that he has forgotten the previous conversation, and, with his mind free of distractions, your chances of communicating are greatly improved.

Rogers' Tips on Timing

1) Don't try to discuss important subjects with people when they are extremely busy or distracted, unless you really have no other choice.

2) Don't try to discuss important subjects with someone when *you* are extremely busy or distracted. There are really very few subjects that won't wait five minutes until you collect yourself.

3) If you deal with the same people over and over, learn to spot their daily mood swings. Some people are morning people, some are afternoon types. Some are ogres on Monday morning; some are at their best then. Try to discuss sensitive issues when others will be responsive and receptive.

LISTENING: THE KEY TO
PSYCHORELATIONS

A conversation is a partnership, a dual relationship between the person who is speaking and the person who is listening. Communication breaks down when the speaker speaks without an awareness of whether or not the other person is listening. It also breaks down when the listener fails to show an interest and a sensitivity to what is being said.

You can't play tennis effectively unless you concentrate. So, too, you cannot completely absorb what is being said if your mind is distracted by what you will order for dinner tonight or that stunning dress you saw in the window of Bonwit's when you went out to lunch earlier in the day.

I always know when my associates are not listening to what is being discussed at an office meeting. There are those who stare into space or doodle on a pad. They file their fingernails, pack a pipe, or light a cigarette. If I ask them to write a report on what transpired, they are hard pressed to do it. They have been hearing, but they haven't been listening. The true listener looks directly at the speaker and follows every word he says. He may not trust himself to remember the points that are made, so he makes notes. The listener comes out of the meeting with infinitely more knowledge than the fingernail filer and, because success is related to learning, is far ahead of the nonlistener.

Most of us *hear,* but we don't *listen.* We are so anxious to speak the moment our friend pauses for breath that we don't digest what he says.

The following is an example of how a lack of listening can detrimentally affect the whole process of communication. One day, a client and I were in his sumptuous Park Avenue office with a *New York Times* reporter who was interviewing him. The reporter sat with pen and pad in hand, asking the questions that would result in what I hoped would be a favorable article.

As the interview progressed, I became increasingly uncomfortable. The journalist was asking questions, but my client wasn't answering them. He just plowed ahead, intent on what he had to say, completely ignoring the reporter's questions. To me, he sounded as though he were reciting Lincoln's "Gettysburg Address" at a Rotary Club convention. I could sense the journalist's annoyance. He was obviously not interested in what my client was saying; he wanted answers to his questions.

At one point the journalist gave me a quizzical look. He said nothing, but I sensed he was asking for my help. "I'm not communicating with this guy at all," he seemed to be saying. "He's not listening to my questions, and I'm not getting the story I came for." I knew it was time to interrupt, and I did.

"Excuse me, John," I said. "Mr. Frankel came here to get a specific story and he's not getting it. I suggest that you listen to his questions and give him direct answers."

The reporter squirmed in his seat, embarrassed. John started to glare at me, but then let out a hearty laugh. "Henry's right," he said to the reporter. "I guess I had a fixed idea of what I wanted to say and I've been so intent on getting my own points across that I must admit I wasn't listening to your questions. Let's start all over again. This time I'll listen to what you ask me and give you direct answers."

The interview went very well from then on, and the reporter wrote an article that reflected accurately what my client had said.

Psychorelations involves your relationships with people, and if you hope to impress them, you must *listen.* You probably think you will impress them by *talking.* But, in fact, you will impress them more by *listening.* Although it is a great gift to be able to entertain people, to be fascinating, it can be an even greater accomplishment to make someone else feel that *he* is fascinating.

I was sitting in my New York office one day. It was late morning, and I reminded myself that I didn't have a lunch date. I dialed a number.

"Are you free for lunch today?" I asked.

"Henry, you know I never go out for lunch. I'm chained to this desk," she replied.

"Not today. We haven't seen each other in months and I insist that you take an hour out of your life and have lunch with me."

She laughed and said, "Okay, you've sold me."

At one o'clock that afternoon, Helen Gurley Brown, editor of *Cosmopolitan* and one of the most prominent women in the United States, was seated with me at "21."

Before we even had a chance to order, Helen asked, "Well, Henry, how is your book coming along?" I told her that it had begun to sell nicely and that I was pleased with the reaction it had received. That prompted me to ask her about her own work and her husband David's new movie, which she answered briefly and concisely before countering with another question about my daughter, who had been ill. After a half hour of this, I became aware of how much I was enjoying myself.

Lunch over, we walked out onto a sunny Fifty-Second Street. As we parted, Helen said, "It was such fun, Henry. I love having lunch with you. Call me on your next trip to New York, and we'll do it again."

"Of course I will. We always have so much to talk about."

As I walked back to our office, I thought, "I like Helen. She's so bright." As I ruminated on the pleasant luncheon, I analyzed why it had been an enjoyable experience.

The one reason, I concluded, was that we had communicated. She invited me to talk and then listened as I did. I did likewise. We maintained eye contact, and by my facial expressions and an occasional "uh-huh," or "I see," she knew that I was interested in what she was saying. She showed the same attentiveness while I was speaking. She gave me a chance to express myself. I did the same for her. We had a rewarding and fulfilling conversation that day because both of us maintained a proper balance of speaking and listening.

LEARNING TO LISTEN

There are hundreds of courses given in high schools and colleges throughout the country that teach students how to speak fluently, effectively, clearly, articulately, and positively. I don't know of any school that teaches a course on "How to Listen."

I believe that I listen better and remember more than most people because I often make notes during a business meeting.

When I have lunch with a client, an associate, or a business contact, invariably points are made, information conveyed, names mentioned that I will want to use in the immediate future. In fact, I don't understand the business person who does not make notes. How does he remember everything he should remember?

A few years ago, I had a meeting with Imelda Romauldez Marcos, the first lady of the Philippines. She is a fascinating, brilliant, voluble woman. I listened intently for the first few minutes of our conversation, trying to absorb everything she was saying, but it became apparent to me that I faced impossible odds. She was saying too much too rapidly for me to fully grasp it all.

When she paused for a moment, I said, "Pardon me, Madame Marcos, do you mind if I make notes on what you're saying?"

"Not at all," she replied. "I would be flattered if you did."

I became a reporter. I looked at her intently, at the same time scribbling notes on what she said. The meeting went on for four hours. I could never have absorbed even 10 percent of the conversation if I had not listened intently and made notes.

Mrs. Marcos subsequently became our client (this was long before the Aquino assassination) and to this day when the subject of her philosophy arises, I still refer to the notes I made the day we first met. More important, I am confident that my relationship with Mrs. Marcos stemmed from that first meeting when I inadvertently made a favorable impression because she quickly recognized my interest in her by my taking notes.

Being a good listener does not necessitate being a passive listener. If you are a good listener, you will give as well as take. If you are listening intently, questions will come to mind. When the speaker pauses, ask them. Even though you may allow him to carry the bulk of the conversation, an occasional relevant comment makes you an active participant. Your comments are as important as your questions, because, without them, it would be an imposition on the speaker to keep asking him questions. Comments are your way of contributing something to the conversation while simultaneously making the other person feel important.

There are several other ways that you can demonstrate attentiveness. Look the speaker in the eye. Don't let anything or anyone divert your attention. Nod in agreement when he makes a telling point. Interject an occasional "Oh?" or "Yes, of course!" If the conversation begins to lag, you can always pick it up again by asking appropriate questions. Appropriate questions, I warn you, can only come if you are really listening. If your mind is wandering, and you bring it back into focus with an inappropriate question, it will not only prove to be embarrassing for you, but insulting to the speaker—the very person you have been anxious to impress.

Rogers' Rules for Listening

1) Think about what is being said.
2) Blot out all distracting thoughts from your mind.
3) Concentrate exclusively on what the speaker is saying.
4) Look him straight in the eye.
5) Let him know that you're listening by asking occasional appropriate questions.
6) Don't interrupt his train of thought.
7) Make notes on what is being said under proper circumstances.

COMMUNICATION MEANS SENSE
AND SENSITIVITY

Communication is nonexistent if there is a lack of sensitivity between two parties who have a need to communicate. Husband
and wife, employer and employee, parent and child, worker and
co-worker must be sensitive to each other's needs. How can we
communicate with the Soviet Union if we are insensitive to its
philosophy, its political system, and its problems? How can an
employer communicate with his employees if he is not perceptive
about who and what they are and what makes them tick? Are you
insensitive to the needs and interests of someone who is important
to you? Is that person insensitive to your needs and your interests?
Do you think that it might be time to talk it out? Do you think
that you may have been ignoring or covering up this problem for
too long? Is it time for sensitivity, talking, listening, communicating?

Personal communication breaks down and relationships deteriorate when there is a reluctance to talk out a problem. Problems
do not disappear if you hide them. They only get worse. Husbands
and wives don't talk out their problems, and the result is an
ever-increasing divorce rate. Employers don't communicate with
their employees, employees don't make their needs clear to their
employers, and industrial chaos and dissatisfaction are the results.

Why do two people have so much to say to each other before they
are married, and so little to say shortly after the wedding? Why does
the employer turn on all his charm when he is trying to convince
someone to join his firm, and then turn cool and indifferent once
the person becomes an employee? The reason is that once the
period of wooing is over, *we all have the tendency to retreat to our
own needs and interests.*

For many years, my partner Warren Cowan and I profited from
the relationship we had with David, our business adviser and attor-
ney. Recently, however, our relationship with him had begun to

deteriorate. He wasn't returning our phone calls as promptly as he always had in the past. Requested memos that would normally have been on our desks in two days were now taking two weeks to arrive. Every other day I walked into Warren's office, or he would walk into mine. "Have you heard from David?" I would ask. "Did that memo come in from David yet?" Warren would ask. With every "no" each of us would go back to his office, wondering and worrying about what was happening to our relationship with a man whose friendship and counsel we cherished.

One day, I said to Warren, "The situation with David is getting serious. Let's do something about it."

Warren thought for a minute. "You're right. There's a problem. Let's get it out in the open. There's obviously been a communication breakdown between us. Maybe he's just as annoyed with us as we are with him."

A few days later, David, Warren, and I sat in my office during lunch hour with sandwiches and iced tea in front of us. I broke the ice.

"David, we have a problem."

"I know," he replied, "do you want to get someone else to represent you?"

"Hell no, that's exactly what we don't want. We want you, but there's obviously something wrong, and we would like to get to the bottom of it. We always communicated very well with each other, but we don't anymore."

We waited for David to respond. After a moment he said, "I'm glad we're talking. You're right. Our relationship has been deteriorating in recent months, and it's time we got it all out."

Warren, David, and I talked together quietly for an hour. He had some grievances about our behavior. We had some complaints about his. We became aware of what had been troubling him, and we told him what was bothering us. Each grievance and each complaint was minor in itself but together they had grown into a Frankenstein monster that could have destroyed a valuable relationship.

David continues to represent us because we spotted our problem and talked it out.

How sensitively are you communicating in your job? Do you have a good relationship with your boss and the people you work with? Test yourself.

Have you studied them, and do you study their needs and reactions? Do you communicate with them in terms of their interests —or yours?

Do you complain that people don't cooperate with you, that you can't get them to do what you would like them to do? It may be that you are trying to force your point of view on them and are ignoring theirs. Most people would never admit it, but it's possible they are not *understanding* what you are saying to them, that you are not getting through.

People are not going to work effectively with you just because you snap your fingers or push a button. You must motivate them by communicating with them effectively. You can accomplish this by learning what they want, what their needs are, so that you can talk to them in terms of their own interests. Everyone you work with is a distinct individual, not necessarily thinking as you do. Each person has his own ideas, his own point of view, and you will be more successful at your job if you get to know him and learn to communicate with him, in terms of his own interests.

Do you speak clearly and succinctly? Are you certain the other person is listening? Do you show interest? Do you give him your complete attention when he is talking? I hope that by now you understand what very few people do—that speaking and listening are not synonymous with communicating. Personal communication is a long and complex process, and, if you hope to achieve any degree of success in your lifetime, it is essential that you understand it, be conscious of it, and give it the highest priority in your relationships with the people who comprise your world.

Communicating with people is the key to psychorelations. Psychorelations is the key to your public image and your public image is the key to your success.

Rogers' Rules for Communicating

1) Stop, look, listen, think, and feel! Communicating involves not only speaking and listening, *but* sensitivity to the sensitivities of others.

2) Think of the other person's needs and interests before your own.

3) Don't sweep your communications problems under the rug—talk them out.

4) Fight the normal tendency to take long-standing relationships for granted—keep communicating. Communication is more difficult to maintain with long-standing relationships than with new ones.

5) Watch for the signals that communication may be breaking down.

8

Taking over

CHIEF EXECUTIVE OFFICERS aren't born, nor are vice-presidents, general managers, or entrepreneurs who run their own businesses. Most of those who hold responsible positions in today's world started at the bottom and fought their way to the top. They schooled themselves, trained themselves, or were trained by their superiors until someone tapped them on the shoulder and said, "You're the one for the job." They started on the assembly line, in the mailroom, or as a gofer. The road from gofer to chief executive officer is long and arduous, but there is probably no better way to learn a business. When I reminisce with a group of friends about our early lives and mention that my first job was as an office boy, no one seems surprised. Most of them started the same way.

I started as a five-dollar-a-week office boy. My son-in-law Mike Medavoy, now executive vice-president of Orion Pictures, started his career in the mailroom of Universal Pictures. Lew Wasserman, chairman of MCA, was an usher in a Cleveland movie theater. Helen Gurley Brown was a secretary for fourteen years before she wrote *Sex and the Single Girl* and subsequently became editor of

Cosmopolitan. Robert Peterson, owner of Peterson Publishing Company and recently named by *Forbes* one of America's "Richest Four Hundred," began his professional life in the publicity department at MGM Film Studios. Very few successful people start at the top, or even in the middle.

THE FIRST BIG PROMOTION: YOU'RE NOW RUNNING THE MAILROOM

The major difference between the gofer and the chief executive officer is that no one works for the gofer, but everyone reports to the CEO. The climb up the ladder from mailroom to corner office really starts the day you are chosen from a group of mailroom boys —and girls—and are appointed head of mailroom operations.

This is your first step toward a management position and it is the day that the first big change takes place in your business life. You now have a staff! Yesterday your performance was measured by the performances of the others in the mailroom who have now become your responsibility. You must now motivate them to do better, because your own future is dependent on how efficiently everyone performs.

BECOMING A TAKEOVER PERSON

You must develop a plan not only for yourself but for the others as well. You must organize your staff into a smoothly operating team. Before your promotion, it didn't matter whether you swept the floor first or delivered the mail.

But now it's different. As a young person who has come this far —from just another guy or gal in the mailroom to mailroom supervisor—you want management to notice you and prepare you for the next, more important job that opens up. You must do the job better than your predecessor ever did. This calls for planning—both for you and for your staff. Staying an hour later at the end of the day in order to get all your work done is no longer the answer. Now it is also your responsibility to make certain that everyone else gets his work done.

It immediately should become apparent that there are certain things you don't know how to do. For example, other people had previously been responsible for operating the telex, the copying machine, and the postage meter. They will remain someone else's responsibility, but you will want to learn those basic tasks very quickly.

You're thinking ahead. Suppose you're the last one in the mailroom one night and the boss asks you to send out a telex. If you don't know how, it will have to wait until morning, and the boss will be annoyed. If you do, score another point for you. He will remember that you're the person who helped him. Your first responsibility, then, is to learn what everyone else in your department does, and how to do it yourself in case the need arises.

Once you know what everyone else's job entails, it is time to develop your own style. There is no one way to become an effective takeover person. There is no one way to manage a business that involves supervising three or thirty or three hundred or three thousand people. Harvard Business School will give you one set of answers, Stanford another. Every successful executive will give you his own formula. Each formula seems to contradict the next. This should not bother you. There is never only one way to do anything.

Warren Cowan and I successfully operate the fourth-largest independently owned public-relations firm in the United States. We have completely disparate styles. We are living proof that there is no one way to be a *takeover* person. I have three or four people report to me. Warren has at least ten. I prefer to have one-on-one meetings with clients. Warren prefers to have one or more of our associates with him. I write innumerable letters and detailed interoffice memos. Warren writes very few. He is at his best late in the day. I am at my best early in the morning. I like seven-thirty breakfast appointments. He doesn't. He entertains at restaurants. I entertain at home. We are both very good salesmen. He comes on very strong. I am told that I undersell. Each of us has his style and each of us is successful in his own way.

EDUCATING YOURSELF TO TAKE OVER

The transition from handling your own responsibilities to taking on responsibility for the work of others is most difficult. We have discovered time and time again that a competent account executive, responsible for three or four clients, finds it difficult to adjust his work habits when he is asked to become an account supervisor. He knows what to do himself. He knows his own priorities, and has the abilities required to perform as an account executive. When we ask that person to move up to account supervisor with three account executives reporting to him and responsibility for fifteen clients rather than three or four, rarely does he have the know-how and the confidence necessary to handle his new job.

Most new managers are reluctant to admit that they need guidance. Don't be one of those. Yell for help, but don't assume that will be enough. It will take much more than someone's guidance and counsel to give you the knowledge required to become an efficient manager. Most successful executives get to the top not only by working at the job that has been assigned to them but by educating themselves in the management role.

Observe the executives in the company. Study them coldly and objectively. Who is doing the best job? Who is the most effective? Who doesn't seem to be making it? Why?

As you look at each executive, begin to rate each one positively and negatively. Gradually, a pattern will evolve. You will admire certain traits in some people. You will be critical of the behavior of others. "Management" is happening every day all around you. Learn from it what you can.

How to Win Friends and Influence People by Dale Carnegie, first published in 1936, is still the most valuable "how to be successful" book I have ever read. I have also gleaned valuable insights from Michael Korda's *Success* and his best-seller *Power;* also *Skills for Success* by Adele Scheele. America Management Association holds seminars throughout the country regularly, and they also publish books and pamphlets that can be helpful. The Dale Carnegie Institute is worth investigating. *Success* magazine runs articles every month offering advice and guidance and their advertising also features courses, seminars, and more books that can assist you in achieving your goal.

Check out your local college or university. Many offer extension courses in management and business administration. Larger corporations often provide support and incentives for continuing education. This can take the form of tuition assistance, paid time-off if class hours overlap the business day, or the promise of a raise or promotion on successful completion of course work. The intellectual stimulation of the outside world can inspire you to take a fresher look at what's happening within your organization.

For a quickie guide to becoming a good supervisor, read Kenneth Blanchard's *The One Minute Manager* (Morrow, $15.00). Here are noted some techniques that have worked well for me over the years. Remember, however, that these are only the methods that have been effective in *my* experience. If a procedure doesn't work for you, change it. Develop your own executive style. After all, *you're* in charge!

Rogers' Supervisory Suggestions

When you are asked to become a supervisor:

1) Determine in advance how much supervision each of your subordinates requires. Some need a lot, some just a little.

2) Devote the major portion of your time to supervision. Begin to phase out your personal responsibilities and turn them gradually

over to those who report to you. Above all, don't fall into the trap of doing both your work *and* theirs. Doing their work is not your job.

3) Set up with each of your subordinates a short- and long-range plan for each of his responsibilities, preparing with him a weekly and monthly timetable for the completion of each assignment.

4) Work with each of your people to set up weekly and monthly priorities. Put the plan on paper so they know exactly what is expected of them and when.

5) Meet with them at least once a week to determine their progress, and help them in areas where they need help.

6) Show them constructively where they make mistakes but don't berate them for their errors.

7) When they have problems you can't solve, ask to have a meeting with your superior. Don't be reluctant to bring the problem upstairs.

8) Meet with your superior each week, tell him about your successes and failures—and ask him for guidance on how you can do better.

COMMUNICATING FOR RESULTS

I have heard this complaint a hundred times: "I feel like I'm cooped up in a cage. I never know what's going on outside of my own office. My boss never tells me what's on his mind. He never criticizes and he never gives me a compliment either. Does he know that I'm alive?"

The people who make those complaints do not work for well-managed companies. Communication—continuing communication—is all important between a manager and his employees. If it exists, chances are that everyone is better off: Your employees will have the pleasure of feeling minimal anxiety because they will know precisely what you want and don't want. You will have the satisfaction of knowing that you've reduced the chances of error due to misunderstandings. Make it clear to your people what you expect of them. Explain to them what they are supposed to do, when they are expected to do it, and what you consider to be a good job. Spell it out—on paper and in person. Come to an agreement with each of your people so there will be no misunderstanding or recriminations later on.

Rogers' Conclusions on Communicating for Results

1) Tell your associates what you have on your mind. When you keep them guessing, they become insecure.

2) Explain what you expect of them. Give them goals to shoot for, so that their standards become as high as yours. Better yet, develop goals together.

3) Encourage them to bring you their problems. Frustration is eliminated when they know there is someone to turn to when they have a need.

4) Don't surmise that they know as much as you do. Supervisors have a tendency to talk in shorthand, not realizing their vocabulary is different from that of their subordinates. Spell it out.

5) Write it—then explain it verbally. Many people don't comprehend written communication. After you have sent a memo of instruction, follow it up with a personal meeting where you discuss it line by line.

THE AUTOCRAT AT THE CONFERENCE TABLE

Should the executive be an autocrat or should he rule democratically? I believe that a business, or an office within a business, cannot be run by committee. Managing is not a democratic process. It cannot be done by consensus. But autocracy doesn't work either.

My advice to you is that, as an executive, you should seek advice and counsel from your associates. Listen to them. Don't give them lip service—or should I say "ear" service? Question your associates; listen to their opinions.

Once you have weighed the counsel you have received, then make your own decision. Everyone isn't going to agree with you, but someone has to have a sign on his desk that says, "The buck stops here." In this case, it's you. Once your decision is made, you must make one more move before the issue is closed. If you have taken your associates' advice, tell them your decision and thank them for their input. If you have decided to go in another direction, give them the courtesy of an explanation. Otherwise, they will be left feeling patronized by you. This will give you the best of what both autocracy and democracy have to offer.

Rogers' Do's and Don'ts on Decision Making

1) Seek the counsel of your associates. One or more of them may have an insight into the situation that has not occurred to you.

2) Be objective in giving them all the pros and cons. If you favor one point of view in your presentation, you can't get their honest opinions.

3) Listen and consider objectively. If you have already made up your mind, then you are wasting your time and theirs in asking for advice.

4) Don't come to an immediate decision. Tell them you want to think it over. If you come to an immediate decision, they will believe you had already made up your mind before you called them.

5) Explain your decision-making process. Once you have decided, explain fully how you arrived at your decision.

6) Thank them for their advice—particularly those whose position you did not take.

MAKING TIME

Another frustration that plagues the success-driven person is lack of time. Success eludes him because he is unable to find the hours that it takes, and he finally gives up the struggle. Nonsuccess, he rationalizes, will give him the time he needs to do what he wants or feels he must do.

One day a friend of mine put it in proper context. "To hell with it," he said. "I'm going to relax. Trying to be successful is too tough. I never have time to do the things that really interest me, and it's not worth the sacrifice. I don't spend enough time with my children; my golf handicap went from nine to sixteen in the past year. And I can't even get to read *Time* or *Newsweek*. I've decided to settle for where I am now. I'm not looking for a better job because I'm determined to take the time to do what I want to do."

My friend wasn't asking for my advice, so I didn't offer it. His decision to give up the struggle and become a nonsuccess person because he didn't have time to do the things he wanted to do was simply a gesture of resignation. There must have been other reasons, for he could have found the time for a growing career and a fulfilled personal life if he had stopped to analyze where and why he was spending his time. I have no quarrel with my friend for opting out. My criticism is that he wasn't honest with himself about *why* he opted out.

FINDING THE TIME FOR EVERYTHING

We can all find the time to do what we want to do. Have you ever noticed the way a truly successful person—it could be your boss, your best friend, or maybe just an acquaintance—conducts his life? Though he walks purposefully, he never seems to be in a hurry. He always has the time to talk to you, even though you may not be very important in his life. Don't you wonder how he finds the time to not only see you, but everyone else as well? He seems to get through life effortlessly and with comparatively little harassment, with time to handle his job effectively, time to spend with his family, time for community activity, politics, charity work, and even time for regular vacations. Are you perhaps one of those who, in contrast, never seems to have time for a casual lunch with a friend? Does your family complain that you don't spend sufficient time with them?

In this book I ask you to do many things you have never done before—things that will require extra effort. Does this prospect discourage you? Are you saying to yourself, "But I don't have time to fit one more item into my overcrowded schedule"? Forget that kind of talk. You will learn how to find the time to do everything you really want to do.

You must reorganize your life-style and discipline yourself so that you will have the time to do everything you want to do—*most*. You may find the answer by looking at some of the people you admire. Your boss? Your wife? Your best friend? There must be one or more people around you who seem to have a knack of having the time to do everything they want to do. Talk to them. Ask them. Watch them. Discover their secrets. There is an old adage that says, "When you want something done, give it to a busy person." I see proof of that around me every day.

I can cite hundreds of cases where important, successful people are able to handle their jobs, their civic, community, and charitable activities, and still exercise and have time for their families, too. How do they do it? Their lives seem to be more complex and more demanding than yours, but they are able to accomplish more than you do. They never seem to fret that they don't have time for a vacation because they always do. They also have time to attend the theater, read, and spend time with their friends.

The answer? They have organized their lives better than you have. They don't waste their time. They don't spend three to four hours a night watching sitcoms on television. They have learned how to do the important things first. They have structured twenty-four hours a day so that they have time to do everything they want.

Corporate leaders are ideal examples of the point that the busiest men always have the time to take on another task if it serves their purpose.

Dr. Franklin Murphy, at the time he was chairman and chief executive officer of Times-Mirror, a multibillion-dollar company, was also president of the Los Angeles County Museum of Art and served as a member of the board of trustees of the Ahmanson Foundation, Carnegie Institution of Washington, J. Paul Getty Museum, and National Gallery of Art. He was also on the board of directors of Bankamerica Corporation and Ford Motor Company, and was heavily involved in a myriad of other businesses, charity, art, and community activities.

Rocco Siciliano is chairman and chief executive officer of TICOR, a Los Angeles-based, diversified financial services company. In addition to this job (which consumes eight to ten hours a day), my friend Rocco also finds time to serve on the California "blue ribbon" Commission on Government Reform, be cochairman of the National Academy of Public Administration, trustee of the Committee for Economic Development (New York and Washington, D.C.), and also serve as a member of the board of directors of Southern Pacific Company, Pacific Lighting Corporation, and American Medical International.

Howard Allen is president of Southern California Edison Company. He is currently vice-chairman of the Los Angeles Olympic Organizing Committee and in addition to his Edison directorship, Allen currently serves on the boards of California Federal Savings and Loan, Republic Corporation, ICN Pharmaceuticals, Inc. Pacific Southwest Airlines, Computer Sciences Corp., MCA, Associated Southern Investment Company, Mono Power Company, the Los Angeles Civic Light Opera, the Los Angeles County Museum of Art, the Los Angeles County Fair Association, Pacific Coast Electrical Association, the California Council for Environmental and Economic Balance, and National Conference of Christians and Jews. He was a director of the Los Angeles Area Chamber of Commerce from 1969 through 1981, having served as president in 1978 and as chairman in 1979.

Over the years I have used men such as these as my role models. I admire their ability to accomplish so much, and consequently I have sought to emulate them. In addition to my position as chairman of Rogers & Cowan, I am chairman of the Center Theatre Group of the Los Angeles Music Center, a member of the board of governors of the Performing Arts Council of the Los Angeles Music Center, a member of the board of trustees of the Los Angeles County Museum of Art, board of directors of the Los Angeles Area Chamber of Commerce, vice-chairman of the American Film Institute, cochairman of the Private Sector Public Relations Committee, United States Information Agency, a member of the executive committee and chairman of the Public Relations Committee of the President's Council for International Youth Exchange.

I have a happy marriage with my wife Roz, children, grandchildren, and a fulfilling combination of business, family, and public life.

I have found the time to do what I really want to do, and have been able to accomplish it by laying down a few simple rules for time management.

Rogers' Hints for Making Time

1) Study your time habits. For a day or two, write down what you are doing at fifteen-minute intervals. Do you lose time in long phone calls? Does it take forever to get dressed? Determine where you have been frittering time away.

2) Add real time to your day. Get up earlier. Take a shorter lunch. Is there a faster route to the office? Can you work on the train or in the carpool? Would it help to hold your phone calls for an hour in the morning?

3) Make your "to-do" list into a schedule. Put the "must-do" items at the top.

4) Establish deadlines for yourself. Estimate how much time a particular task will require and try to stick to it.

5) Determine what you want to do that you haven't had time to do. Take active steps toward it. Reserve theater tickets; make a plane reservation; sign up for tennis lessons. Give yourself enough advance notice to make room in your schedule.

MANAGING YOUR TIME AS WELL AS THEIRS

Every executive discovers at the outset that managing his own and his associates' time effectively is one of the keys to his success. Once you determine what is really important for you to do, then it will be time to determine priorities for your associates. As you get into your new takeover job, you will discover that very few of your people are working efficiently or to their full capacity, and you will be appalled at the amount of time that is being wasted. It is essential, therefore, that you set priorities on your own time so that you will be in a position to help your associates set priorities on theirs.

Priorities at this point are more important than they were before. You are now susceptible to having your priorities dictated by the priorities of others. Everyone wants to see you. Everyone has a problem you are called upon to solve. Everyone has pressures they expect you to relieve for them. You must determine your own priorities and get them to fit theirs to yours without giving them the impression you don't care. Here is an area where you must use your psychorelations skills.

You must be the master of your own time. Your associates will need your help. Meetings will have to be held. Your boss expects your attention, too. First you must decide what time you need for yourself. When do you just sit and think? When do you dictate your letters and memos? You must handle all those solo items and still leave yourself the hours necessary to lead your troops and practice the art of psychorelations.

The biggest problem you will face is to give your associates the time they need with you and still leave yourself sufficient hours to do what you must do.

It is difficult to defend yourself against "drop-in" meetings, but you must do it. There was a time when I was so anxious to prove to my associates that I was always available to them, that I encouraged them to "drop in anytime." When they did, I gave up whatever I was doing myself and devoted my time to them. That proved to be a trap. I would never get my own work done. I don't discourage the practice, but now I say, "I'm jammed up now but I'll come to your office just as soon as I finish what I'm doing." I don't trust my memory so I ask my secretary to remind me. In that way I am able to handle my own problems as well as those of my associates.

I ask my associates in advance how much time our meeting will take. Then I fit them into a time during the day when I know I can give them the attention they need without distraction. If they reveal that the subject will take more than a few minutes, I suggest we have breakfast together, lunch if I'm free, a drink after office hours, or occasionally meet on Saturday or Sunday. Normally, however, the meeting takes place during the normal working day. When an associate arrives, I greet him, get up from my desk and move to an upholstered chair on the far side of my office. He sits opposite me. The atmosphere is relaxed but I politely cut him short if he starts a gossipy conversation. We get to the point quickly, and I keep my responses crisp and to the point. I try to keep the conversation on target, and find that in five, ten, or fifteen minutes we have solved the problem, developed the plan, or dispensed with the business at hand. We then take a moment or two for niceties before he leaves.

By planning and organizing my day in advance and by setting a time frame for the meeting so that it does not run on interminably, I have given my associate the attention that he needs, without upsetting my own timetable.

TO EACH HIS OWN

I know a successful business executive who has two lunch appointments at his club every day, one at noon and the next at one o'clock. I often have a breakfast appointment at seven-thirty and another at eight-thirty. Some executives never go out for lunch, preferring to continue working through the day with a fifteen-minute respite for an order of cottage cheese, fruit, and a glass of milk. You have to find your own best way of getting all your work done.

Recently I telephoned Marvin Traub, president of Bloomingdale's, and asked him for an appointment. We chatted for a minute or two about which of us got started earlier in the morning, and we finally agreed that I would meet him at seven-thirty on Thursday morning in his office. "Can we handle it in fifteen minutes?" he asked. "We can and we will," I replied. As an exponent of time and priorities, I respect the other person's schedule. I entered Marvin Traub's office at seven-twenty-eight and left at seven-forty-five, having finished my business with him. Another gentleman was waiting to see him. I walked from Bloomingdale's to my eight-o'clock breakfast appointment at Sixty-Sixth and Park. That handled, at nine-fifteen I arrived at my office at Forty-Second Street and Lexington Avenue ready to start my day's work.

I don't expect you to spend your day the way Marvin Traub and I spend ours, but, if you plan ahead what must be done each day, allocate a specific amount of time for each meeting or solo task, you will learn that you can get everything done.

Rogers' Hints on Time Management

1) Set priorities on your own time. Don't fall into the trap of keeping so busy doing the nonessentials that you don't have time to do what is important.

2) Set priorities on your associates' time. Make certain that they are doing the same.

3) Defend yourself against "drop-in" meetings. They will kill your day.

4) Set a time limit on each appointment. A meeting can go on interminably unless you set a limit at the outset.

5) Plan your day before it begins. Know in advance just what you expect to accomplish on any given day.

FIND A MENTOR/ROLE MODEL

I have recommended that you observe the executives in your company in action. As you do this, you will discover several you admire and respect for certain qualities that attract you. It could be management ability, charisma, skill with people, quick reaction time in crises or facile public speaking and presentation. These individuals are *role models* for you to emulate, people whose skills you would like to develop and enhance in yourself.

There will probably be a number of people with these qualities; by seeking them out, discussing their abilities with them and indicating your desire to learn from them, one (or more) may become your mentor.

You can use (in the best sense of the word) your mentor to help you reach heights that you couldn't otherwise achieve. Everyone needs a push, everyone needs a helping hand, but most of us are reluctant to ask someone for advice and support. I had a number of mentors in my early days in business, and Rogers & Cowan might never have reached its present size and stature if it had not been for people who took me under their wing.

In Chapter 1 I gave credit to Charles Feldman for helping launch my business in the early 1940s. He never referred to me as his protege, but because he permitted me to spend time with him in both his office and home, I learned a great deal about how to handle clients. He was then recognized as one of the three or four most important motion picture agents in the industry, and I studied his tactics carefully. I listened to the way he spoke with his clients on the telephone. I watched how he treated them in his home. I was sensitive to the way he worked with his associates. He became my first mentor and once he was aware that I was emulating him and learning from him, he became instrumental in getting me many important clients in those early years of my business career.

Five years later, I latched on to my second mentor. By that time, I had acquired some of Charlie Feldman's polish and knowledge in client relations, and that may have been the reason a business manager named Bo Roos took to me. He liked me (maybe psychorelations was already at work) and he was more overt than Feldman about imparting his business knowledge to me. He talked to me about his clients and what he did for them. He explained to me how he managed to deal with their idiosyncrasies and how he retained their good will. Bo Roos was the second person from whom I learned that the ability to develop personal relationships with your clients was just as important as doing a creditable job for them. Psychorelations was working for me at a very early age.

Roos's personal interest in me translated into approximately 25 percent of my income at that point in my career. I can think of no specific reason for his adopting me. We were friendly acquaintances but not good friends. Evidently he sent me his clients because he trusted me, because I would do the best possible job for the people he represented and because I would remain loyal to him. The qualities he perceived in me were, I believe, qualities I developed from my association with Charles Feldman.

At one point the following clients appeared on our roster who were clients of Bo Roos: Red Skeleton, Fred MacMurray, Lloyd Nolan, Robert Preston, Johnny Weismuller, Patric Knowles, Mitchell Leisen, Frank Borzage, James Stephenson, and Edgar Kennedy. Some of them have long since been forgotten, but in the late forties and early fifties they comprised a formidable list. So much for what two mentors did for me.

In 1969, a brilliant young man named Robert Marston left our firm to go into business for himself. I always liked and respected him and didn't argue with his decision to strike out on his own. Bob had a big advantage. He had a mentor. Through me he met Dan Lufkin, a young, astute investment banker and one of the principals in the distinguished Wall Street firm Donaldson, Lufkin, Jenrette. They became good friends and at one point when Bob expressed his ambitions to Dan, he was offered financial backing, contacts, and whatever other assistance he might need in starting a public-relations firm. Robert Marston Associates did very well right from the start, and today is recognized as one of the most successful firms in the country. Bob and I have stayed in touch, and although I knew Lufkin had been of tremendous help to him, I always surmised that he had a financial stake in the business and that was one reason why he had always pushed the Marston firm with his friends and his associates.

Recently, I sat next to Dan Lufkin on a plane flying from New York to Los Angeles. We started talking about our mutual friend. "Did you ever hear the story about us?" he asked. I said that I had always been curious but had never been told the story behind the story. Lufkin then revealed that he had offered to invest $100,000 in the not-yet established Marston firm. Bob, according to Lufkin, wrestled with the temptation for a number of days and finally turned down the offer. He had decided to try it on his own without financial assistance. Dan was so impressed with Bob's independence and determination that he helped him even more than if he had actually had a financial stake in the business.

Why should anyone want to be your mentor? What's in it for him? Mentors like to help others, but not for entirely altruistic reasons. Not only do they get self-satisfaction from helping someone else become successful, they also win points with their superiors for being a keen judge of character and for improving the skill level within the company. On an even more self-serving (again in the best sense of the word) level, they are building a cadre of loyal supporters in the up-and-coming ranks, who will help them in their struggle to the top and serve as an information pipeline on how things are going at the bottom.

You don't have to be young and inexperienced to have a mentor. I have had many over the years, and still have no qualms about seeking advice and counsel from those who are more experienced than I. I would often solicit the advice of Ben Sonnenberg, a legendary public-relations practitioner whose home in Gramercy Park in New York City contained one of the great private collections of furniture, paintings, sculpture, silver, copper, and brass. He would invite me to his home for tea, and he would talk for hours as I plied him with questions about his extraordinarily successful career. He would sit there, a short, plump, bald man with a walrus mustache, wearing a four-button suit, vest, a starched detached collar, and a flowing black silk tie—a figure out of the Victorian Age—and tell me how he had emigrated from Poland as a little boy, become a Broadway press agent, and with mentors such as Bernard Baruch and Herbert Bayard Swope, had eventually became rich and famous through his public-relations representation of major corporations. At one point I asked him why he was willing to give me so much of his time. He smiled owlishly and answered, "Don't you know that when you seek someone out for advice, you have given him the supreme compliment?"

But how will you find a mentor?

In a large corporation it is comparatively easy. Some companies have career guidance counselors who are waiting to help you. Others don't but there are many people in middle management who will be willing to give you advice and help you along the way. In small companies, or for the individual entrepreneur, it's not so easy. Basically, the young person must look to an older, more experienced person for guidance. A young doctor can seek advice from a seasoned professional and probably get it. A young artist can always count on advice from an older person who is already successful.

Look around you. Consider approaching one of your role models. Pick one and walk into his or her office and ask whether he or she would be kind enough to answer a question or help you solve a problem. (Remember your timing—pick a moment when they are not jammed up with more pressing business.)

Note the reaction. You may be given a cool, distant, impersonal response. He or she might say, "Don't bother me. I'm busy." If something like that happens, you know that he's not your man—or woman. Try again, and again, and again. Eventually, someone will say, "Sit down. Tell me your problem." If you feel that this might be the beginning of a meaningful relationship, go back a few days later with a second question. If you are met with a similar warm, caring response, you may have found your mentor. If not, keep looking.

You are probably asking, "What good will a mentor do me?" If you are like most people, including me, you'll admit that you don't know all the answers. You never will. But a mentor will start by giving you some of them. He'll help you get through the political maze of the business world with less anguish, less pain, and fewer mistakes than if you were to do it entirely on your own. He will, over a period of time, answer questions such as these:

Is it time to ask for a raise?
How should I present myself when I ask for it?
How do I solve this work-related problem?
How do I position myself to get a better job?
How can I impress my boss?
How can I impress my coworkers?
What positive moves should I make to enhance my position in the company?

These and many other questions will besiege you as you build your career and you will find it comforting to have a more experienced person standing by your side, willing to help you find the answers.

BE A ROLE MODEL FOR YOUR SUBORDINATES

Just as you are learning from your own mentor, realize that others will be using you as a role model, and that consequently, your work habits will become those of your subordinates. If you are not working at your maximum efficiency, don't expect anything better from them.

No matter how many times you say, "Don't do as I do, do as I say," they will still emulate you. If you get to the office at ten, don't expect them to start slaving away at eight. They might punch the time clock at eight if that's the time your office opens, but you'll find them wasting time between then and when you arrive on the scene. If there were a gauge for measuring productivity, you would soon discover that the wheels start grinding down when you leave the office at four o'clock to get in nine holes of golf before dinner. You're the leader, and they're looking to you for leadership.

In our company, we open at nine in the morning, but you will always see six, eight, or ten publicists and office personnel working in their offices at seven-thirty or eight o'clock. We close at six, but at seven, you will still see lights burning. Walk in on a Saturday morning or a Sunday afternoon, and you will always hear the clattering of a typewriter, or two or three. No one asks our associates to work beyond the prescribed hours.

They are emulating the leaders of the firm, who have set the example for them. Your work habits must be exemplary because the results you get from your associates will be in direct proportion to your own output. When you were a youngster, you played follow the leader in the schoolyard. Today, follow the leader is being played in your office every day but now the game is much more important than when you were a kid.

Rogers' Mottos for Mentor/Role Models

1) *Your personal appearance should be beyond reproach.*   Your associates will try to look better if you look your best at all times.

2) *Your personal behavior should be beyond reproach.*   They will be well spoken and well mannered if you are.

3) *Your work hours should be punctual and well ordered.*   They

will be emulating you, so don't expect them to exert themselves if you leave at three to play tennis.

4) *Keep your meetings short and your telephone calls even shorter.* They will accomplish more during the day if they note your well-organized work habits.

5) *Acknowledge their accomplishments and share your successes with them.* They will do the same with their peers and subordinates with a resultant high morale in your organization.

6) *Grace under pressure,* one of John F. Kennedy's favorite phrases, is something to be remembered at all times. They won't blow their tops nor will they panic if you don't.

7) *Encourage them to seek you out for advice and counsel.* You are the father or mother figure and if they need you, it is essential that you make yourself available to them.

8) *Show them that you are personally interested.* A birthday card, a box of candy, or a box of cigars at the appropriate time builds morale in the organization.

9) *Be helpful.* Show them how to do their jobs more efficiently but don't do it for them.

10) *Compliment and criticize as outlined in previous chapters.* Always use tact and diplomacy at appropriate times.

HIRING THE RIGHT PEOPLE

When the final tally is made of your success or failure as an executive, it will be determined to a great extent by the people you hire to work with you.

Take your time about hiring. Your success in your new position may be dependent on the new people you bring on board. Get input from others. Check out references. Don't depend on resumes. Don't make a decision based on your first impression. We all have a tendency to hire people without first defining the role we want to fill. Spell out the job, pinpoint the qualifications required, and then check out the man or woman you are considering, point by point.

The right person for the right job is hard to find. You must interview many prospects before coming to a decision. Weigh one person's qualifications against the other's. You will be fortunate if you are able to hire people who are already winners. It is more likely, however, that those you add to your payroll will be potential winners.

Just as you needed help at the outset, it is then your responsibility to train them, work with them, and encourage them so that they can realize their full potential under your leadership. Too often, well-qualified aspirants are brought into a firm and left to fend for themselves. Occasionally, one of them will struggle to the top strictly on his own initiative, but too many of them don't make it because they don't receive the requisite guidance, direction, inspiration, and training. You will be a better executive, you will become more successful, if you spend a certain percentage of your time helping your people do their job better. Don't do their jobs for them, even though you can do it better than they can. Point the way, and then let them do it in their own way, which might not necessarily be yours. Once your people have been properly trained, let each of them find his own road.

Rogers' Takeover Road Map

Consider the contents of this chapter as merely a road map. I have given you only a few guidelines to help you get started. You have just finished the first fifteen minutes of what should be a multiyear study program if you are serious about becoming a truly outstanding takeover person. I leave you with a number of observations on what some of your goals should be. You should learn to:

- Know where you are going and how to get there.
- Behave in a way that you will be believed and trusted.
- Encourage and help those who work for you.

- Delegate authority.
- Avoid passing the buck. Assume responsibility for the actions of others.
- Communicate effectively with your associates.
- Be guilty of errors of commission rather than omission.
- Encourage innovative thinking and treat it with respect.
- Praise your people immediately and tell them what they did right.
- Criticize your people immediately and tell them what they did wrong.
- Seek the advice of your associates, but explain your decisions to them if you don't accept their suggestions.
- Do unto your associates what you hope they will do unto you.

9

Perspective and priorities

THOUSANDS OF BOOKS have been written on the subject of how to become successful. Few, if any, have been written on how to remain successful. It's easy to be a failure and it's not too tough to achieve some modicum of success. But it takes a superhuman effort to remain on top. Those who have not yet experienced the six-figure job, the beautiful home, three cars in the garage, and a membership in the most exclusive country club, cannot conceive why appurtenances don't automatically bring peace of mind, freedom from fear, joy and happiness. "Just give me a chance at them," you say, "and I'll enjoy every minute of my life." Unfortunately, you are no different from anyone else. If and when success is yours, you will face the same pressures and insecurities that others do.

Then why bother struggling for success? What's the point of it all if there's no joy once you achieve it? Because there *is* joy and satisfaction and fulfillment if you learn to live with success, if you learn to handle it; and you can only do this by preparing for success in advance.

FEAR OF SUCCESS

One day it was only your own success that was involved. If you didn't succeed, it would not be catastrophic. You were only responsible for yourself. Today you are an executive. Maybe the lives, the careers, the success or failure of five people are dependent on what you do. And maybe it's not five, but fifty or five hundred, or five thousand.

Are you worthy of taking on such responsibility?

You begin to question yourself the moment you have your success. The day you leave the secretarial pool to become an executive secretary, the day you move from the mailroom to become an assistant to an assistant account executive, the day you become a vice-president. It is the moment when you agree to take on added responsibility, when you are no longer invisible in the company and you suddenly realize that others are watching you. You are being evaluated. That is when you experience the first *fear of success*. It happens to everyone. The $400,000-a-year executive in the billion-dollar conglomerate who is promoted from president and chief operating officer to chairman and chief executive officer also experiences this fear. He has handled his rise to prominence very well up until this moment. Is he capable of taking over the top position in the company?

Can you handle success once you have achieved it? Whether you are a secretary or a CEO, the answer depends on your ability to overcome the fear of success by anticipating and then learning to cope with the problems that will beset you—and they will. Such problems can get the best of even (and especially) the most successful people.

You probably had the same feelings of puzzlement and sadness that I did when you read that John Belushi had died from an overdose. I kept asking myself "why?" Here was a brilliant entertainer who in a few years rose from obscurity to stardom. If anyone had it made it was he. But he could not handle it. He didn't die because of a bad break, an accident, or a stroke of fate. He couldn't live with success, and if he hadn't died that day in the way he did, it would have been another day in another way. He was bent on self-destruction.

The pressures of show business are obviously enormous. Do you remember Marilyn Monroe, Judy Garland, James Dean? They couldn't handle it either. Music? Jim Morrison of The Doors, Janis Joplin, one of our greatest contemporary singers, Brian Wilson of The Beach Boys, who has been fighting a drug problems for years. For them, too, success was too much.

Business? There are thousands of cases. Sharply focused in my mind is that of John DeLorean. He had the ability to raise hundreds of millions of dollars to design, manufacture, and market a revolutionary new automobile, the DMC. Married to the beautiful Christina Ferrare, with angelic children, a multimillion-dollar apartment on New York's Fifth Avenue, a ranch in Paloma Valley in southern California, and the whole world ready to embrace him, DeLorean couldn't take it. It was too much for him.

I knew Burt Kleiner, a Beverly Hills investment broker. He was recognized as a brilliant talent in the financial community, and made millions of dollars through creative financing. He became a collector of contemporary art, and won the respect of the Los Angeles establishment when he donated much of his collection to the Los Angeles County Art Museum. He couldn't handle success either. He became involved in a number of questionable deals, and one day he left town and was discovered soon after living the life of a beachcomber in a Mexican fishing village.

Stanley Goldblum was a client of ours in the early days of the Equity Funding Corporation. We didn't relate to each other very well and he discharged us after a short time. I watched while he became enormously successful in his financial dealings. Then one day someone blew the whistle on him. Equity Funding Corporation went down in one of the worst financial scandals of the twentieth century. Stanley Goldblum went to jail. The pressures of success were too much for him.

Once you realize that there are pitfalls to be avoided, you will be in a better position to deal with them.

THE PITFALLS OF SUCCESS

Success can easily go to your head. You say, "Oh, that could never happen to me." Success and power, with all the perquisities they bring, can also bring newly acquired conceit and arrogance. "Look what I've accomplished," says Mr. or Ms. Success. "That proves I'm better than anyone else."

Success can also have the opposite effect. You can become consumed with guilt. "I don't deserve this," you say to yourself. "I've just been lucky and any day now it will all disappear and I'll be right back where I started!" If that happens to you, you will soon find yourself on the psychiatrist's couch.

Suddenly your marriage is on the rocks. You and your spouse were once the epitome of compatibility. Today you no longer have anything in common. What happened? Your life has broadened, you have new interests, new friends. Your life has changed but your spouse's hasn't. He/she is left behind. Is it your fault? What's the difference? Your marriage is finished.

"What happened to Joe? He doesn't have time for his family and friends anymore!" Haven't you heard that said about someone you know? They may one day say it about you. You will get so wrapped up in the success syndrome that you will forget your friends and your family and leave them behind.

"I can't stand the pressures. They're getting me down," is a common complaint of the successful person. Life used to be simple, but now it is more complex. There are great demands on your time, problems pile upon problems, and the responsibilities are a hundred times greater than you ever imagined.

LEARN TO MANAGE YOURSELF

I remember my early struggles very well. My future mother-in-law wouldn't allow my wife of forty-six years to marry me until I bought her an engagement ring. A one-carat ring cost $400 in those days and I had barely 400 cents. "He can't afford to marry you if he can't afford to buy you an engagement ring" was the edict that came down from on high. Tears and pleadings and entreaties were of no avail. I was twenty-two, madly in love, and desperately yearned to marry that gorgeous creature who had said yes to my proposal. I decided that maybe I would win $400 in a gambling casino.

One night, after dropping off my soon-to-be fiancée, I detoured before going home and went to the Clover Club, an illegal gambling joint on the Sunset Strip in Hollywood. I had $20 in my pocket and, believing that God smiled on young lovers, was certain that I would have $400 in that same pocket before the night was over. I came close. The dice were hot, I was in love, and at one point I counted $250 in chips in front of me. It wasn't enough.

I kept playing and the result was predictable. I arrived home at 5:00 A.M. with thirty-five cents, but I survived. I finally borrowed four hundred dollars from a trusting friend and bought Roz the diamond ring. She wears it today.

I had many, many personal, business, and financial crises in those early days.

Stuttering, as I mentioned earlier, was a serious problem. The telephone remained a nemesis and every personal encounter proved to be an emotional, near-traumatic experience. In fact, at one point in the 1940s I sought out the speech therapist I had worked with back in New Jersey when I was in my teens. He helped me considerably but the problem still remained.

The business was excruciatingly slow in building. From 1937, when I got married, up to and through the early war years it was difficult for me to support Roz and our two children. Finally there was a breakthrough. I got more clients, convinced them to pay higher fees, and by the time we bought our home in 1945 for $36,750 (we still live there) the financial pressures began to ease.

I managed to handle all those problems with no great strain, but when I began to experience the first signs of success, coping with life's problems became more difficult. When I had simple responsibilities, I had simple problems. If I was late in paying the forty-dollar monthly installment on my Pontiac, I didn't give it a second thought. When dinner for the two of us cost five dollars, it didn't bother me that I would go without lunch the next day because I had completely run out of money. When a client was three months late in paying his hundred-dollar monthly fee, it didn't give me sleepless nights. I had few judgments to make. I didn't have to be innovative, creative, or inventive. There was no need to be competitive because I was a long way from realizing any degree of position or reputation. I had no fear of success because there was still no success.

It was when I first began to feel that I had a real chance to make it that I began to develop a fear of success. The responsibilities were greater. The challenges were greater. The stakes were higher. I had never really thought much about success or failure. Once I found myself on the road to success, it became apparent that I was also subject to failure. I became frightened.

It was when the tempo of life picked up, when my personal and business life became more complex, when friends and acquaintances intruded themselves (with my consent and acquiescence, of course) into my life, therefore complicating it even further, that the problems began to mount. I was torn, pulled by conflicting forces, confused as to priorities and what I should and should not do. It's not too difficult to figure out why the pressures continued to mount. The president of a billion-dollar company has more problems than Henry Thoreau had at Walden Pond.

I was and am no different from others, who, when they finally make it, discover that success brings with it problems that were nonexistent before. Making money doesn't eliminate problems—it compounds them. Getting a better job, moving up the ladder of success, doesn't simplify your life—it complicates it. You will find that you will be working more and enjoying it less. You will ask yourself, "What the hell am I working so hard for? What am I getting out of it?"

All this can be avoided if you start now to prepare yourself for the price that must be paid for success, and learn to manage yourself.

In order to *manage yourself*, you must develop a *perspective* on your life. You must also establish a list of *priorities* by which you run your life. Once you have done that, you'll be able to handle the pressures and responsibilities that could prevent you from enjoying your success, without the agonies and frustrations many have come to accept as their normal life-style.

ESTABLISHING A PROPER PERSPECTIVE

One reason you may be having trouble handling the pressures and responsibilities that everyone faces is your inability to distinguish between important and unimportant problems. Do all the annoyances, frustrations, and aggravations that plague you really merit the importance you attach to them? Is it worth getting angry because the rain is pouring down this morning and you can't find your umbrella? Is it catastrophic if the school bus is late and your children ask you to take them to school? Is it tragic if the corn flakes are soggy rather than crisp? Are these annoyances really worth the Tums and the aspirin tablets that you take every morning?

Marriages are broken, partnerships are dissolved, children leave home, lovers quarrel, faces are smashed in barroom brawls, all because *people are unable to establish a perspective on what is and what is not important in their lives.*

Stop and think. Isn't it true that *most of the things that aggravate you are unimportant* if you look at them in relation to the total context of your life?

I was a victim of not maintaining a perspective on my life. I feel compassion for the successful business executive who starts to drink heavily. I empathize with the career-minded men and women who find it difficult to cope with their responsibilities.

There was a point in my life when I was in a constant state of depression and annoyance, and it was getting me down. Every day brought another unpleasant experience with my business colleagues and my family, and, every day, my stomach seemed to ache more and more. As time went on, I discovered that a double shot of vodka or scotch was helpful. The pain would start up shortly after one of my regular run-ins with an associate over some trivial matter. Two or three of these incidents occurred every morning. By the time I went off to a lunch date, my stomach was churning like a dishwasher.

At lunch one day with a friend, I turned to the waiter: "A double vodka on the rocks, please."

My luncheon companion looked up from the menu he had been scanning. "Since when?" he asked.

"Since when what?"

"Since when a double vodka on the rocks?"

There was a moment of silence. "I just can't seem to relate to people anymore," I said in what was becoming a rare moment of candor. (My psychorelations skills had left me.) "I seem to blow up at the slightest provocation, and it depresses the hell out of me. The depression gives me an ache in my stomach and the vodka relieves the ache. Then I get into another argument, my stomach aches again, and then I'm ready for another vodka. I've even been thinking about giving up my business."

"Why? Is business bad?"

"No, in fact, business is very good, but it just isn't fun anymore. I don't get the satisfaction out of it I once did."

"Why not? If business is good, why aren't you enjoying it?"

"Because I just can't cope anymore," I repeated, as if that in itself were a sufficient explanation.

"Have all those people changed that much over the years?"

"N-o-o . . . I guess not."

"If you can't cope with people in your business, you probably can't cope with your family either. Am I right?"

"Ye-e-e-s-s-s," I replied thoughtfully.

"Well, if you can't cope with people in your business and your family, and you admit that they haven't changed, and you're thinking about giving up your business because you can't cope, did you ever think that *you've* changed, that there's probably something wrong with you?"

I didn't answer him. I thought for a moment. (Where had I lost psychorelations?)

"Maybe there is," I finally said. "I never thought of it before. What do you think it is?"

"I have no idea. Why don't you figure it out for yourself and forget about giving up your business until you do."

I went home early that day. Roz wasn't there. I undressed, put on a robe, and slid into my favorite chair. Where should I start this self-analysis, which I knew I needed desperately?

My father came to mind. I remembered that he had once left my mother and moved into a motel because he had found rust at the bottom of the family coffee pot. I recalled how foolish I used to think he was for so frequently losing his temper over trivia. Now I was following in my father's footsteps. I, too, was getting aggravated and depressed about minutiae. My wife annoyed me; my business partner annoyed me; my son disturbed me—for a hundred reasons—as did my daughter, my business associates, and my friends.

When I am thinking about a problem, I find it helpful to make notes. I got up from the chair, went to my desk drawer and pulled out a yellow lined pad and ballpoint pen. I sat down again, pen poised.

What should I write? I wasn't sure. I thought for a moment. "I must find a place to start. Okay, let's try this: I'll start by listing each plus and minus in my life—the good things and the bad. I'll start with the plusses." My list began:

I am healthy.
My family is healthy.
I have a flourishing business.
I love my business.
I love my wife.
My wife loves me.
I love my children.
They love me.
I have no financial problems.
I am well respected in the community.

I kept writing and writing. I started a second page. I suddenly stopped. The point was made. I knew I could have filled six pages if I kept going. I started a new page. The minuses:

My wife smokes too much.
My daughter forgot my birthday.
My partner interrupts me when I'm talking.

The list became less important and more ridiculous as I wrote down each new item. I picked up the first list, looked at it, picked up the second list and looked at that. I started to laugh. I had always thought of myself as a reasonably intelligent man. I wasn't acting that way. I was acting stupidly.

I was a man who had made it in life and was about to throw it all away because I had never realized how good my life was. Why had I been so blind to the long list of important plusses? What was wrong with me? A big word hit me. I could see it written in six-foot-high letters on the wall of my dressing room:

PERSPECTIVE

I had simply lost my perspective. I had never thought about what was and what was not really important. This is probably true of most people. We tend to assume that our feeling of something being missing is due to our not yet having achieved the goals we are striving for. Then, when those goals are met and contentment still eludes us, we are faced with figuring out why. In my case, I discovered that I did not appreciate all the good things I had and was deriving little, if any, pleasure or gratification out of my very successful life. I was exaggerating every minor annoyance out of proportion. I thought back over all the unpleasant incidents that had given me stomachaches over recent years. Each one was minuscule in comparison to the good things that comprised my total life.

I took up pad and pen again and proceeded to write a plus-and-minus list for all the people who had caused my annoyances. I started with Roz. In this case, I started with the negatives. I wrote down three items. Then I moved to the plus side. When I got to number thirty-three I crumpled up the sheet of paper and threw it on the floor. Then I started with my partner Warren. Then my son. Then my daughter. Then my business associates who had annoyed and frustrated me. In each case it was just about the same. The ratio was ten to one, ten plusses to one minus.

There was nothing wrong with the people in my life. *There was something wrong with me.* Was it serious? Not really. I had simply never analyzed my life that way before. Most of us, in fact, *don't* consider our particular perspective until it goes awry. And those of us for whom such an occurrence is new may not immediately recognize what has happened. We trudge on, confused malcontents. If this condition persists too long, it may give way to new and far more serious problems as our cheerlessness starts to alienate those around us. Now I could see on the sheets of paper in front of me that I had allowed the few unimportant minuses in life to outweigh all of the important plusses. I had been accentuating the negative rather than the positive. I had forgotten what Dr. Norman Vincent Peale had written about the power of *positive* thinking (Ballantine Books, 1982, $2.75).

I got up from my chair and went to the telephone. I dialed my friend with whom I had had lunch.

"Thanks for the advice," I said.

"I didn't give you any advice. I merely told you that there might be something wrong with you and not the people who were bothering you. I told you to think about it."

"Whatever you said, it worked, because I think I found the answer. We'll have lunch again next week, and I'll tell you all about it."

That insight changed my life. I no longer get easily annoyed, nor do I slip into fits of depression. When something does disturb me, I reaffirm my perspective. I examine how consequential the situation is in relation to my total life. It is usually something on the bottom of my priority list and not worth getting riled up about.

I now feel better about myself. I realize that I had a serious problem that could have ruined my entire life, but fortunately I was able to figure out what it was and how to solve it.

Rogers' Perspective on Perspective

1) The easiest way to keep your perspective is not to lose it. Take stock of yourself regularly. Use landmark occasions—your birthday, the new year, the first day of spring—any date that is easy for you to remember.

2) Think about yourself *in writing*. You may wish to keep your notes to refer back to in the future.

3) Be specific in listing the positive and negative aspects of your life. Look at the negative; is there anything you can do—any action you can take—to improve things?

4) List the most important people in your life—at home and in the office. Enumerate their good and bad qualities. Would it help to discuss those aspects that bother you?

5) You don't suddenly lose your perspective all at once; it ebbs away little by little. Successful people have a tendency to fume and fret. When I lose patience with the petty annoyances of the daily business wars, I remind myself of how much worse it could be. One good way to keep your perspective is to:

Count Your Blessings

If I have problems with clients, I remind myself it is better to have problems with clients than to have no clients at all.

If I have problems with my associates, I remind myself that it is better than having no public-relations business and no associates.

When our switchboard operator fails to answer my call after the first or second ring, I remind myself that business must be booming if she cannot handle all the calls.

If I return to my office after a day's absence and find that the pile of papers is eight inches high and that I must return thirty-seven telephone calls, I say, "How would I feel if no one telephoned me or no one wrote me a memo or sent me a letter?"

Some would say this is a Pollyanna attitude, but I don't agree. It is the proper perspective for the person who realizes that success is as or more difficult to handle than failure.

SETTING PRIORITIES

You must separate the significant from the insignificant, eliminate the insignificant, and then handle the significant in proper order of importance.

Success often brings with it intense frustration over your inability to handle the responsibilities heaped on your shoulders. You toss in bed at night and groan, "I can't handle it all. There's so much to do." One answer to your sleepless nights is to learn to set priorities for yourself.

Setting priorities is the logical extension of establishing and then maintaining your perspective. You determined your perspective by separating the important from the unimportant aspects of your life.

With that done, you may find that you are still dissatisfied because you are still not getting the pleasure out of life you have always wanted. You are not doing those things you really want to do. You are not seeing the people you would like to see.

My experience is a good example. I had finally established a better perspective on my life, but still I was far from attaining the goals I had set for myself.

For years I was disturbed when I woke in the morning to find that tomorrow had become today, and what I had planned to do yesterday had not been done at all. Every day repeated itself. Every day I was faced with unrealized goals and unsolved problems. I was working under pressure and with continuous frustration. I was busy, busy, busy, but I was never satisfied with what I was doing, because it all seemed so unimportant.

The pile of papers on my desk seemed to get bigger and bigger instead of smaller and smaller. The really important things never seemed to get done. Always an early starter, I would begin to work at seven or eight in the morning and would continue until six in the evening with barely a half hour for lunch. Still, that stack of papers never seemed to disappear.

Compounding my frustration was the fact that I thought I was very well organized in my work habits. I rarely forgot what I had to do. I carried a pad in my pocket and made notes to myself all day long. I kept a pad of paper next to my bed, and, if I woke up during the night, I would make a note of something I wanted to do the next morning. Whether going to the office for a day's work or to a black-tie dinner party, I always carried a notepad and pen.

At regular intervals each day, I would put all those notes together on one piece of paper. Sometimes I would do it in the evening, before I went to bed, or before I had breakfast in the morning. Sometimes I dictated the new notes to my secretary before we got started in the morning. She would take the list of notes that had not been crossed off the day before, type up the new notes together with the old, and present me with a clean page, or pages, of items. I would have a complete picture of the things I knew had to be done. Included were calls to be made, calls to be returned, memos to be written, letters to be dictated, correspondence to be answered, meetings to be held with associates, meetings with clients, ad infinitum.

I always felt I was a well-organized business executive, but I still couldn't get my work done. Why?

I found the answer at six-fifteen one evening as I was about to leave my office. I had arrived at seven-thirty that morning and had not stopped to breathe from the moment I had made my first telephone call to our New York office. I stood up from my desk and paused for a moment to take a quick look at my "to-do" list. I was pleased to see that most of the items had been crossed off. For a moment it appeared to be a satisfying day. Then I looked at the list again. I counted. Twelve items remained. I looked at them, read each one, then looked at the list that had been crossed off. Suddenly I had a feeling of frustration. The twelve uncrossed-off items were much more important than those that were completed. I had spent eleven hours at my job and had accomplished very little of what was important to me and our company. Genuinely annoyed by this time, I sat down at my desk again and studied the list carefully. Then came the great awakening.

Again, my problem could be summed up in one word: *priorities*. My priorities were screwed up.

It then became apparent to me for the first time that I had a tendency to postpone the substantial and essential matters that required my attention and to keep busy ten to twelve hours a day with piddling details, which were of no importance in the running of our business.

I would scan my "to-do" sheet every morning. Invariably, I would start to make an unimportant phone call, dictate an inconsequential memo, or meet with one of my associates about something so insignificant that it did not call for a meeting. I always began my day with the "unimportant"—never the "important." I would start out with some seventy-five or hundred items on the sheet. At the end of the day, I would proudly note that fifty-six or sixty-two or seventy-eight had been checked off, yet I always went home with a nagging feeling that something was wrong. And there was. Out of those original seventy-five or one hundred items, there were only a half-dozen really important matters that had to be handled—and they seldom were. Why?

As I analyzed my own behavior and the habits that had become ingrained over the years, I noticed that each of the five or six important tasks would always be time consuming, requiring considerable amounts of effort, thought, and decision making on my part. I concluded that I apparently hadn't wanted to face up to the responsibilities of doing the important things because I was afraid that I might fail. I delayed the moment when I had to confront a problem and solve it. I avoided making the decision that was required. *I always had time to take care of trivial details because they prevented me from facing up to the significant issues that should have taken precedence.* I don't believe, in retrospect, that I realized what I was doing. No wonder I felt I was accomplishing nothing!

I decided then that my list of things to do was not enough: I was organized but not properly organized. The list reminded me of what I had to do but *not the sequence I should follow.* It didn't establish *when* I should do *what.* I knew then that if I wanted to discipline myself, I would have to structure my "to-do" list every day in *order of priority.*

Each morning I now list in capital letters the five to ten items that I feel *must* be handled that day. The less-important items are put at the bottom of the page in lower-case type. The priority matters are handled first. Now that I understand why I had been avoiding them, they present no problem for me. When I finally get around to handling the comparatively nonessential items on my list, they take one-half to one-third of the time they formerly took. Why? I previously had prolonged the minor matters because I could thereby postpone when I had to face what should have been the priority items.

Rogers' Priorities on Setting Priorities

1) Setting priorities for yourself is the logical extension of establishing a proper perspective.

2) Distinguish between what is really important and what is not.

3) Ignore the unimportant until the important matters are handled and out of the way.

4) Don't concern yourself with trivia. You will discover that most of it won't get handled and it doesn't matter.

10

The benefits of failure

"THE BENEFITS OF FAILURE" may sound like a paradox, but it isn't. Everyone has failures, and you are no exception. The good news is that you can actually benefit more from your failures than from your successes.

I will emphasize that again. *You can benefit more from your failures than from your successes.* If you absorb only this one aspect of psychorelations, I will have helped you become a more successful person.

It is only normal human behavior to chastise yourself for wrong moves. Most of us acquire this attitude early in life and carry it to our graves. Unfortunately, however, it prevents us from achieving our greatest success potential, and most of us don't know how to lift this load from our shoulders.

Start fresh and:

Stop dwelling on your failures.
Stop worrying about strikeouts.
Stop punishing yourself for your mistakes.

In this chapter, I will discuss *failures, strikeouts,* and *mistakes.* In order to understand the distinctions, I shall first give you a number of definitions and analogies.

Failure is "the act of failing; a falling short, nonperformance, deterioration, bankruptcy." The synonyms include *nonfulfillment, abortion, vain attempt, go under, lose the day, throw in the towel, downfall,* and such slang words as *flop, bomb, dud, washout.*

Keeping these words as reference points, let's look at what I consider to be *failure:*

When I fail to get the job I applied for.

When I get a failing grade on a test.

When I set out to run four miles and stop at two.

When I give a speech that is greeted with boos or silence.

A *strikeout* is a calculated risk that didn't work out. When you are at bat, you take three hefty swings at the ball and miss each time —that's a strikeout. When an attempted field goal doesn't sail between the goal posts, it's a strikeout, in my book, and when the hockey puck misses the cage, that's a strikeout, too.

A *mistake,* in contrast, is an error, a blunder, a misunderstanding, a slip, or a misinterpretation.

Show me the person who claims he never made a mistake and I'll show you a liar. We are all human beings and we all make mistakes. But the difference is that only some of us profit from them. Those who do, go on to success; those who don't, fall by the wayside.

Being able to tell the difference between a failure, a strikeout, and a mistake is a vital part of keeping your *perspective.* Although failure is the most serious of the three, it is important not to blow any of them out of proportion, making them more catastrophic than they really are.

Joan Crawford, at one point in her career, was branded as "box-office poison," a failure, by the theater owners of America, and was subsequently fired by her long-time employer, Louis B. Mayer, head of MGM Studios. She didn't bemoan her fate and sink into obscurity after this devastating setback. She knew that she had once been acclaimed as one of the world's greatest movie stars and was determined to regain that distinction. She convinced Warner Bros. to give her the title role in *Mildred Pierce* and went on to her greatest achievement by winning the Academy Award for her performance in that film. A few years later, she returned to MGM in triumph.

Great men and women are not born great—they make themselves great. One of the attributes that makes them great is their refusal to accept failure and their refusal to allow those failures to color their views, diminish their will, undermine their struggle for success, or impede their ability to force self-doubt, self-deprecation, and self-debasement out of their minds. They force themselves to forget the failures of the past and look forward to the successes of the future.

PUBLIC-RELATIONS PEOPLE DON'T DWELL ON FAILURES

Those of us in public relations learn very quickly that we cannot dwell on our failures. The very nature of the public-relations profession calls for a continuing cycle of failures as well as successes. The campaign we plan so carefully may backfire on us for reasons we cannot anticipate. Of course, we have our successes. If we didn't, we would have long ago been forced to look for another way to earn a living; but we never allow our failures to get us down.

Several years ago one of our most important clients was Edgar Bergen. Mr. Bergen, the great ventriloquist, had gained fame and fortune with his sidekick Charlie McCarthy. Now it was time to introduce Charlie's new pal, Mortimer Snerd, to a waiting world. We decided to make the big announcement to the press at a Sunday brunch reception at the magnificent hilltop home of Edgar and his beautiful wife Frances.

"Are you sure that the press will show up on a Sunday?" asked

my distinguished client. "Of course they will," answered the confident public-relations representative.

Based on my assurance, Frances prepared to entertain fifty press
correspondents that still-remembered warm sunny afternoon. Tables were set up in the garden, adorned with exquisite imported
damask tablecloths. Out came the best silver, the buffet tables were
piled with eggs, four different varieties of toast, ham, bacon, and
sausage, orange, grapefruit, cranberry, and apple juices, Danish
pastry, and gallons of coffee. Our press releases were ready. Charlie
McCarthy's dress suit and top hat were freshly cleaned and pressed.
Mortimer Snerd was hidden from view until the moment when he
would be unveiled.

At twelve noon we were ready. At twelve-thirty we were still
waiting. At one P.M. it became apparent that no one was going to
show up. Finally, three relatively unimportant journalists arrived.
One of them was D.O.A. (drunk on arrival). It was time for well-
founded embarrassment. There were many explanations. None of
them satisfied the Bergens or me. It was a Sunday. No one wanted
to give up their weekend for what we considered fun, but what
journalists obviously considered work. We blew it.

It was one of our biggest failures. Frances and Edgar were lovely
about it. They didn't complain about the humiliation they suffered
from the aborted nonpress event, but I knew I had lost face with
them. Despite their disappointment in me, I didn't dwell on my
failure. I didn't make excuses or put the blame on anyone else. I
knew that in order to regain the position of respect I had once had
with the Bergens, it was important that I prove myself with them
once again. We staged a press conference a week later at the Beverly
Hills Hotel. All the invited media attended. We finally accomplished our objective, and were soon back in their good graces. We
continued to represent Edgar Bergen and his friends Charlie and
Mortimer for many years after that shameful episode.

I was in my mid-twenties, struggling to get a foothold in Hollywood, when I first learned that if I really wanted to be successful
I must learn to accept some failures as inevitable, learn not to let

them get me down, and learn something from each knockdown.

In the publicity business, verbal communication is essential, yet the telephone absolutely terrified me. I knew that my future lay in my ability to communicate with people, and realized that Western Union or the mailman couldn't do it for me. It was essential that I talk to people on the telephone, but I dreaded the thought because I stuttered. I didn't speak too badly when I met with someone in person, but, like most stutterers, I would panic and mentally begin to stutter the moment I realized I had to use the telephone.

On this particular day I was to call Marlene Dietrich, one of the most glamorous women in the world. Her representative, Charles Feldman, had recommended me to her when she asked him to suggest a publicist. His secretary called to tell me that Mr. Feldman had spoken with Miss Dietrich and that she was now waiting to hear from me.

I reached for the telephone. Then I stopped. I knew exactly what would happen when I dialed the number. A voice would answer. Maybe it would even be the recognizable sultry tones of Marlene Dietrich herself, asking, "Who's calling?"

Then would come the problem. I would be unable to answer the question. I would *not* be able to say my name. It would take an interminable length of time for me to say "H-H-H-enry." It would take even longer for me to painfully get out "R-R-R-ogers." I panicked as I considered the possibility that Miss Dietrich would hang up when she heard strange noises coming from her receiver.

I suddenly remembered that just the other day I had made a call with very little difficulty. "H-H-H-enry R-R-R-ogers" had come out quite easily with only the slightest stutter. "Why do I keep worrying about the failure calls?" I asked myself. "Why can't I concentrate on that successful call I made to Dick Powell the other day? I hardly stuttered at all. I'm going to call Marlene Dietrich right now, and I'll think only about my successful conversation with Dick Powell."

I reached for the telephone again. Finally, I started to dial, saying over and over again, "Dick Powell, Dick Powell, Dick Powell."

"Yes?" queried the voice on the other end. I recognized Marlene

Dietrich's voice. "M-Miss D-D-Dietrich," I said, "this is H-H-Henry R-R-Rogers. Charlie Feldman asked m-m-me to call you."

I had done it. I had actually said my name, gotten out the first sentence without any great tragedy.

"Yes, Mr. Rogers. I've been expecting your call. I would like to see you. Can you come by this afternoon at five for tea?"

"Y-y-es, I would l-l-ove to," I replied. She gave me her address and said, "I'll see you at five," and I heard the receiver click.

CONCENTRATE ON YOUR SUCCESSES

I learned a lesson from that telephone call to Marlene Dietrich and I have never forgotten it. I learned to overlook my failures and concentrate on my successes.

My early years in the business were hampered by fear of failure. I not only avoided making telephone calls, I was also reluctant to meet personally with a prospective client. Whenever I spoke with one, I would remember the client whom I didn't get. I would remind myself of the times when I stuttered badly or spilled a drink on the floor or dropped pipe ashes on the sofa. Every business meeting thus became a chore to be avoided; in those first few years I had to steel myself to set up appointments. I neglected many opportunities and even broke appointments with lame excuses because I was *afraid*. My telephone call to Marlene taught me to approach every meeting, every encounter, with a positive rather than a negative attitude. It worked for me then, and it still does.

If past failures are preventing you from attaining your success potential, learn from my experience. Forget your failures. Think only about your successes.

I can hear some of you saying, "But I've never had any successes to look back on. I can only remember the failures I've had in my life."

I don't accept that. You're putting yourself down because you don't recognize the successes you've had. The first step you took as an infant was a success. Learning to read and write was a success. Graduating from school was a success. Finding a spouse, or a lover, was a success. And, by thinking positively, you'll be able to remember many others.

DON'T TAKE FAILURE PERSONALLY

Your failures are not necessarily someone else's victories. The world is not out there cheering for your downfall, although there are surely days when it feels like it. Just as you wouldn't take an associate's failure as your success (would you?), don't assume that your failure is a win for the other guy. It is important not to take failure personally—it's not a kick in the ego or any other part of your anatomy. You will be much healthier—and more successful—if you accept failures as part of life, learn from them what you can, and proceed to the next challenge.

Many years ago, my ego was dealt a devastating blow. For a number of years I enjoyed a very close warm relationship with Danny Kaye. I was his public-relations representative and traveled with him on his UNICEF trips to different parts of the world, and on his engagements with symphony orchestras on behalf of Musicians' Pension Funds. We literally spent hundreds of days together; I was proud that one of the world's greatest entertainers had chosen me not only as his public-relations representative but as his friend as well.

Then one day it was all over. We were in New York. The night before had been a fiasco. Danny had been named "Man of the Year" at a March of Dimes dinner at the Waldorf. He hadn't wanted to accept the honor because it was against his policy, but one of his associates had talked him into accepting it and making an appearance.

We had advised him against accepting because he had confined his charity appearances for many years to his role as U.S. ambassador to UNICEF and we felt that he should not depart from this policy. Yet, other minds prevailed and we were given the responsibility of making certain that the event was successful.

The key to the success of any "Man of the Year" benefit is the roster of names who appear on the dais. Danny had accepted the honor because he had been assured that sharing the dais would be such luminaries as Nelson Rockefeller, David Rockefeller, Averell Harriman, Jacob Javits, Mary Lasker, and a dozen other distinguished personalities. Instead, to our chagrin, we arrived to find that the dais was occupied by a group of borscht-belt comedians. Danny was seething. It was not what he had expected, but he kept smiling through the evening. He never said it, but I knew he blamed us because Nelson Rockefeller and Averell Harriman did not show up to pay tribute to Danny Kaye. It was up to us to make certain that the dais was a prestigious one. I loved Danny and still do, but I always wondered how he expected me to tell Senator Javits and the mayor of New York where to spend their evenings.

The next morning the axe fell. He called me first thing. "Henry," he said, "I've decided that my relationship with Rogers & Cowan must come to an end. You have been wonderful for me all these years, but I don't want to have public-relations representation for a while. I certainly appreciate everything you have done. Rogers & Cowan is the best. I don't intend to hire anyone else to replace you, but let's wind it up at the end of the month."

I am usually highly critical of my own performance, more so than I am of my associates', but in this case I couldn't fault myself. I was powerless to do anything about it. Danny had crossed Rogers & Cowan and me out of his life.

"Okay, Danny," I replied. "We'll finish up the few things that are pending and we'll wrap it up at the end of the month."

I called Warren and told him what had happened. "Do you mind if I call Danny and try to straighten it out?" he offered. "Maybe your time has run out with him, and it's time for a new face. Let me take a crack at him."

"Of course I don't mind. Go ahead. If you can get him to change his mind, great!"

Ten minutes later Warren called back. "I think I did it. I convinced him not to be hasty and that he and I would get together as soon as he gets back to Hollywood."

I congratulated Warren, but I do admit that I was jealous. Danny wouldn't let me try to reason with him but he had listened to Warren. He had even agreed to postpone our discharge until the two of them had a talk. They did and it was obviously a successful talk. Danny agreed to remain as a Rogers & Cowan client, provided that Warren represent him rather than Henry. He made a proper decision, for now, some twenty years later, Danny Kaye is still our client and Warren is still his "man."

There was a time in my formative years when the Danny Kaye incident would have had a devastating effect on my ego. I might have accepted that Danny's preference for Warren Cowan over Henry Rogers was advantageous to our business, but my own insecurities in those early years would have made it impossible for me to accept it on a personal level. I would have been unable to accept the rejection graciously; I would have fretted over my personal failure. Fortunately, by the time this incident occurred, I had become more mature, and better able to accept the fact that setbacks and failures are an inevitable part of life.

STRIKING OUT MEANS YOU'RE IN THERE SWINGING

In my first conversation with a new client I explain our philosophy of doing business: "We are in a creative profession, and we are not infallible. In order to be creative on your behalf, we will act rather than react. We are aggressive, not passive. We make events happen. We don't wait for them to happen. We go to bat many times, but we don't break into tears when we strike out. We just go to bat again and, because we do, our creativity is never stifled. By taking that attitude we remain capable of always giving you our best efforts."

My advice to my business associates for many years has been, "Let's be guilty of errors of commission rather than omission. You'll never be successful in this business if you're unwilling to take a chance."

That philosophy was developed over a period of many years, and is based on the premise that if you expect to hit a home run you must swing at the ball. But you must also realize that you may strike out.

When I talk to a new associate about our philosophy, I always give him/her a number of examples. I explain that for many of our clients we prepare a monthly activity report. The client may be critical of it but it is better than not preparing a report at all. At least the client is informed of what we are doing on his behalf and knows what he is paying for. It is better to open yourself up to criticism for something you did than for something you didn't do.

Our co-mission/o-mission policy is at work all the time. We try to acquire another public-relations firm. It doesn't work out. We have no regrets about trying. We have a problem. We try to solve it. We don't, but we tried. We pursue a prospective client. He rejects our proposal. We're disappointed but we know that if we keep trying we will win out in the end. We strike out a lot, but we also hit a lot of home runs.

DON'T LET YOUR STRIKEOUTS
GET YOU DOWN

Lee Iacocca struck out as president of Ford Motor Company. His boss, Henry Ford, fired him and there were many who thought he was finished in the automotive business. But he didn't worry about his strikeout. He took over the top spot at Chrysler and steered that near-bankrupt company back to success.

In a few years Iacocca came from the bottom back up to the summit of the American corporate world, higher than he had ever been before.

Victor Kiam, chairman of Remington Products, also struck out. Just a few years ago he was running Benrus Industries, a publicly held company. He overextended his credit with the banks; the banks became nervous about his managerial style and finally asked him to resign from the company. Victor is another executive who doesn't worry about striking out, and he soon found another situation that appealed to him. The Remington electric razor was a tiny subsidiary of Sperry-Rand, the billion-dollar conglomerate. Victor knew that this infinitesimal division had been losing money consistently for a number of years, and he also knew how he could turn it into a moneymaker. With the help of a few financially astute friends, Victor convinced Sperry-Rand to sell him the business with no money up front. Remington Products is now a multi-million-dollar-a-year business, showing substantial profits. So, every time you see Victor Kiam in a Remington commercial telling you that he liked his electric razor so much that he bought the company, remember that he is another person who didn't worry about strike-outs.

No one will criticize you if you keep trying, and you should not criticize yourself too severely for missing the ball when you swing at it. We all strike out frequently, but it took me a long time to learn that the person who keeps going up to bat again and again eventually hits a home run.

I truly believed in my early years that each strikeout was an irreparable blow to my struggle for success; I was not paying attention to the experience of those around me.

Richard Zanuck and David Brown were responsible for two huge financial disasters at Twentieth Century-Fox: *Tora! Tora! Tora!* and *Hello, Dolly;* yet they came back a few years later with *Jaws,* one of the greatest successes in the history of motion pictures.

Many years ago, Clark Gable insisted to his MGM bosses that he appear in a movie entitled *Parnell,* playing an Irish statesman in a role that was totally out of character for him. The film was one of the worst flops ever. Gable tried again and again and, not too much later, eagerly accepted the role of Rhett Butler in the immortal *Gone With the Wind,* which won him everlasting fame in movie history.

General Foods, Procter & Gamble, General Mills, and Ralston-Purina test new products constantly. Ninety percent of them fail, yet these companies keep trying again and again until at last they hit the one winner that makes up for all the losers.

With all these examples in front of me it is now incomprehensible why striking out became such a devastating experience for me. At first, I fantasized all the time that I was up at bat and the ball was coming at me with bullet speed. I swung hard. Crack! The bat connected solidly, and I watched the ball rise and rise higher into the air. I tossed the bat aside and jogged casually around the bases as the tiny white sphere sailed majestically over the right-field fence. Sixty thousand fans cheered and applauded. I had done it again. I was the Babe Ruth, the Willie Mays, the Hank Aaron of the public-relations world. And, at the beginning, events bore the fantasy out.

Overnight my world changed. My perfect record was over. I began to lose important clients (what had happened to my psychorelations skills?). We sold our business to a publicly held company for a block of stock that we expected to make us independently wealthy. The price of the stock dropped from sixteen dollars to ten cents a share. It was a humiliating, painful and costly experience. It took five years before we were able to buy back Rogers & Cowan and become profitable once more, but in the meantime I lost confidence. I felt that I had lost my touch.

I was consumed by self-pity. My self-image, which had been at astronomical heights, dropped lower and lower, and my depression became deeper and deeper. I resented everyone around me and finally resented myself more than anyone else. I had been kicked in the rear end by life and couldn't take it. I had accepted success as my just due, but I was incapable of dealing with failure.

NOBODY LIKES A CRYBABY

One night as I arrived home for dinner and grumpily made myself a drink, I scarcely noticed my wife watching me warily. There was an ominous silence. I flopped into my favorite chair, noisily opened the evening newspaper, and buried my nose in it. Suddenly I felt the newspaper being torn from my hands, and there was Roz, grim and angry, standing over me.

"Oh no you don't," she said. "Not tonight. You're not going to sit there again as you have night after night, feeling sorry for yourself."

"Leave me alone. Let me live with my own problems." I grabbed for the newspaper. She stepped back. It was out of my reach and I didn't have the strength or the will to get up and pull it away from her.

"I won't leave you alone. I'm sick and tired of your being a crybaby. You're acting like a spoiled kid. You're going to listen to what I have to say."

"Do I have to?" I asked wearily, wishing desperately that she would just go away.

"You're damned right you have to. I'm not going to let you throw away your life and mine too."

I remained quiet while my wife told me off. "I know why you're in this state of depression. You just can't take any kind of setback. Are you going to live this way all your life? Don't you know that your life, and mine, and everyone else's is a constant series of ups and downs? You have more than you ever dreamed of having, yet you're complaining. When things are going along smoothly you're all smiles and you get cocky because you really believe that you deserve clear sailing 365 days a year. Suddenly when there's a little downturn, you turn your face up to the sky and indignantly proclaim, 'God, you can't do this to me!' "

She talked for twenty minutes. When she was finished, I stood up and said, "Thanks, that was very helpful. Now I'm going out for a walk to think about what you've told me."

"Are you angry with me?" she asked.

"No, of course not, I needed that. You've given me a new perspective. Just give me some time to work it all out."

I walked down the driveway, reflecting on the long years that had brought me to this depressing state.

"Roz is right," I said to myself. "What the hell right do I have to really believe that there would never be any setbacks? Where did that feeling of invincibility stem from? Probably from the first few successes. I thought I had the magic touch and couldn't make a mistake. Then my security began to crack, and I just couldn't cope with it.

"The trouble must have started when I began to expect perfection from myself. The better I got, the better I wanted to be. The faster I ran, the faster I wanted to run. I accumulated success after success and never realized that they couldn't continue all my life. I've had more successes than I ever expected to have, and I'm going to stop complaining right now."

I walked back into the house with a rueful smile on my face. I told Roz she was right. She had taught me a lesson. It is time for you to learn yours.

EVERYONE STRIKES OUT

Let me tell you right now, in as strong terms as I can—everyone strikes out. Willie Mays, Hank Aaron, Mickey Mantle—everyone —you and me included. Did you know that Babe Ruth struck out more times than he hit home runs?

The key here is to realize that striking out is *not* a black mark against you personally. It's an honest attempt to achieve a goal that, due to circumstances, is not attained. The fact that you went to bat should make you proud. You must realize that you're not going to win every game. If you keep going up to bat, if you keep swinging at the ball, you'll eventually hit a home run.

IT'S OK TO MAKE MISTAKES— JUST DON'T REPEAT THE SAME ONES

Successful people all admit to their numerous mistakes. But rarely, if ever, do they make the same ones twice. Each mistake is an opportunity to learn, each error in judgment an opportunity to gain another shred of knowledge, each false start another brick laid on the foundation of success.

Fred walked into my office one day, dejected and disconsolate. "I really put my foot into it this time," he said. He went on to explain that he had made a serious mistake in dealing with one of our clients, and he was now flagellating himself.

Fred is one of our most competent and efficient young executives. He was punishing himself needlessly, and I decided that it was time for me to give him some senior statesman-type advice.

"Sit down," I said, "and listen to the guy who has made more mistakes in this company than anyone else—me."

His head was hanging low, practically between his knees. He raised it and looked at me quizzically. "You're kidding me. I've never seen you make a mistake."

I laughed. "That's because you haven't known me very long. Of course I have. I try not to make the same mistake twice, so by this time there aren't too many more left for me to make. You don't know about my long history of faux pas. Did you ever hear what happened to me at Doyle, Dane, Bernbach many years ago?" He shook his head and I began to tell him the story.

"This was in the late fifties, when advertising agencies were hiring public-relations firms to publicize the television programs their clients sponsored. It was a new, challenging opportunity for growth in our business. Spending more than half my time in New York, as I did then, had paid off handsomely. We were already representing shows sponsored by Procter & Gamble and General Foods.

"We were scheduled to make a presentation to Doyle, Dane,

Bernbach, one of the best advertising agencies in the world. We had developed an excellent presentation, and a half-dozen DDB executives were seated around a conference table waiting to hear what I had to say. In those days, however, I was too insecure to present a plan verbally. Instead, my practice was to distribute copies of the document to everyone present, suggest that they read it and ask me questions as they went along.

"As each of them turned to the first page, Mr. Doyle spoke up: 'Excuse me, Henry, there seems to be a problem. I believe you've given us the wrong presentation. Here, take a look at this,' he said as he handed it back to me. I looked and silently asked God to allow me to sink through the floor. Printed in gold letters on the cover of the presentation, which Mr. Doyle, of Doyle, Dane, Bernbach had just handed me, was 'A Public Relations Presentation to *Benton & Bowles* Submitted by Rogers & Cowan.'

"I instantly knew what had happened. Earlier in the day we had made a presentation to Benton & Bowles, another fine advertising agency, for one of their new Procter & Gamble-sponsored shows. I had put a number of leftover copies back into my briefcase. The B&B presentations were in one pocket of the briefcase, the DDB copies in another. When I walked into the DDB conference room, my hand inadvertently went into the wrong pocket, and I had distributed the wrong presentation.

"I apologized. They saw my discomfiture, saw the sweat break out on my forehead, tried to laugh it off. I retrieved the wrong copies and distributed another set—this time the right ones. They read through the plan as I had requested. Was it my imagination or were they unenthusiastic? Their questions were brief, my answers were laconic (I hadn't recovered from the shock). It seemed an interminable length of time before Mr. Doyle stood up, shook hands with me, and said, 'Thank you for your time. We'll let you know.' Two of our New York associates were with me. They were more embarrassed than I, because they were embarrassed *for* me. After all, I was their role model. I was the young man who had come from Hollywood and was conquering Madison Avenue. I had lost face in their eyes but they couldn't very well tell me that. We all tried to laugh it off as we walked back to the office but it wasn't funny. I had made an inexcusable, careless mistake. I knew it and they knew it.

"I wondered whether I had gotten away with it, but I hadn't. A few days later we received word from DDB that our presentation had been rejected and another firm had been engaged. Was it rejected because of my mistake? I'll never know. But the aftermath was something that is important for you to remember.

"I eventually realized that the DDB rejection was good, not bad for me. If they had said yes, it would have told me that I could get away with carelessness. Now I knew that I had to pay for careless mistakes. I determined that I would never make the same mistake a second time—and I haven't. Now when I make a presentation, I make certain there is only one set of documents in my attaché case, and that it's the right set."

By this time Fred was sitting up straight in his chair, his head held high. He just couldn't believe that I was telling him this anecdote, an incident in my life that showed me at my most incompetent.

"That's a great story," he said, "but are you sure you just didn't dream it up to make me feel better? Are you sure that really happened?"

I laughed at his skepticism. "Of course it's true. You just had a bad experience and you're convinced that you're the only one who's ever made a mistake. At this low point in your life you can't believe that your boss, the chairman of the board, has made mistakes much worse than you've ever made. I told you that story for two reasons: to impress upon you the fact that everyone makes mistakes, but more important, that the smart ones are the people who learn from their mistakes and never make the same one twice."

Fred stood up. "Thanks," he said, "I feel better now than when I walked in. You can bet that I'll never make that mistake again."

One evening I was having dinner with a client, and we decided at that moment to telephone another client-friend who could help solve a problem that was troubling us. I excused myself, went to the phone booth to dial the number, and then remembered that the gentleman had an unlisted number that I had forgotten. I returned to the table and explained that I would make the call in the morning. It was certainly not a tragic incident, but I have never been caught short like that again. The following day I bought a tiny, compact notebook, in which I wrote down all the numbers I would ever need if I were not in my office or at home. Automatically now, as I dress in the morning, my telephone directory goes into the back pocket of my trousers.

HOW NOT TO MAKE THE SAME MISTAKE TWICE

It's easy to say, "Don't make the same mistake twice," but how do you do it? I learned a trick that you may have noticed in the two incidents I just related. I *know* that when I go to make a presentation I have only one set of documents in my briefcase, and I *know* I have my little phone book when I go out.

One of the biggest mistakes you can make is to trust yourself to remember. When I attend a meeting I look around me in wonderment when I notice that most people sitting around the conference table are not making notes. How do they remember what's been discussed? How do they remember what decisions have been made? How do they remember who is supposed to do what after the meeting is over? When I ask them they answer, "I'll remember—don't worry—I'll remember." But they never do, because it's impossible. They mistakenly trust themselves to remember. I rarely, if ever, make the same mistake twice, because I don't trust myself to remember and work out some kind of infallible reminder for myself.

Rogers' Hints on Failure, Strikeouts, and
Mistakes

- Success is *persistence*—don't let failures
  deter you from your goal.
- Don't take failure personally.
- Take the calculated risk—a strikeout is better than not trying.
- Learn from your mistakes—take the time to analyze what went
  wrong and figure out how to avoid it in the future.

11

The stress of success

EVERYONE TALKS about it, we all live with it, but few of us know what it is. Stress means different things to different people. It is as difficult to define as it is to find a definition for success.

Robert La Veninga and James P. Spadley in their recent book, *The Work Stress Connection*, define stress as "anything that places an extra demand on you." Dr. Hans Selije, a distinguished authority on the subject, says, "Stress is the nonspecific response of the body to any demand made upon it," while Dr. Donald Tubesing, another authority, states, "Stress is part of everyday life" but "contrary to popular belief, stress is not the pressure from the outside—the divorce, the death, the burned supper, the vacation, the isolation. . . . It is your response to those situations that constitutes stress."

The word *stress* has a negative connotation, but it is an erroneous assumption that stress is necessarily bad for you. It can be good or bad. "Stress," says Dr. Tubesing, "can be a turn-on. It can pump you up, give you energy, supply that zest for living." You don't have to concern yourself about the kind of stress that turns you on. That's healthy.

But, if your ambition is to become successful and remain success-ful, you should be alerted to the possibility that one day you will face what appears to be an insurmountable block preventing you from gaining your objective. Your normal stress, which has been a healthy fact of life and has helped to bring you where you are today, has turned to *distress*—and you're in trouble.

STRESS AND DISTRESS

Let's first consider some simple examples of stress and distress. Getting out of bed in the morning, brushing your teeth, scrubbing your back while you are showering, starting up your car, driving to your job, meeting with your boss, helping your children with their homework are all situations that make a demand on you but in most cases they are pleasurable, positive experiences. They are forms of stress.

But now let's look at the potential for distress in the very same situations I have just described. When you get out of bed, you can't find your slippers. When you start to brush your teeth, you notice your gums are bleeding. Your car won't start, and while you are driving to work, you get into a traffic jam that makes you twenty minutes late for work. Your boss scolds you for your tardiness and that night you find that your children's homework is so difficult even you can't do it.

How you perceive the normal extra demands that are made on you constantly determines your life-style. Do you live your life with stress and distress?

FACING MY OWN DISTRESS

Even though I constantly faced stressful situations in my business for many years, they rarely became distressful. There would be an occasional week or month when the pressures became intense, but if I looked at it from the perspective of a forty-year span, I didn't have too much to complain about. Problems with clients are part of my normal existence and for years I thrived and prospered under the constant tension that is an integral part of the public-relations profession. During all the early years I had been able to handle problems with equanimity. Normal business problems usually rolled off my back. I would go out for dinner in the evening and was rarely disturbed by the dozen different perplexing and often aggravating situations that had plagued me during the day.

The reason for my ability to handle the pressures without too great an effort was that I loved my job. I never thought of going into any other business. In the early days I was offered a job in a motion picture agency. The offer was for much more money than I was making at the time but I never even considered it. I was fortunate that by happenstance I had fallen into a profession that gave me great satisfaction and gratification. I had no interest in being a movie producer, an agent, or an insurance salesmen. I didn't even want to be president of General Motors. I always liked what I did.

Then, one day, only a few years ago, I became aware that my attitude toward my job had changed. It wasn't fun anymore. The stress had turned to distress. Now there was anger, conflict, arguments, and constantly mounting pressures. The distress was perplexing to me because I had always been able to handle pressures before. Why not now? Why couldn't I handle them as easily as I once had?

I was filled with self-doubt, loss of confidence, and self-pity. The pressures, the aggravation, the turmoil, the constant arguments had begun to make my life miserable.

I recalled a day that started with a 7:00 A.M. telephone call from an irate client. When I got out of the shower, I started to fret because I had promised to take my grandson to a basketball game that night but I also knew we had planned going to the ballet with friends. I had to make a decision. It began to rain as I drove to the office, and after running through the parking lot without a hat, coat, or umbrella, I finally arrived in soaked, wrinkled, unpresentable clothes. The day seemed to evolve into a series of catastrophes, each more aggravating than the next. By the time I returned home at seven o'clock, I said, "I've had it. I just can't take it anymore."

However, this day was no different from similar days twenty years ago. The problems were no greater or more complex than they had ever been. My distress was caused by my perception of those problems today versus my perception twenty years ago. I had obviously changed as a person. There was a time that I could handle a day like this easily. Not anymore. Today, I took situations that were just normal incidents and built them into *distressful* situations. The situations were the same. I was different. "That's it," I concluded. And at that moment I found the reason for my inability to handle stressful situations today with the same equanimity as I had yesterday.

I AM RESPONSIBLE FOR MY OWN DISTRESS

People are not responsible for my reactions to situations. *I am responsible for my own distress, my inability to cope. My reaction to what people do or say or to what I do or say* is the key to my problem.

I thus discovered the secret that enabled me to eliminate most of the distress from my life and substitute it with the healthy stress with which I had always lived.

I knew that if I could learn to change my reaction to situations, I could eliminate the distress from my life.

WHEN YOUR STRESS TURNS TO DISTRESS

In order for you to be successful you need a certain degree of stress in your life, but it should be the healthy stress that brings with it self-satisfaction and a certain contentment. Each of us must find the appropriate level of stress that is right for us. Too little is stultifying and will turn you into a vegetable. Too much will give you an overload that will bring on *distress*.

If you don't succeed in finding the proper balance between stress and distress you will be miserable because you are doing nothing worthwhile or equally miserable because you are doing too much.

How will you know when you are heading for an overload condition? It is easily recognizable. You will experience discontent, depression, restlessness, sleepless nights, uneasiness, fatigue. You will begin to get pains you never had before, headaches, backaches, allergies. When the doctor says he can't find anything physically wrong, then you will know you are carrying a stress overload that is about to turn into *distress*. That is the time to stop and do something about your condition.

RECOGNIZING DISTRESS

I was fortunate in that I was able to recognize my stress overload. Try to recognize it in yourself. If you are dependent on aspirin, alcohol, drugs, and sleeping pills to keep you going, it is obvious that you cannot handle the stress in your life. There are other symptoms to look for. Look at yourself. Take inventory. Are you more irritable than you were a number of months ago? Do you lose your temper more readily? Do you get tired too quickly and does your fatigue last too long? Are you depressed, frustrated? Has smoking become a nervous, rather than a pleasurable habit? If these are characteristics of your life today, the odds are overwhelming that you are experiencing negative stress.

WHAT TO DO

Don't expect miracles. Your life isn't going to change overnight. There is no panacea for human suffering, so don't expect an instant cure. Dr. Paul Rosch, president of the American Institute of Stress in Yonkers, New York, states, "If anyone says they're going to give you a stress-reduction program in a day, forget it. It's a scam."

First, *retrace your steps*. How did this happen to you? Where did it start? You lost your job? You were passed up for a promotion? Your spouse walked out on you? A death in the family? You have changed as a person and haven't realized that what brought you satisfaction before now brings you frustration?

Once you have pinpointed the immediate source of your distress, you must alter the environment in which you are living so that your present damaging distress can once again become stimulating stress. Then, you can get back on the road that leads to a successful life. Easier said than done.

A change of environment can be emotional as well as physical. It involves as much what you think as what you do. In fact, it is unlikely that because you now recognize that *distress* is the cause of your problem you will suddenly quit your job and move to another part of the country, or divorce your spouse or kick your boss in the shins. No, it is more likely that your answer is to change some part of your basic outlook on life, and to be ready to experiment with new behavior as well. You may have to change long-standing patterns of thinking and coping that will take time and effort but remember that you yourself have created the tension and anxiety that have come to plague you. If you created it, you can also remove it from your life.

Change Your Habit Patterns

First, I changed my habit patterns. I do as much as I ever did, maybe more, but my life is now structured to keep negative stress at a minimum. For instance, there were many years when I was so anxious to get to my office in the morning that I never had breakfast and didn't even read the morning papers before sitting down at my desk to start the day's work. My excuse was that I never had the time. I would compensate by reading the newspapers before I went to bed at night.

Today, as part of my program to eliminate negative stress from my life, I awaken an hour earlier than was my norm. I walk rapidly for two miles, which takes a half hour. While I cool off, I read sections of the *Los Angeles Times, Los Angeles Herald Examiner,* and the *New York Times.* After shaving, showering, and dressing, I have a breakfast of bran flakes, fruit, milk, and tea, while reading James Reston, Tom Wicker, Anthony Lewis, or William Safire, each of whom I study carefully after I've scanned the rest of the *New York Times.*

Start by Reducing Simple Stress

If most of the negative stress we endure is self-imposed, then, logically, the solutions to it lie within ourselves. I decided that if I had been responsible for my own negative stress all these years, I just might be able to unmake some of it. I did, and in the process I discovered that some formulas for stress reduction are amazingly simple.

When I first arrived in Los Angeles, the skies were clear, as were the roads. Today we suffer through smog-filled days and the traffic is often reminiscent of the worst of New York, Rome, or Tokyo. I hate traffic and as it now takes me almost thirty minutes to get to my office in the morning when it formerly took fifteen, I fretted and fumed for years, arriving every day at my desk in a state of anger and frustration. Then I recognized what negative stress was doing to me and I quickly found a solution. KFAC and KUSC are our classical music stations. I now drive to the office, not really caring about the traffic or the gasoline fumes, because Beethoven, Tchaikovsky, Rachmaninoff, and Wagner transport me into another world for a half hour. I had made my own stress and with the simple flip of a switch, I learned how to unmake it.

Have rude waiters and maitre d's ruined as many expensive dinners for you as they have for me? I could not possibly enumerate the occasions when I left a restaurant annoyed, frustrated, and disenchanted with an evening that should have been pleasurable. Having an evening ruined by an unpleasant waiter is bad enough but when you have just paid a check for $50, $100, or $200, it is logical that negative stress will upset your stomach for hours to come.

I learned how to handle that situation one night while watching a friend, who had learned how to deal with negative stress long before I did. There were six of us at an elegant French restaurant in New York, celebrating the wedding anniversary of our host and hostess, Bill and Clarissa. The waiter was intrusive rather than rude. He insisted on interrupting the conversation. What kind of cocktail did we wish, did we want to look at the menu, what would we want as a first course, and on and on. He was becoming annoying to all of us, and I noticed that tension had started to build around the table.

Suddenly Bill excused himself, and I watched him walk over and talk to the waiter in a low, unobtrusive tone. Then he returned to the table and told us a funny story about a pompous waiter in a European hotel who suddenly became aware that his fly was open. We all laughed. The tension disappeared.

The waiter was never intrusive again. He stood some ten feet from our table and whenever Bill felt that his guests needed service he caught the waiter's eye, and he became all-attentive. I marveled at the change of atmosphere at the table and was curious as to how Bill had, with a thirty-second conversation, changed his anniversary party from a disaster into a triumph.

As we were walking out of the restaurant I asked him. He smiled and said, "I wasn't about to let that son-of-a-bitchin' waiter ruin our evening. I told him very quietly and politely not to come near our table until I gave him the eye, and to seal our bargain I slipped him twenty dollars."

"But how did you come up with that very appropriate story about the stuffy European waiter when you came back to the table?"

"That was part of my getting-rid-of-stress program," he replied.

"All of you were holding your breath when I sat down, waiting for me to tell you what happened. If I had told you, the unpleasantness would have stayed with us all evening, and if I had ignored it and started to comment on Ronald Reagan's press conference this afternoon, that would have also left the shadow of our waiter hanging over our heads. By telling a story about a waiter whose fly was open, I hoped to dispel the tension." He certainly did, and my friend Bill taught me something. We can sit and let negative stress build up in a room—or we can do something about it.

STOP TREATING THE SYMPTOMS

I took a sleeping pill before going to bed because the stress of the day kept me awake at night. At first, I tried counting sheep, but that didn't work. Then I tried to blank everything out of mind, but the blankness lasted only a moment and was supplanted by unpleasant scenes from the previous day. The depressing conversation with a client who complained about one of my associates, my business adviser telling me that I had to cut down on my personal expenses if I hoped to balance this year's budget, the reminder from my wife about the black-tie dinner party the following night, the call from Associated Press asking why our press release arrived at their office an hour and a half after United Press International had received theirs, a local charity asking when they could expect the check I had pledged a number of months before. Nothing let me sleep except the pill.

I would take an aspirin for my headache that started in midmorning and then a double vodka on the rocks before lunch—the result of a stressful confrontation with one of my colleagues. Then came the decongestant I took for my runny nose. I didn't realize at the time that I was treating the symptoms of daily negative stress and was ignoring the causes of my ailments.

Once I learned that my ailments and my sleepless nights stemmed from the negative stress that I could no longer handle easily, I was then able to take positive action to solve the problem. Once I started to develop the strategies that were to eventually lessen the degree of my negative stress, I stopped treating the symptoms.

LESSENING STRESS DOESN'T MEAN THAT YOU CARE LESS

There is a great temptation to be consumed with guilt when you begin to control your life and eliminate negative stress. You say to yourself, "That means I don't care as much—I don't feel as intensely—I'm not as emotionally involved as I used to be." That attitude is a trap to become aware of and then avoid. It's easy for me to say this now, but I did experience great guilt during the first few weeks of my new regimen.

On reflection, it was a silly reaction because getting into the office at eight-thirty or nine o'clock is not a crime. But for me it was such a departure from my normal six-thirty to seven-thirty schedule that I worried.

"Am I slipping?" I asked myself. "Don't I care as much about my job as I used to? Is this the first step to retirement?" Then I remembered the all-important word *perception* and the guilt receded. I now know that by eliminating some of the stress in my life, I arrive at my desk warmed up for an active day just as an athlete has warmed up before he starts to compete. I care *more*, not less.

LONG-TERM STRESS REDUCTION MEANS NEW HABITS

There is no single simple method of stress reduction, because stress has so many causes. Each individual must seek his own solutions. But there are several successful techniques that have helped many people.

First, take responsibility for your own stress and distress. Realize that you alone cause it, and you alone can relieve it. Then, change your patterns. Find new ways to approach both your work and your relaxation. Pursue novelty for its own sake. Try something new. Break out of old ruts. And improve your life by reducing simple stress. Pay the rude waiter twenty dollars and shrug off his interference; rent the car with air conditioning. Be easy on yourself. Don't sweat the small stuff.

But even after you have tried some new patterns and made the easy stress-relief decisions, there will be plenty of stress left. This will only be relieved by adopting new habits over the long term. I have tried many approaches to stress reduction and will share them with you. But remember that these are techniques that have worked for me; you may have to find other, perhaps analogous ways of coping with your stress.

Here are eight stress-reduction techniques to consider:

1) Talk positively to yourself.
2) Buy a new hat.
3) Learn to say "no."
4) Beethoven, not memos.
5) Relax before dinner.
6) Meditation.
7) Exercise.
8) A Walkman and Heavyhands.

Talk Positively to Yourself

I talk to myself constantly. Don't you? I've been doing it ever since I can remember. I may be rehearsing what I'm going to say to a business associate who is due in my office in five minutes. When I drive to the office in the morning I talk to myself about the client meeting I expect to have at ten; I plan the approach to the conversation I intend to have with my partner at lunch; the telephone call I will make to my wife later in the day about our plans for the evening; and the subjects I expect to bring up for discussion at an executive committee scheduled for that afternoon.

I have found that talking positively to myself about stressful situations has proven to be enormously successful. It is important, I decided, that my perceptions of each stressful situation be based on positive messages I give myself. I fell asleep in the barber chair and the barber gave me a terrible haircut. My natural inclination was to rant and rave about what I realize was a ridiculous, unimportant matter. I stop and say, "Oh, what the hell, I can live with it. It will grow back in a week or two." When I look at myself in the mirror the next morning, I have already conditioned myself. I laugh and say, "You're a silly sight, but it's good for you. You've become too egotistical about your appearance anyway."

I arrive home exhausted after a trying day. I've already decided to have a quick dinner and go right to bed. I am greeted at the door by my wife who says, "You might want to shower and change. The Murphys and the Sperlings are coming to dinner at seven-thirty." I had forgotten.

My first inclination is to moan and groan, but I don't. I just grunt. Walking up the stairs, I start talking to myself. "A hot shower will make me feel better. I'll have a vodka and tonic before they arrive and that will pep me up. By the time they get here, I'll be in good shape." I talk to myself. That is one way I keep my perception of stressful situations in a positive light.

Buy a New Hat

Many years ago it was an acknowledged fact that a woman relieved the pressures of her life by buying a new hat. After she had had a serious argument with her husband, or had lost twenty-six dollars in a bridge game, or finished a screaming session with her daughter, Mrs. Jones would take herself off to the local millinery shop and let off steam by buying a chapeau. I have always remembered the mythical Mrs. Jones and I have figuratively followed in her footsteps.

When I feel the pressure building up at the office, even though no one particular issue is especially important, I get up from my desk, walk six blocks to Carroll & Co., and buy a new tie. I contend that I have as many ties in my closet as does Mr. Carroll in his entire shop, but I don't have an ulcer. (Of course, neither does he!)

Learn to Say "No"

I have learned to say "no," but it took many years. I no longer accept every invitation to social, civic, or charitable events. I always thought I would miss something important if I said "no." Now I realize that my quiet evenings at home are more important to me and more relaxing than my stressful evenings on the town. I no longer show up at every meeting I am asked to attend. By saying "no" I have reduced my stress.

Beethoven, Not Memos

For many years my business stayed with me while I was driving my car. I came close to killing myself a dozen times because I found I could not drive and write reminder notes to myself simultaneously. When I began to develop my stress-less program, I changed my driving habits. I now play classical music on my car radio as a diversion. If the commercials begin to irritate me, I use my audio cassette player.

Relax Before Dinner

I never go directly to the dinner table when I arrive home in the evening. I know that I need a half hour of relaxation before soup or salad is placed before me as a first course. I have a drink, sometimes nonalcoholic, and watch the evening news on television. If it has been a particularly difficult day, I watch the "McNeil-Lehrer News Hour" after the network news, so it's eight-thirty before I'm ready for dinner. Although our cook frets about the lateness of the hour, and my wife complains that I am causing her to suffer from malnutrition, I allow myself this little indulgence.

Meditation

For a number of years I meditated. Many friends had told me they had found meditation an effective method for combating negative stress. I enrolled in a Transcendental Meditation course and after a number of weeks of experimentation discovered that the twenty minutes twice a day of reciting a mantra was helping to achieve my objective. It gave my mind a rest, a short vacation from worry and aggravation, freedom from the responsibilities of my job and my family. Everything I was doing at that time to relieve my mind and body from negative stress was working. I felt better and better, and after two years I gave up TM. Although I no longer practice, I recommend it to everyone. You can find out about it from your friends or a local TM center, or your local library has a number of books on the subject.

Exercise

For years I have been told that I must exercise. I have been told that I should build up my stamina so that I could withstand long-term negative stress. My doctor keeps telling me that walking or swimming will tone up my muscles and keep me trim. He tells me that I will sleep better and that my endurance will increase. "But, doctor," I reply, "exercise is such a bore!" And for years I exercised infrequently and intermittently. I played golf for many years, but always regarded that as four hours of socializing with friends and acquaintances rather than a period dedicated to toning up my muscles. I tried an exercycle for a time, and even though I watched "Today" or "Good Morning America" while my legs went up and down and up and down a thousand times, I still found it to be tedious and irksome. I swam on and off—mostly off. I did it for a few weeks at a time, ten laps, twenty laps, and then the sheer boredom of it got to me, and I stopped. For a time I walked about two miles every morning. That didn't last long either. It was boring.

A Walkman and Heavyhands

Then I bought a Walkman. Maybe music would relieve the boredom, I thought. I put the headphones on my ears, the equipment in my pocket, and set off to the strains of a classical piece, or, at times, a Neil Diamond or a Barbra Streisand audio cassette. That helped.

One day I came across Heavyhands and "Hooked on Classics." Heavyhands is what its creator, Dr. Leonard Schwartz, calls the ultimate exercise system: AMF developed a set of hand weights to accommodate Dr. Schwartz's regimen, and they can be purchased at one-, two-, three-, and up to five-pound weights. He prescribes exercises you do with these weights as you are walking or jogging. Then came "Hooked on Classics," an audio cassette of classical compositions, speeded up in tempo so that it is perfect for rapid walking. At last I found the exercise that I believe I can live with for the future. I've been at it for a year now, so if you see a strange creature walking up the quiet streets of Brentwood at daybreak every morning with headphones, an audio cassette player in his pocket, wildly pumping or swinging scarlet-colored Heavyhands, don't think it's a *Star Wars* character come to life. It's me, exercising my body and relaxing my mind, and relieving myself of some of the negative stress that had built up from the day before.

My walking habit is the best solution I have found to reducing stress in my life. Perhaps it will work for you, too. But if it does not, keep trying other techniques until you find one suited to your own particular needs. If you are going to live the stressful life, you don't have a choice.

Rogers' Rules for Coping with Stress Overload

Don't try to transform yourself overnight.   There are no quick solutions to your problem.

Take one step at a time.   It is a slow process but if you take each problem as it comes, you will eventually start to successfully cope with life again.

Get ready to change your habit patterns.   If you want your life to improve, you must change the way you think and what you do.

Set new long-term goals for yourself.   Stop living your life aimlessly. Diversion from one way of life to another has therapeutic value.

Remember the power of positive thinking.   To lessen stress, think about the good things in your life, not the bad. Your wine bottle is half full, not half empty.

Change the way you relate to people.   Your problem may stem from your inability to resolve interpersonal conflicts. The answer is *compromise.* Learn to be more satisfied with less than total victory. Think about psychorelations.

Stop thinking exclusively about yourself.   Stress will be lessened if you devote yourself to new activities and new people.

Stop evaluating yourself.   Learn to tolerate and accept your own shortcomings, and stop concerning yourself with self-worth.

12

Is that all there is?

FROM AGES twenty-five to seventy-five, millions of people in our country ask themselves the same nagging, worrying question: "Is that all there is?"

They are depressed and unhappy, convinced that life will always remain as dull as it is today, and that it will never get any better, any richer, or any fuller.

The people I am referring to are not the unemployed, the under-privileged, or the manual worker in a boring job. No, they are the upper crust of our population, the people who are looked up to in their communities as among the few who have made it to the top. They have the best jobs in town. They play golf at the best country clubs, drive the most expensive cars, and live in the loveliest homes. Yet, they are the ones who get up every morning, look at themselves in the mirror, and ask "Is that all there is?"

Something seems to be missing. They feel that life has deceived and cheated them.

Often the boss doesn't understand why his subordinates appear to be much more content with their lives than he is. After all, he reasons, he drives a Lincoln Continental and they drive VW's. How can they be happier than he? As Yul Brynner pondered in Rodgers and Hammerstein's *The King and I,* "It's a puzzlement!"

SUCCESS IS NOT MONEY

In our history, the word *success* was always related to money. The more money you made, the more successful you were. The larger your home, the happier you were. The bigger your automobile, the more respect you enjoyed from your neighbors. But this has been a uniquely American trait. The more civilized Europeans and Asians learned a thousand years before we did that success is more closely related to the quality of *life* than to the quantity of material possessions.

ARE YOU ASKING THE QUESTION?

Are you the father of two healthy, happy children and married to a wonderful woman? Do you live in a beautiful home, lead a comfortable life, and get up every morning with the gnawing question, "Is that all there is?"

Are you a successful career woman who has an intelligent man madly in love with you? Are you, too, asking, "Is that all there is?"

If you are, you should understand that there are millions like you: male, female, young, middle-aged, married, single, who, having reached a higher station in life than they ever dreamed possible, are also asking the question. You are different from them, however, because you are about to discover that the answer is *"no."* You are about to learn that there *is* much more out there. Your future is brighter than you thought it was. Life can be as full and as rich and as satisfying as you hoped it would.

If you are *not* asking the question, if you are not one of those I have just described, read on anyway, because there is a better than even chance that one day in the future the question will plague you, too. Discovering the answer today can save you years of anguish in the future.

THE DREAM OF SUCCESS

Many of you have already discovered that the reality of success does not match the dream of success. You have achieved the goals you set for yourself many years ago, and now you are wondering where is the satisfaction everyone told you to expect. You have all the material evidences of success, but emotionally you're worse off today than when you first started, because there's nothing to look forward to. You have more than you ever hoped for, but you have nothing.

How do I know all this? Because it happened to me.

ALREADY SUCCESSFUL

In the mid-fifties, Henry Rogers and Warren Cowan were already recognized as the leading publicists in Hollywood. We represented a formidable list of movie stars, producers, directors, and motion picture production companies. We had substantial incomes and lived glamorous lives. We entertained in our homes the greatest film personalities in the world, and, in turn, were entertained by them.

As part of our job, we lunched frequently at the movie studios, surrounded by beautiful women and handsome men. We walked onto the sound stages where motion pictures were being filmed so we could meet with our clients between scenes. Who could want anything more out of life?

I did not discount the pleasures of working with Joan Crawford, Frank Sinatra, Judy Garland, Dick Powell, June Allyson, Rex Harrison, Fred MacMurray, John Wayne, Red Skelton, Lana Turner, Gary Cooper, and a hundred more; nor did I complain about the lunches I had in studio dining rooms while Spencer Tracy, Katharine Hepburn, Clark Gable, and Cary Grant sat at nearby tables. But I had a gnawing sense that something was missing.

I awakened with a groan one morning and shuddered at the prospect of going to work. I was approaching middle age, and I was dissatisfied with my life. Self-doubts had been building up over a period of months. I got out of bed, went to the bathroom, looked at myself in the mirror, and said, "I'm halfway through my life; everyone tells me that I'm successful but so what? I thought I would be feeling greater gratification for what I've accomplished, but I feel very little. *Is that all there is?*"

FEELING SORRY FOR MYSELF

I felt sorry for myself. "I'm taking care of everyone," I groaned, "but there's no one taking care of me." How ridiculous! I should have been grateful that I needed no one to take care of me, but I didn't learn that until later on. I realized that I was getting older and that I was at a critical point in my life. I was depressed, confused, and resentful. I really had nothing to complain about, except for my state of mind. I reminded myself of an expression I used many years before to describe people who didn't appreciate what they had: "He's crying with a loaf of bread under each arm." I was that person now but it didn't help to tell myself that there was nothing to cry about. It didn't stop me from speculating day after day that there must be something more to life other than what I was feeling.

I knew I faced a monumental challenge. Fearful as it was, I felt it was something I had to handle myself. I felt very lonely. I even decided not to talk it over with my wife. She seemed so occupied with our children and our home that I didn't want to burden her. When she became aware of how disconsolate I was and asked me what was wrong, I dismissed it by saying, "Nothing, I'm just depressed. I'll get over it."

I thought that getting away from the normal routine of home and office would help. One day I told Roz that I wanted to go to Palm Springs for a couple of days—alone. She was worried about my state of mind, but so was I. I checked into a motel, and sat there for a week thinking and thinking, trying to figure out what was wrong with me. Once I ran into some old friends who invited me to have dinner with them that night. I declined. I didn't want to talk with anyone. I wanted to be alone. I stayed for a week, and returned home in exactly the same miserable mood as I was in when I left.

A few weeks later, I went away again, more depressed than ever. This time I went to Balboa, a beach resort only fifty miles away, and checked into a shabby rooming house. You would expect me to now tell you that I then proceeded to drink a bottle of whiskey and pass out, but it was worse than that. I didn't even take solace in alcohol. I just thought, and walked, ate a hamburger, walked again, slept restlessly, and thought some more.

My whole life, my career, my marriage, my relationship with my children, were in crisis. It was important that I take some kind of action or this depression would continue indefinitely. I would have to move ahead or sink deeper into self-pity, ruining my own life and that of my family as well.

But, what did "move ahead" mean? Where did I want to go? What was my problem? What was really wrong with my life? On the surface it looked as though I really had it made. What was wrong with me?

Advice from Artie Shaw

One day I was discussing the problem with a friend, Warren Bennis, professor at the School of Business Administration at USC, when he suggested I track down a book titled *The Trouble With Cinderella* written many years ago by Artie Shaw, long recognized as one of the great jazz musicians of the twentieth century. I had only read the first few pages when I realized that my problem was not unique. In the very first paragraph Shaw wrote:

I've been traveling along this highway for quite a while now. Looking back at where I started out it seems to me that I've come a considerable distance. Of course there's no way for me to tell how much actual progress I've made. Progress is a word that has no meaning unless you can measure how far you've come in terms of where you want to end up; and I haven't the vaguest idea of where I'm heading.

That was my problem. I didn't have the vaguest idea of where I was heading.

Shaw continued:

At the moment, though, I'm in a bad fix. I've come to a dead stop. I'm going to have to make some kind of decision before I can get going again because this isn't like any other place I've been in up to now.

I identified with that completely. Then, reading further, I finally came to the point that eventually led me to the solution to my problem. Shaw said to me:

I feel that there is a point in Everyman's life when he should take inventory, look back over what he has done with his life up to that point, and then decide whether he wants to continue along the line which has brought him to the point where he is, or go off into some other form of activity more suitable to his real needs as a growing, developing human being rather than a cleverly contrived automaton devised for the purpose of doing the same tricks over and over again. . . . I believe this whole job of self-appraisal and consequent reorientation can only be done out of the conscious realization that any change—absolutely any change at all—will be an improvement.

He had summed it up. I needed a change—but why and what?

I DIDN'T LIKE THE VIEW

I had climbed to the top of the mountain everyone talks about. I had attained my objective, all right, but I didn't particularly like the view. Life was more exciting, more challenging, when I was struggling to get to the top of the mountain than it was when I finally got there.

That was it, I decided. That was my problem. *Life was more exciting when I was struggling to get to the top of the mountain than it was when I finally got there.*

The fact of success had not matched the fantasy of success. I remembered that a sense of disillusionment had descended on me the moment I realized I was a successful man. I remembered reading once that the disappointment experienced by the man who gets what he wants is not too different from the disappointment felt by the man who doesn't. I knew now that the statement was true, at least for me.

I said to myself, "You're on top of the mountain and you're unhappy. You were happy when you were climbing so the answer to your problem, Henry, is to find another mountain to climb." Logical? I thought so. But—what mountain? Where was there another one? The Hollywood publicity business was all I knew. I couldn't suddenly become an architect, an engineer, or a physicist. What new mountain loomed so tall that it would make me jump out of bed enthusiastically again, as I once had every morning, eager to get to my office?

LOOKING FOR ANOTHER MOUNTAIN

Now at last I was on the way to a solution. I felt better already.

I paced the living room night after night, thinking about what changes I wanted to make in my life—what new mountain I wanted to climb. During the day I went through the motions of doing my job but I was still in a desultory state. Warren would ask me what was wrong, but I wouldn't tell him either. Again my only reply was, "Oh, nothing. I'll be all right. It's nothing." Nothing? It was everything. It was my whole life.

How About New York?

The days, weeks, and months of long nights and painful days finally came to an end. I had gone to New York and was walking up Fifth Avenue on my way to an appointment. I breathed deeply the diesel fumes from the exhaust pipes of the succession of buses that were causing an apparently impenetrable traffic jam. The sidewalks were crowded with pedestrians who jostled and pushed me until I discovered that it was simpler to walk in the street. "Not like peaceful Beverly Hills," I said to myself. I looked at the crowded stores, stared at the towers of Rockefeller Center, admired the beauty of St. Patrick's Cathedral, saw the lush green of Central Park a few blocks ahead, and then it hit me.

I had made a success in Hollywood. How about New York? How about going back to my roots? Years before I had fled the deadening, humid summer heat and the numbing winter cold of New Jersey and New York for the mild sunny climate of southern California. At the time I loved the change I had made in my life. Now the pleasures of beach, mountains, and clear skies had become unimportant to me. The cement canyons of Manhattan beckoned. The board rooms of Madison Avenue, the theatrical wizardry of Broadway—the whole, new lively world of New York became my mountain.

There was an untapped movie business in New York just waiting for the public-relations firm that was aggressive enough to go after it. There were actors, actresses, and filmmakers and movie companies that preferred to headquarter in New York rather than Hollywood. But most important, there were television and New York-based corporate public-relations challenges as well. Maybe we could build a business in these two new areas as we had done in the Hollywood motion picture industry. Maybe we could and maybe we couldn't, but the challenge was there.

New York was the new mountain I had been looking for. I knew now what I had to do. Just as years before I had cultivated agents, lawyers, and business managers, pounding the pavements of Hollywood Boulevard day by day in order to get a foothold, I was now ready to start all over again, 3,000 miles away, pounding the pavements of Madison Avenue.

THE DECISION THAT CHANGED MY LIFE

"Suppose," I asked myself, "I built up a New York business and became dissatisfied all over again?" Well, that was nothing to worry about immediately. Right now I had to pack my mountain-climbing clothes, buy a new pair of pavement-pounding shoes, and head East. Years before my father had said to me, "Let's go West, son." Now I was saying, "Let's go East because that's where the new mountain is."

The decision I made that day changed my life. I never again asked myself, "Is that all there is?"

In New York we started slowly, renting desk space in a small advertising agency, with one young man as our New York representative. We then took a hotel suite that served double duty for me as living quarters and office. We began to get a number of New York-based clients and finally decided we could afford our first real office on Madison Avenue, above a Longchamps Restaurant between Fifty-Sixth and Fifty-Seventh Streets. Business was starting to roll.

For many years I had enjoyed the delicious assortment of sweets that Hollywood had to offer. Now, New York was the site of my new candy store. When I went to see Ed Ebel at General Foods in White Plains, Tom McDermott at Benton & Bowles, Lewis Titterton at Compton Advertising, Sam Thurm at Lever Bros., and David Foster at Colgate-Palmolive, I received the same satisfaction I once got when I met with clients and prospective clients at RKO, Universal, Columbia, MGM, and Twentieth Century-Fox all on the same day.

Then there were the out-of-town trips to Cincinnati for meetings with Procter & Gamble, to Pittsburgh for Westinghouse, Minneapolis for General Mills, Chicago for Sears-Roebuck. Each city and each company presented a challenge, and each challenge brought with it a new fulfillment. The climb wasn't steady. I would take one step forward and then slip back two. There were also good years when I would take two steps forward and only slip back one. But the climb was fun and exciting.

ANOTHER CHALLENGE, ANOTHER MOUNTAIN

It was in the mid-sixties that I began to think about yet another mountain. It came about when, through a series of circumstances, I was asked in January 1966 to serve as press liaison officer for Prince Philip's upcoming tour of the United States. When William Heseltine, assistant press secretary to the queen at that time, announced my appointment to that prestigious post, I received a barrage of publicity in the London press.

The *Evening News* banner headline read THE MAN WHO WILL "MANAGE" PRINCE PHILIP. The *Daily Express* headlined EXCELLENT! JUST WHAT THE PALACE NEEDS. Robin Douglas-Home wrote:

> Three great rousing royal cheers this morning for Prince Philip. His decision to accept a professional American public-relations firm to handle publicity for his tour of The United States is the best thing that has happened to royalty since the invention of the camera. I know the idea to employ the firm—Rogers & Cowan, which handles some of Hollywood's top stars and *Playboy* magazine—came from Variety Clubs In-

ternational. . . . But the point is that Prince Philip himself approved of the plan.

When I arrived in London, I hit the front pages again. The *Evening News* blared PRINCE PHILIP'S NEW MAN. Keith Blogg wrote: "This afternoon Mr. Henry C. Rogers, gray-suited athletic-looking chairman of the grand Rogers & Cowan publicity machine, was presenting himself at Buckingham Palace to start work as the first professional to 'handle' a member of the Royal Family."

For the next few months and through the tour that took place in March of that year, Rogers & Cowan was mentioned constantly by the British press. When the trip was over, Warren and I agreed that the time was right for us to open an office in London.

The American motion picture industry had moved into Wardour Street and Berkeley Square. It had become economically viable for the major Hollywood studios to produce films at Pinewood, Elstree, and the other film studios that had been built in the suburbs of London many years before. We knew most of the Americans who were now frequenting the White Elephant, Les Ambassadeurs, and the Connaught, as they had formerly dined at Chasen's, the Bistro, and the Polo Lounge. It made good business sense for us to take advantage of those long-established relationships.

Margaret Gardner, an American journalist who had lived in Paris for many years, worked as a part-time representative for us during the years when the Hollywood studios were making films there. Now that the action had moved to London, it was logical that if we were to establish ourselves as a viable force in that city, it was Margaret who should take up the reins. Easier said than done. She was happy in Paris, spoke fluent French, had many friends there, and loved the Parisian life-style. It took a lot of convincing but she finally agreed to pull up her Parisian stakes and move to London to set up our first international office. I went over to help her get started.

When I arrived in London to aid in organizing the new office, Margaret told me she had just received a call from Warren Cowan who reported that Diana Ross and the Supremes, one of our important clients at the time, were coming to London for their first appearance in Great Britain. It was vital for Margaret to launch them in a big way. She asked me if I had any ideas. I said to her, jokingly, "Maybe we could get Prince Philip and Queen Elizabeth to give a party in their honor."

Margaret told me to stop kidding around. This was a serious matter, and we really had to come up with something new and fresh that would alert London to the fact that Diana Ross and the Supremes were a very important American music group. My joking reference to Queen Elizabeth and Prince Philip gave me an idea. It was time to have some fun with Margaret.

"This is our first day in business here in London," I said. "We haven't even had our first appointment yet. You know me by now. I always like to start at the top. Let's make an appointment."

"Where? With whom?" she asked, a note of apprehension in her voice. She had dealt with me before. I didn't answer her. Instead, I buzzed our receptionist and said, "Diane, please get Buckingham Palace on the telephone."

Margaret jumped up from her chair.

"Buckingham Palace? What do you think you're doing? People don't just call up Buckingham Palace. Especially Americans who are in business for one day."

"Sit down and relax," I replied calmly. "For years to come people are going to ask you how you spent your first day in London. Whom did you see? they'll ask. With whom did you have your first appointment? You're going to answer them very casually. You'll say, oh, it was nothing much. I went over to see Bill Heseltine at Buckingham Palace to discuss the idea of having Queen Elizabeth and Prince Philip give a party in honor of Diana Ross and the Supremes."

Before Margaret could answer, the receptionist informed me that Buckingham Palace was on the line. Margaret looked at me, aghast.

I asked for William Heseltine, press officer for Prince Philip, with whom I had worked the previous year. He greeted me warmly, and made a date for Margaret and me to see him at the palace. At five-thirty that afternoon we were ushered into Bill's office. He offered us a drink and we began our conversation. I told him that I needed some advice. We wanted to do something special to launch Diana Ross and the Supremes in London, and while I knew it was ridiculous to think that Prince Philip and Queen Elizabeth would host a party in their honor, I wondered what he thought of having the Supremes give a concert at the palace for Princess Anne, Prince Charles, and their friends. Very tactfully, he laughed off the idea. "That was a good try, Henry," he said, "but there is no chance. Forget it." I was not at all surprised. In fact, I had never expected a "yes."

Having unsuccessfully concluded our business we left the Palace offices, walked across the courtyard where I had watched the Changing of the Guard as a tourist many years before, and began to stroll back to the Dorchester Hotel.

"Well, Margaret," I said with a chuckle, "we'll have to figure out something else for the Supremes, but at least you can tell your friends that your first meeting in London was at Buckingham Palace."

Margaret laughed. "I must admit that it's quite an impressive way to start up a new business."

What now? Where is the next mountain to climb? As of this writing we have just opened an office in Washington, D.C. Will there be other mountains after that? I'm sure there will. Each one rejuvenates me and gives me a new vitality and enthusiasm.

PERSONAL MOUNTAINS TO BE CLIMBED

But I am getting ahead of myself, because in those early days of anger and frustration I was also as dissatisfied with my personal life as I was with my business.

One day, back in the mid-fifties when I had first asked, "Is that all there is?" I arrived at the office in my usual depressed state, went through the motions of taking care of business, and, at noon, left for a hair-cut appointment before a scheduled lunch date. As my barber started his work, my regular manicurist sat down opposite me, looked up smiling, and said, "We'll have to find someone else to do your nails next week, Mr. Rogers. I'll be away on vacation."

"Where are you going?" I asked listlessly.

Her smile broadened. "Oh, my friend and I are sailing on the S.S. *Liberté*—that's the French Line, you know. We're taking a three-week trip to Europe."

I sat up straight in my chair. The barber pulled back, fearing he would cut off a piece of ear.

"That sounds exciting," I said. I began to question her about her trip. Then, because I knew her well and was confident she wouldn't be offended, I asked, "On your income, I don't understand how you can afford such a trip."

Again she smiled, "Oh, I can afford it. I've been saving up for this trip for years. The only reason I work as hard as I do is to earn money that will allow me to do the things I enjoy doing."

GET OUT OF THE RUT

Driving home that evening I concluded that my manicurist was much more astute than I. Life wasn't a bore to her—she had developed an interest that made it exciting. Each morning when she awakened she looked forward to earning just a little bit more money to add to her vacation nest egg. To me, life was a drag; to her, it was exhilarating.

That night I decided to talk it over with my wife. Over dinner I told her about the conversation I had had with the manicurist. "She's much more enthusiastic about her life than I am about mine. She has something to look forward to. I don't.

"We're in a rut. I don't like it and it's time that we pulled ourselves out of it. We've never been to Europe. Let's plan a trip."

"We can't afford to go to Europe," Roz replied. "We live extravagantly considering your income, and we just don't have the money to take that kind of vacation."

"Well, let's do what my manicurist does."

"What's that?"

"Let's start saving until we do have enough to take a trip. I'm sure that if we put our minds to it, we could go next June."

Out of that conversation came a whole new life-style for us. We concluded that just as climbing new mountains was the answer to my business dissatisfaction, the same answer was applicable to my personal life. We were both in a rut, and the only way out was to expand our horizons, look for new personal, as well as professional, challenges.

We had been living extravagantly. By cutting down on restaurants, home entertainment, Palm Springs weekends, and other incidentals, we managed to put together a fund sufficient to take us to Europe the following summer. We flew to Paris and spent five days there taking in the sights like typical American tourists on their first trip abroad. We picked up a little car in Paris and drove through Switzerland, Austria, Italy, and finally returned to Paris exhausted but exhilarated. We arrived home five weeks after we had left, determined that this was the first step to completely changing our way of life.

We went to museums and art galleries and gradually began to collect modern and contemporary art. We became interested in classical music and started to go to concerts regularly. We tried ballet and opera and decided that we loved ballet and hated opera. I changed my reading habits and switched from best-sellers to the classics, which I had never read before. I began to enjoy all those books that had sat by my bedside unread for years.

We both became interested in charities and community and political work. As the years went on, I continued to look for new personal mountains to climb. I decided to write my first book. It took many years to write, but I eventually had it published. The book led to television appearances and college lectures. That, in turn, led to regular lecture courses, which I gave at UCLA and

USC. Today, thirty years after I first asked the question "Is that all there is?", the thought of asking the question ever again doesn't occur to me. I'm sure I'll never ask it because I know that, for me at least, the answer to enjoying success is to continually seek new challenges, to constantly look for new mountains to climb.

HOW OTHERS HAVE FACED THE PROBLEM

David Finn, one of the world's most distinguished public-relations professionals, dealt with this problem in his book *The Corporate Oligarch*, published by Simon and Schuster in 1969. He agrees with my contention that frequently those who reach the pinnacle of success are dissatisfied with their lives. He writes that even after the successful person has become "rich, powerful, and important in the world," there is something deep within him that is frustrated. He feels that profit and profit alone does not satisfy his desire to devote himself to some worthy calling.

Finn agrees, too, with my theory that looking for another mountain is the answer to the question "Is that all there is?" He told me that "I would be inclined to say that there is no view from the top since there's no top. If one becomes head of a company, president of a university, director of a hospital, or president of the United States, that's only a beginning rather than an end. Achieving a prominent position gives one an opportunity to work toward more ambitious goals. I find that as a photographer I keep working on more and more books as time goes on because I feel a sense of permanence in what I'm doing. . . . The more one accomplishes, the more one wants to accomplish."

Joseph N. Mitchell, president of Beneficial Standard Corporation, states that he too needs more than his business career to make his life complete. "I do share your enthusiasm and drive to follow additional pursuits over and above my primary business," he told me. "I've found new challenges in serving on a variety of corporate, civic, and philanthropic boards and committees. These activities broaden my perspective and provide real satisfaction after I accomplished meaningful results in the business world. There is only one area of activity that I have not pursued as yet and that is politics. Perhaps that will be the next mountain I wish to climb."

Coy Eklund, recently retired chairman of Equitable Life Assurance Company, now spends much of his time serving as chairman of the executive committee of the President's Council for International Youth Exchange. His philosophy of life is such that he will never have to ask, "Is that all there is?" He says, "Winston Churchill said that success entails struggle, sacrifice, and ceaseless effort. And habit becomes well-nigh unbreakable. The bottom line that expresses it for me is 'Work is life, and good work is good life.'

"To be always useful, to contribute, to make life count—those objectives, those guidelines, are continuously effective motivations for most successful people. There is no stopping place short of the grave. The mind, the heart, will have it no other way. I have learned that nobody has it made. That nobody arrives at any plateau of total satisfaction. A divine discontent continues to stare; the sense of life, the sense of being alive, is a force that must be shared."

Becoming satisfied with your accomplishments is one reason for the dissatisfaction one feels once success has been achieved. Henry Moore, one of the world's greatest living sculptors, has never had that problem because he is never satisfied with his work. He always strives to be better. In a recent interview in *GEO*, Moore said:

I've never yet been absolutely satisfied with anything. That is, while I'm working on it. Sometimes if I haven't seen something I've done for a few years and I see it again I am pleasantly surprised. But it's a danger to anyone to become too conceited. It's work itself that stops you from being like that because every new work that one does is a problem. Quite often I'm disappointed when I see something that I don't think is right or I see something happen I don't like and I feel like a parent who finds his child doesn't sing a song right while reciting on the stage. This is the way of working. You do something, you don't like it and you alter it in a way that you might like it a bit better. It's a matter of inventing, discarding, altering, changing, until perhaps another idea comes into your head that you want to try and you decide you've finished with what you've been doing and want to change.

Frank Dale, publisher of the *Los Angeles Examiner*, is involved in a myriad of educational, civic, service, religious, and charitable organizations. He is a trustee of American University and Occidental College, a member of the National Advisory Boards of both Boys Clubs of America and Boy Scouts of America, vice-chairman of Methodist Hospital of Southern California, and a director of the National Conference of Christians and Jews.

George Moody, president of Security Pacific Corporation, finds added stimulation through his involvement with the Hollywood Presbyterian Medical Center, the YMCA, Pomona College, California Museum Foundation, the Colorado River Association, the United States Olympic Committee, and many more.

Norman Barker, chairman of First Interstate Bank of California, is another who enjoys climbing new mountains. In addition to serving as a trustee of the University of Chicago, Occidental College, and the Los Angeles County Museum of Art, he serves on the board of directors of Carter Hawley Stores, Carnation Company, Lear Siegler, Southern California Edison, and the Los Angeles United Way

Every successful businessman I know is involved in various activities over and above his primary career responsibilities. That is the reason these men are never prompted to ask, "Is that all there is?"

REACH FOR NEW HEIGHTS

If you are asking yourself, "Is that all there is?"—it is time for you to reach for new heights. It is time for a change. It is time for you to recognize that the gratification and satisfaction you expected to feel when success was finally attained might not be there after all.

The moment has come for you to redefine the word *success,* to realize that it should mean inner peace and contentment rather than just material possessions. It is time to think positively about yourself and to understand that, if you wish to, you can start your life all over again.

Start With Your Job

Let's start with your job. Are you in a rut the way I was? Do you no longer get a kick out of it? Are you no longer anxious to get to work in the morning? Maybe there is something you can do about it. You have probably never studied the characteristics of the company you work for, nor studied the opportunities that may be awaiting you. Look for them. Are you waiting for your boss to decide what your next move should be—if any? That's a mistake. Make your own decision about how your present job can be made more important, or what new job you would like to have, and then go after it.

Plan Your Own Career

Too many of us wait for someone else to plan our careers for us. Have you ever thought that you can possibly influence your boss to help you move into the new area that interests you? Have you ever studied your employer, his strengths and his weaknesses, and decided how his traits can be used to your advantage? We talked about psychorelations and the role it plays in success. Now is the time for you to begin to play the game and determine for yourself how you can move ahead in your company using your present job as a base. If you decide you can go no further in your present job, then begin to look around.

Back to School?

Consider going back to school. What's wrong with that? There must be a night school not too far from your home. There are numerous opportunities; you must look for them, and if nothing works out, you will at least have made the effort. It will give you more satisfaction than you have today.

LOOKING FOR A NEW DIMENSION

Changing your life so that you get more enjoyment from it may not happen without trial and error. Before you make your first move, study what your life-style is today. When you get home from the office, do you usually have dinner and then watch television until it's time to go to bed? Do you go out two or three times a week, usually with the same people? Your first step might well be to meet some new people. Where do you find them? Do you know your next-door neighbor? Have you ever spent any time talking with that person who works in the office next to yours? Did you meet a charming woman at the market this week? Is there someone at the PTA or the Elks Club who might interest you?

There are opportunities all around you to meet new people. Seek them out, have a drink, invite them over to dinner, suggest you get together for coffee, go to a movie with them. You might not find them any more entertaining or amusing than the people you already know and, if that's so, the time may have come for you to take a good look at yourself. The reason for your lack of interest in them is that their interests may not be yours.

Think about what activity might give your life added meaning. Spectator or participant sports? Collecting—whether it be stamps, memorabilia, first editions, or match covers? Macrame, weaving, embroidery? Cards—bridge, gin rummy, poker? Horse racing—or horse breeding? The world of art? The world of music?

If you find that all this searching still doesn't satisfy your urge for something new, don't get discouraged. It has taken you many years to establish your habit patterns. Don't think that you're going to develop a whole new series of patterns that will instantly give you a fresh outlook on life. Keep looking. Eventually you will discover the new interest that will bring you to the point where you will no longer ask yourself, "Is that all there is?"

DON'T YOU DARE BUY ANOTHER "SUCCESS" BOOK

You have now read and I hope assimilated my theories on psychorelations. I hope I have made clear to you my conviction that using psychorelations skills can be your key to success and a better life in the years ahead.

I have pointed you in the direction of a goal titled *success.* Will you set out to reach that goal or will you put this book on a shelf and forget everything you just read? If you do, you have wasted your time and your money. Do you have other "how to be successful" books on that shelf? Might you buy still another the next time you browse through your neighborhood bookstore?

Diet books are always on the best-seller list because the same people keep buying them. Go into the homes of hundreds of thousands of overweight people and you will find their bookshelves piled high with *The Atkins Diet, The Scarsdale Diet, The Pritikin Diet,* ad infinitum. The people who own them are still overweight. What's the explanation for this paradox? Are the diets ineffective?

No, there's nothing substantially wrong with the diets. There's something wrong with the people who go on the diets. They don't have the will to practice what the book preaches. After a few weeks of diligently following the rules, they fall back into their old eating habits again. When they regain the weight they had fought so hard to lose, they blame it on the diet. "That diet doesn't work for me," they say. They're wrong. A diet book won't help a person who won't help himself.

If you wish to help yourself, there is no point in buying another success book. This one can help you if you have the will and perseverance to practice some of the guidelines I've laid down. All of them don't necessarily apply to you, but I'm sure that a number of times you read a chapter or even a paragraph and said to yourself, "That's me."

Will and *perseverance* are the key words. If you decide that success is important to you and that it is time to do something about it, start by repeating those two words to yourself over and over again, day after day.

I started by asking you to think of yourself as a political candidate, and I repeat it now. You are running for office. Are you worried about whether or not you are fit for the job?

Don't think of this campaign as a new burden you have placed on your shoulders. Make a game out of it. I have found that making a game out of everything that requires an extra effort is the best way I can achieve my goals. Just recently, I decided to start swimming again every day and to go on a diet. I didn't particularly relish the thought of either one, but I knew I could do it if I made a game of it. I taped a slip of paper on my dressing-room mirror and wrote in bold letters—*will power*. Every morning when I get out of bed I see the written reminder of what I have to do that day. Every evening, with great satisfaction, I put a check mark by the reminder. I haven't missed yet. It's a game that is working for me.

Make up your own game that will inspire you and give you the incentive to keep you going. Getting started is the toughest part. Your excuse for not starting may be, "I have had the same behavior and habit patterns all my life. How can I possibly begin to change now?" The answer is: *The only way to break an old habit is to start a new one.*

Off with the old, and on with the new, but don't try to digest the contents of this book all at once. Don't try to make a number of drastic changes in your life all at the same time. It is physically and emotionally impossible. Take one step at a time. Take one chapter at a time. Decide whether or not it is applicable to you. And if it is, work on it until you feel it has become part of your life-style. Then go on to the next chapter.

Are you having second thoughts about all of this? Are you worried about it? Are you concerned that so far you have never been able

284 Rogers' Rules for Success

to follow through on anything? If so, let me try to instill in you the will to do it this time.

I want you to think about the great satisfaction you will have if you can say to yourself one day soon: "I decided to pursue psychorelations. I developed a program to better myself. I persevered at it —and I made it. I am a different and a more successful person than I was yesterday and I'm proud of what I accomplished."

Admit it—won't you get a great kick out of being able to say that to yourself one day?

Formulate the goals you wish to achieve, both in your professional and your personal life. List them on a sheet of paper and carry them with you at all times. Read them every day, and keep reminding yourself what you must do in order to achieve those goals.

A note of caution. Make sure your goals are realistic. Don't develop a program for yourself that is not within your abilities and talents to attain.

If you are saying to yourself, "I can't do it," you really mean, "I won't do it"—or "I'm afraid to do it." Do you remember the chapter that deals with striking out? Does it apply to you right now? Are you afraid of striking out? Are you afraid of failing? Go back and read Chapter 10.

If you strike out, it won't be a tragedy. At least you gave it an honest try. Trying in itself will make you more successful. Most people are content with their lives. They are in a rut and don't have the will to even try to get out of it. Not you. If you have come this far in pursuing psychorelations, it means that you have come into this world to succeed—not to fail. You *will* succeed if you keep trying and trying and trying.